THE PAGODA WAR

by the same author

THE ULSTER CRISIS

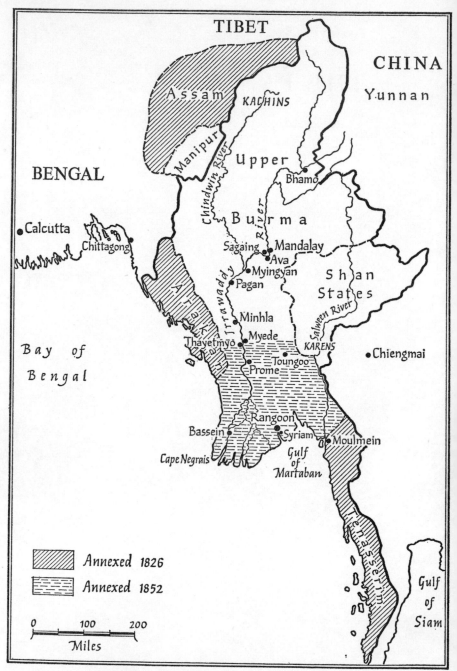

1. Burma, showing places mentioned in the text

THE PAGODA WAR

Lord Dufferin
and the fall of the Kingdom of Ava
1885-6

by
A. T. Q. STEWART

FABER AND FABER
3 Queen Square
London

First published in 1972
by Faber and Faber Limited
3 Queen Square London WC1
Printed in Great Britain by
Ebenezer Baylis and Son Ltd
Worcester, and London
All rights reserved

ISBN 0 571 08722 1

For
ANNA

ACKNOWLEDGEMENTS

This book owes its origin to serendipity. While I was reading through the Dufferin correspondence, for quite another purpose, my curiosity was aroused about the campaign which inspired Kipling's famous and familiar lines, and which nevertheless seemed to have been almost completely forgotten. When I began to look for information on the subject, I discovered to my surprise that very few books had been written on any aspect of Anglo-Burmese relations. Fortunately their quality is in inverse proportion to their quantity, and I must at once acknowledge my debt, in understanding the background to my material, to such books as Miss Dorothy Woodman's *The Making of Burma*, Professor J. F. Cady's *History of Modern Burma*, and above all to the work of Professor D. G. E. Hall.

Extracts from the Dufferin Papers in the Public Record Office of Northern Ireland are reproduced by permission of the Marquess of Dufferin and Ava and of the Deputy Keeper of the Records. Crown Copyright material from unpublished sources in the India Office Library and India Office Records appears by permission of the Controller of Her Majesty's Stationery Office. I am grateful to Lady Napier for allowing me to publish quotations from the correspondence of her father, the late Field-Marshal Sir George White, V.C.

My thanks are due to Miss Joan Lancaster, the Deputy Librarian of the India Office Library and Deputy Keeper of the India Office Records; to Mr. Brian Trainor, the Deputy Keeper of the Records in Northern Ireland; and to the Librarians of the Queen's University Library, the Linenhall Library, Belfast, and the Belfast City Libraries, whose staff, under very difficult circumstances, assisted my research in every possible way. I am indebted to friends and colleagues for much help, advice and encouragement, in particular to Professor Michael Roberts and Professor J. C. Beckett of the Department of Modern History in the Queen's University of Belfast, to Dr. J. G. Simms and Dr. H. E. Shields of Trinity College, Dublin, and to Dr. D. J. Crawford, Mr. W. H. Crawford, Mr. Kenneth Darwin, Mr. J. W. Gracey, and Mr. J. W. Vitty. Mr. J. L. Lord read the whole book in typescript and in proof, and made many valuable comments, from which I have been able to profit. None of these bears responsibility for opinions expressed, or for any remaining errors.

A brief word is needed on orthography. I have used the spelling of Burmese names now generally accepted by Western historians; but most of these names were spelled differently in 1885, and in direct quotations the original form is preserved. Thus King Thibaw appears in quotations as Theebaw, or Thebaw (the spelling favoured by *The Times*), Supayalat as Soopayalat, the Taingda Mingyi as the Tynedah Mengyee, and so on. I have, however, adhered to the familiar spelling of names like Irrawaddy and Rangoon, where the older forms have been fixed by usage.

A. T. Q. STEWART

The Queen's University of Belfast,
October, 1971

CONTENTS

ILLUSTRATIONS

PLATES

*Photographs taken by Colonel W. W. Hooper from the India Office
Library: 5, 6, 8, 9, 10, 11, 13, 14 (from* Burmah, *a series of photographs*

ILLUSTRATIONS

illustrating incidents connected with the British Expeditionary Force. . .
J. A. Lugard, London, and Thacker, Spink & Co., Calcutta).

From the Mansell Collection: 4, 7, 12.

MAPS

PROLOGUE

One morning in February 1890, David Masson, the Professor of English Literature at Edinburgh University and the author of a standard life of Milton, waved a copy of the *Scots Observer* at his students and shouted 'Here's Literature! Here's Literature at last!' His excitement was caused by some grim verses entitled 'Danny Deever', about the hanging of a soldier for the murder of a comrade. It was the first of Rudyard Kipling's *Barrack Room Ballads*, which were within a few weeks to make their author, then just twenty-four and quite unknown in England, a world-wide celebrity. Not since Byron had any English writer risen so swiftly to international fame. In the eighteen months following, Kipling also wrote two novels, *The Light that Failed* (his enemies called it the Book that Failed) and *Naulakha*, and the short stories which were published as *Life's Handicap*. It was a prodigious arrival and Kipling might be forgiven for dispatching a telegram to his parents in India which read 'Genesis, xlv, 9'. His first name was Joseph, and the verse runs: 'Haste ye and go up to my father and say unto him, Thus saith thy son Joseph: God hath made me lord of all Egypt; come down unto me. tarry not.'[1]

In the spring of 1890 the *Ballads* created a literary sensation as they appeared one by one—'Tommy', 'Fuzzy-Wuzzy', 'Loot', 'The Widow of Windsor', 'Gunga Din'—until in June there appeared one which was to be remembered most of all:

'*By the old Moulmein Pagoda, lookin' lazy at the sea,*
There's a Burma girl a-setting, and I know she thinks o' me;
For the wind is in the palm trees, and the temple bells they say:
Come you back, you British soldier; come you back to Mandalay!'

Kipling's enormous popular success did not disarm the literary critics. On the contrary, they vied with one another to inflict upon him wounds the scars of which he carried for the rest of his life. But for some reason even the most rancorous of his detractors made an exception of 'Mandalay'. The embittered Francis Adams, who could not make up his mind whether Kipling was merely 'a clever journalist', or an 'ill-educated, promiscuously receptive, little-brained second-rate journalist', found this poem alone 'instinct with the lyral cry, with the note of "the tears of things", the eternal voice of human regret'. A hundred years hence, he predicted, someone might be searching in the British Museum for any other work by the man who wrote 'Mandalay'. Robert Buchanan, whose article *The Voice of the Hooligan* set the tone for much Kipling criticism since, thought that 'Mandalay' had a real melody and a certain pathos; Richard Le Gallienne considered it the best of the ballads, though made of the very refuse of the language.[2] Half a century later, George Orwell, who had his own good reasons for not being enthusiastic about Burma, or British imperialism or Kipling's moral and aesthetic outlook, declared bluntly that unless one were a snob or a liar it was impossible to say that no-one who cares for poetry could get any pleasure out of the lines:

'For the wind is in the palm trees, and the temple bells they say,
Come you back, you British soldier, come you back to Mandalay!'[3]

There were never any misgivings among the general public. Kipling, as was his habit, composed 'Mandalay' to a tune that was running through his head—an old waltz. The ballad was almost immediately set to music both in England and in the United States, and it has been sung ceaselessly since. Few young men of twenty-four have written verses which are so widely known throughout the English speaking world, and which have given the language a phrase so evocative as 'the road to Mandalay', or a concept such as 'East of Suez', which politicians have elevated into an aspect of national policy.[4]

It is all the more astonishing, therefore, that the impressions so vividly recollected in 'Mandalay' were received in one day, 15 March 1889, when Kipling made a brief visit to Rangoon. He was on his way home to England via the United States in the company of his friends Professor and Mrs. S. A. Hill. Hill, a scientist at Muir College in Allahabad, was married to an attractive American girl, and Kipling was at that time very much under her spell. They had first met at a dinner-party two years earlier, and she had on that occasion written to her sister in America: 'I've met an unusually interesting man with the uncommon name of Rudyard Kipling. . . . Mr. Kipling looks about forty, as he is beginning to be bald, but he is in reality just twenty-two. He is animation itself, telling his stories admirably, so that those about him were kept in gales of laughter. He fairly scintillated . . .'[5]

At the beginning of the cool season of 1888 Mrs. Hill fell seriously ill with meningitis, and when she recovered, her husband decided to take her on a sea-voyage across the Pacific, and then on to her home in Pennsylvania, where her father was the president of a college. Kipling was already planning to return to England, and was saving money for the journey; when the Hills invited him to travel with them, he accepted at once, and George Allen, his employer on the *Pioneer*, commissioned him to write a series of letters of travel for the paper, a series which was to become *From Sea to Sea*.

They left Calcutta on 9 March 1888, and five days later stopped at Rangoon, where they went ashore to see the Shwe Dagon pagoda. Kipling was intoxicated by the sounds, smells, and colours of Rangoon, especially the colour, 'lilac, pink, vermilion, lapis lazuli, and blistering blood-red under fierce sunlight that mellows and modifies all.' They were colours he was to remember vividly in a London fog. Next day the three friends travelled eastward across the Bay to Moulmein, where 'Aleck' Hill, a keen amateur photographer, set up his tripod and began to photograph elephants at work in the timber yards,

> *'Eliphants a-piling teak,*
> *In the sludgy, squdgy creek,*
> *Where the silence hung so heavy you was 'arf afraid to speak'*

and then the ancient pagoda, hung round with bronze bells. 'I should better remember what the pagoda was like', Kipling recalled, 'had I not fallen deeply and irrevocably in love with a Burmese girl at the foot of the first flight of steps.'

Leaving this 'far too lovely maiden,' Kipling began to climb the pagoda steps, and turning round looked upon a view that made him rejoice to be alive. 'The hillside below me and above me was ablaze with pagodas. . . . Far above my head there was a faint tinkle, as of golden bells, and a talking of the breezes in the tops of the toddy-palms. Wherefore I climbed higher and higher up the steps till I reached a place of great peace, dotted with Burmese images, spotlessly clean. Here women now and again paid reverence. They bowed their heads and their lips moved, because they were praying. I had an umbrella—a black one—in my hand, deck-shoes upon my feet, and a helmet upon my head. I did not pray—I swore at myself for being a Globetrotter, and wished that I had enough Burmese to explain to these ladies that I was sorry and would have taken off my hat but for the sun.' Kipling recorded every image with precision and clarity, and stored it away in his mind for future use—the gilt Buddhas in the side-temples, the little palms that grew out of cracks in the tiled paving of the court, the big palms above, and the great bronze bells that hung at each corner of the pagoda for the women to smite with stag-horns. A year later, lonely and ill in London, despite his sudden literary success, he was haunted by the memories of that day, and the voices of the wind-blown bells.[6]

The local colour for 'Mandalay' was thus gathered in the space of a few hours. But that is only part of the story. Though the scene is Moulmein, the title is taken from the Burmese capital, some 635 miles to the north, and the allusion is to the British military expedition which took the road to Mandalay some five years earlier. The road to Mandalay was in fact a river, the Irrawaddy, which ran from north to south through the whole of Burma, and on whose waters Kipling gazed for the first time in 1889, though he had often pictured it in imagination. It seems strange that the fall of the Kingdom of Ava should be celebrated in these verses which are so well-known, while no detailed account of the campaign has even been written.

I

THE VICEROY

At the end of 1884 India had a new viceroy. Frederick Temple Hamilton-Temple Blackwood, Earl of Dufferin and Baron of Clandeboye was an Irish aristocrat with large estates in the north of County Down. Then in his sixtieth year, Lord Dufferin was a proconsul of vast political experience who had been Governor-General of Canada and British ambassador at St. Petersburg and at Constantinople. His appearance and manner very much suggested the studied aloofness of one born to privilege and wealth. Flowing hair, worn shorter as the century progressed, a full moustache and a neatly-trimmed imperial beard gave his strong features a patrician cast; his eyeglass and slow lisping habit of speech heightened the impression of detachment, and those who met him for the first time often thought him affected and artificial in manner. Beneath this exterior, however, he was a sensitive and sympathetic man, with considerable charm and a quick Irish temper. His affectation and his reserve on first meeting others owed much to self-consciousness on account of the impediment in his speech. On occasion throughout his public career he was to betray a hyper-sensitiveness to criticism or ridicule, against which his background and education, and a long exposure to political and diplomatic life, might have been expected to armour him.

Dufferin was the only son of Price Blackwood, the 4th Baron, and Helen Selina Sheridan.[1] His mother was the eldest of three beautiful and famous sisters, grand-daughters of Richard Brinsley Sheridan, the author of *The Rivals*. The youngest, Jane Georgina, married the 12th Duke of Somerset, and she it was who was crowned the Queen of Beauty at the Eglinton Tournament of 1839. The second sister, Caroline, married George Norton and parted from him in a famous divorce suit of 1836 in which Lord Melbourne was cited as co-respondent: she was the original of Meredith's *Diana of the Crossways*, and the publication of the novel in 1885 revived the calumny that she had betrayed to *The Times* the secret of Peel's intention to repeal the Corn Laws. The eldest sister married Price Blackwood, then a naval captain with little money, in 1825, when she was only seventeen. To escape the disapproval of the Blackwood family, the young couple went to live in Italy, and it was in a house in Via Maggio in Florence on 21 June 1826 that Frederick Temple Hamilton-Temple Blackwood was born. In later years he would remark that he enjoyed the rare distinction of remembering his mother's coming of age, the more vividly in that he spoiled the occasion by eating some laburnum seeds in the garden. 'My mother and I were young together in the reign of George IV,' he would tell his friends. 'We shared our youth.'[2]

Helen, Lady Dufferin, was a witty and accomplished woman, and like her sister the Hon. Mrs. Norton she had literary ability. Her songs and verses, collected and edited by her son, included the once popular ballad *The Irish Emigrant*. For more than forty years she lavished devotion on her only son, and had it returned by him. On his twenty-first birthday she gave him a Roman lamp in silver, as a symbol of her love, inscribed with the words 'Fiat Lux' and a poem. And in 1850, six years before her death, he had built for her Helen's Tower on the highest spot in the park at Clandeboye, commanding a view across Belfast Lough to Antrim and across the windy expanse of the North Channel to the Mull of Kintyre and the Isle of Man. On its walls are inscribed poems in her praise, including Tennyson's lines:

> *'Helen's Tower here I stand*
> *Dominant over sea and land*
> *Son's love built me, and I hold*
> *Mother's love in lettered gold . . .*
> *Would my granite girth were strong*
> *As either love, to last as long.'*[3]

Price Blackwood had inherited the Dufferin title and the Clandeboye estates from his uncle Hans, Lord Dufferin, in 1839 and died two years later (through a chemist's error in mixing a prescription). His son, then at Eton, succeeded to the title and the estates at the age of fifteen. He went up to Oxford in 1845 as a Gentleman Commoner of Christ Church. His attachment to Oxford remained strong throughout his life, and his biographer Sir Alfred Lyall records having seen him for the last time in October 1901, leaning over Magdalen Bridge 'looking down the stream towards the sunset, absorbed, as it seemed to me, in the remembrance of bygone days'.[4]

After Oxford Dufferin had gone into politics as a whig, and in 1849 Lord John Russell had conferred an English peerage upon him. Dufferin had chosen to sit in the House of Lords, instead of acquiring his political education in the Commons, and though he was ambitious his temperament was not suited to the cut and thrust of parliamentary debate. Moreover the Irish land question produced in him a conflict of loyalties. While still an undergraduate he had travelled from Oxford to Skibbereen in Co. Cork and seen at first hand the effect of starvation and typhus during the Irish Famine, and he never forgot the experience. But when Gladstone, the leader of his party, began some twenty years later the systematic destruction of the Irish landlords as a class, Dufferin was pulled in opposite directions. Gladstone he respected and admired, but he confessed that he hardly ever left his presence without feeling his face burn with irritation at his ignorance of Irish conditions.

Dufferin never succeeded in reconciling the conflict of emotion and loyalties posed by Ireland and her problems, and for most of his early manhood it seemed likely to thwart his political ambitions. From the arid waste of Irish controversy he escaped at last, fortuitously, into the world of diplomacy, where his considerable abilities had fuller expression. In 1860, after the massacre of Christians in Damascus, and the consequent intervention by the great powers, he was sent to Syria by Lord Palmerston as the British representative on the commission then set up, and achieved there a notable diplomatic success. Yet he was to wait another ten years before he received another appointment in which these qualities could be displayed. In the meantime he had a spell as Under Secretary at the War Office and the India Office, and when Gladstone formed his first ministry in 1868 he was made Chancellor of the Duchy of Lancaster and Paymaster-General. At forty-two he was still a minor member of the government.

He had, however, crammed into those years a considerable amount of varied experience, including exploration. In 1854, following that casual and privileged tradition available to young noblemen with a taste for adventure, he had sailed to the Baltic and witnessed the naval engagements between the Allied and Russian fleets, and as the guest of Admiral Napier he had taken part in the siege of Bomarsund. Two years later, he sailed his little 80-ton yacht *Foam* on a 6,000 mile voyage through the Arctic seas to Jan Mayen island and Spitzbergen, a voyage that admitted him to the select circle of Arctic explorers and made him a literary reputation, for his account of it, *Letters from High Latitudes*, has run through many editions, and in 1910 was included in the Oxford *World's Classics*. To the end of his life, sailing remained Dufferin's favourite recreation.

In 1870, after the passing of Gladstone's Irish Land Act, Dufferin began to dispose of his estates in Co. Down, keeping only the Clandeboye demesne and Helen's Bay, and soon afterwards he told Gladstone of his intention to resign from politics and retire to Clandeboye to write a history of Ireland. He did not resign, however, and in 1872 he allowed his name to go forward for the post of Viceroy of India, after the assassination of Lord Mayo. Lord Northbrook was chosen instead, but a month later Dufferin was appointed Governor-General of Canada.

In 1862 Dufferin had married Hariot Rowan Hamilton of Killyleagh in Co. Down. The Hamiltons and Blackwoods were neighbours and kinsfolk, for the fortunes of these two families of Scottish planters had been strangely intermingled. The Blackwoods were first to come to Ulster about 1576, having associated themselves too closely with the policies of Mary Queen of Scots, and they obtained lands along the shore of Belfast Lough. In James I's reign, Sir James Hamilton, who had gained great influence with the king, was granted by royal patent certain castles and lands of the O'Neills 'in Upper Clandeboye and the Great Ardes'. In 1610 he acquired by dubious means the demesnes of the Barony of Dufferin, and finding an old Norman castle at Killyleagh had made it 'ane very strong castle: the lyk is not in the northe'.

A macabre crime perpetrated there by Lady Alice Moore, involving the murder of her husband, the 3rd Earl of Clandeboye, and the destruction of his father's will, led to a protracted lawsuit at the end of the seventeenth century, as a consequence of which the Probate Court in Dublin divided the Hamilton properties equally between two Hamilton heirs, one male and one female. Even Killyleagh Castle itself was mathematically divided, the keep being awarded to Gawn Hamilton, and the gatehouse and part of the battlements going to Dorcas Hamilton. It was an inconvenient arrangement, made worse when Dorcas Hamilton married Sir James Blackwood, and throughout the eighteenth century it created a good deal of friction between the Blackwood and Hamilton clans.

It fell to Lord Dufferin to heal the quarrel when he came of age in

1847. Declaring that he would not 'keep a man from his own front door' Dufferin not only handed over to his future father-in-law the gatehouse and walls of Killyleagh Castle, but restored the keep in the extravagant style of one of the châteaux of the Loire, so that to this day its fairytale towers take the traveller by surprise when he comes upon them among the gentle drumlins of Co. Down. In return the Hamiltons agreed to pay Dufferin a peppercorn rent: they presented him with a golden rose and a golden spur in each alternate year. These tributes, manufactured by Messrs. Elkington of London, graced Dufferin's dinner tables in many parts of the world, from St. Petersburg to Simla, and provided his guests with a ready source of conversation, for years after he had married the eldest Hamilton daughter.[5]

It was an extremely happy marriage. Throughout his public career, Hariot Dufferin strengthened her husband's self-confidence by the very singleness of her devotion. His nature was sensitive, and there was always within him an element of unsureness, at odds with the outward ease and elegance of his manner, which her shrewd and sensible counsel helped him to master. Her nephew, Sir Harold Nicolson, has recorded that even as a child he was conscious of 'some quality in their relation-ship which was deep and strange'.[6] She would cease speaking at once when he appeared, and she never referred to him by his Christian name; in her diaries he is always 'Dufferin' or simply 'D'. Such deference was securely based on deep affection, as was Dufferin's demeanour to-wards his wife. His eyes lighted up with pride when she entered the room, and even when he was over seventy he would bring a blush to her cheek by paying her some small compliment on her appearance. Though essentially a shy woman, Lady Dufferin had a serenity and dignity which abundantly fitted her for the social position she was to occupy as wife of the Governor-General of Canada and the Viceroy of India. Formidable towards anyone who seemed likely to menace the proprieties of Victorian society, as defined in the light of an Ulster upbringing, she was otherwise tolerant of human irrationality and possessed of a shrewd sense of humour.

The seven years which Dufferin spent in Canada were very happy and successful ones, and he is remembered as a popular Governor-General. The political tasks which faced him were daunting, chief among them being to smoothe down the troubles which followed the consolidation of the dominion. It was for just such patient but firm diplomacy that Dufferin was suited by temperament and aptitude. His method, wrote

Nicolson, was 'to sandwich his resolution between two layers of charm'.[7] He was unrivalled in the art of conciliation, and he could often by his candour and humour lead contesting parties to appreciate the difficulty and delicacy of his own position as the representative of the Imperial government, and enlist their aid in finding an acceptable solution. He prepared his ground carefully, and proceeded very cautiously until he found the essential principle involved; having made his mind up on that principle, he acted with speed and resolution. The art of diplomacy, he once said, was to turn the corner of a brick wall, rather than to run your head against it.[8]

When Dufferin returned from Canada in 1878 Disraeli (now Lord Beaconsfield) offered him the post of ambassador to Russia. Again it was a situation which called for Dufferin's special qualities, for the Russians were smarting under the humiliation imposed upon them by the Congress of Berlin, and the Czar Alexander II held Great Britain largely responsible for robbing him of the spoils of the Treaty of San Stephano. Dufferin, who was not identified with the Conservative Government's policy, accepted, after some considerable hesitation. Gladstone was anything but pleased at what he considered this desertion, and when he came to power in 1880 he left Dufferin at St. Petersburg, though it had been expected that he might offer him either Ireland or India. Dufferin did not hide his disappointment, for St. Petersburg was an uncongenial embassy. 'I should have thought', he wrote home, 'that my seven years in Canada, and the additional year I have spent here in keeping the peace between our Foreign Office and the Emperor, might have deserved a better reward than a further term of exile in an Arctic climate.' But at least he kept his country from war with Russia, even if it meant that he spent more time in soothing the Foreign Office than in soothing the Russians.

On 13 March 1881, Dufferin had a brief conversation with the Czar at a military review; a short time later, after he had returned to the embassy, taken off his uniform and begun to read a newspaper, he heard 'a violent report like a cannon'. It was the explosion of the bombs which assassinated Alexander II. Dufferin reached the Winter Palace at the same time as the doctor and the priest, and was told by the Grand Duke Vladimir that the Emperor was dying. He at once returned to the embassy and telegraphed the news to the Queen and the Government. His last diplomatic function in Russia was to attend the Prince of Wales at the investment of the new Czar Alexander III with the Order of the

Garter. Queen Victoria telegraphed that she held Dufferin 'personally responsible' for the Prince's safety.[9]

In the same year Dufferin was transferred from St. Petersburg to Constantinople. At the Porte he had to deal with exceptionally complex and delicate diplomatic problems, and after Arabi Pasha's rising in Egypt he was sent to Cairo in charge of the British Commission there, entrusted with the task of drawing up a scheme for the government of the country. In outmanoeuvring France, the other power implicated, and in securing virtual control of Egypt after Sir Garnet Wolseley's defeat of Arabi Pasha at Tel-el-Kebir Dufferin was credited with the Machiavellian subtlety of English diplomacy, but in reality accident played a large part in the course and timing of these events. The Dufferin Report, published in 1883, established the principle that Egypt could never be ruled directly from London, and the system he advocated worked for thirty years. His handling of Egypt made his reputation as a diplomatist.

Such was the man appointed Viceroy of India in 1884. It was a task which called for all his diplomatic skill, for once again he was to pour oil on waters which others had troubled into a storm. Lord Ripon, his predecessor, was a sincere and optimistic liberal who had outraged the Europeans in India by what seemed to them his excessive partiality for the aspirations of the educated Indian classes, who now had their own press, clear political objectives and, in an as yet inchoate form, a political organization. Ripon's policy had raised their hopes to fever point. The storm in the Anglo-Indian community had broken with the Criminal Procedure Amendment of 1882, generally known as the Ilbert Bill, which would have made it possible for Europeans to be tried by Indian magistrates. Even Gladstone had thought it unwise for Ripon to introduce such a bill in the midst of so many other, and less controversial, reforms. When Ripon intimated that he would be glad to be relieved of his post, the Secretary of State, the Earl of Kimberley, saw an opportunity to put into the position someone more amenable to his own cautious and progressive ideas.

Dufferin was carefully coached by his friend and mentor, and Kimberley indicated very clearly the lines which he was to follow. He was, above all, to restore tranquillity in Indian life, and allow the Government to pay more attention to imperial matters. For the meantime reforms that were exclusively in Indian interests were to be postponed. Yet it was in 1885, the first year of Dufferin's viceroyalty, that the Indian National

Congress was founded, and it is his domestic policy which now attracts the attention of historians.[10] Whether or not he handled India's internal problems with success is a matter for debate, but there is no doubt that he felt more at home in external policy, and during his period of office he was confronted by two crises, one at each extremity of the vast Indian Empire.

In the spring of 1885 he received the Amir of Afghanistan at Rawalpindi. The Amir had been a firm ally of the British, and Dufferin wished to bind him even closer, in order to offset the very threatening advance of the Russians towards the key fortress of Herat. Preparations were made to entertain the Amir on a very lavish scale. Thirty-six tents were put up for guests and the Viceroy's staff, forming a wide street the length of which was broken with fountains and rockeries; and at the top of the street a tent palace was erected for the Viceroy, with Persian carpets, sofas and armchairs. The street had water laid on, and lamp posts, telephones and a post office, complete with waiting messengers on camels. Unfortunately the weather broke on the day of the Amir's arrival, and incessant rain turned the street into a quagmire. The Shamiana, or durbar tent, collapsed, the state procession of fifty elephants had to be abandoned, and the Amir made his entry in a closed brougham, while a military band played:

> *For he might have been a Roosian*
> *A French, or Turk or Proosian...*
> *But in spite of all temptations*
> *To belong to other nations*
> *He remains an Englishman.*

The Amir Abdur Rahman was described by Sir Alfred Lyall as 'a stout, burly man dressed in a black uniform coat, decorated with two diamond stars, with long black boots, and an astrachan cap; a prince of frank and even bluff, yet courteous manners . . . a man of some humour in jokes, with a face occasionally crossed by a look of implacable severity, the look of a Louis XI or Henry VIII that is now never seen in civilised life.'[11] The Amir had indeed brought with him his executioner, clad in red velvet and carrying the implements of his office, an axe and a strangling rope; yet he puzzled the Europeans by spending one whole morning arranging cut flowers in forty vases.

On 30 March, while the Amir was still at Rawalpindi, news came that the Russians had attacked the Afghan frontier posts at Penjdeh. There was at this point a serious risk of an Anglo-Russian conflict, for Dufferin was already committed to a policy of defending the Indian frontier in Afghanistan should the Russians attack Herat. The Amir and the Viceroy went into grave consultation in a dripping tent. After a lengthy exposition of the British view of the situation, Dufferin told the Amir that British troops might be sent to help him defend Herat, but the Amir said that his people were ignorant and suspicious and would resent the soldiers. Then, said Dufferin, he would have to make the best terms he could with the Russians, and he would have to give up Penjdeh. To the Viceroy's astonishment, the Amir insisted that he had never made any claim to the Penjdeh district, and that the Russians had not therefore violated his frontier. Once he was sure that the Amir did not want the assistance guaranteed by his treaty with Britain, Dufferin left the tent to telegraph this welcome news to Gladstone and the Cabinet. Subsequently an Anglo-Russian commission demarcated the Afghan frontier. The incident represented the limit of the Russian incursions into Central Asia. Dufferin was instructed to invest the Amir with the Star of India. He also received a sword with a Damascus blade and a gold hilt set with diamonds, bearing the inscription that it was presented to the Amir 'by his friend the Earl of Dufferin, Viceroy of India'. He vowed that he would use it to smite any enemy of the British Government.[12]

Among the journalists at the Rawalpindi Durbar was a young reporter with a sharp eye for the colour and excitement of the event. It was the most important assignment Rudyard Kipling had so far been given, and he was determined to prove himself worthy of it. The magnificent preparations, the arrival of the Amir, the military displays and the atrocious weather were described graphically and at length for the *Civil and Military Gazette*. But Kipling also carried away precious material that he was to use later in his stories and verse. He had been one of those who had gone up to Peshawar and on to Fort Jumrood, at the entrance of the Khyber Pass, to see the reception of the Amir at the frontier. With a boyish hope of adventure he had wandered alone into the Pass, turning back only when a tribesman fired a rifle shot at him. Strange as it seems, this was Kipling's only visit to the North-West Frontier, but it powerfully excited his imagination; when Lionel Dunsterville (the original of 'Stalky') came to India in 1886, Kipling proudly related the experience to him, describing the tribesman as 'a narrow-minded sort of cuss who couldn't appreciate the responsibilities of journalism'. Kipling worked so hard reporting the durbar and the Penjdeh crisis that he became ill. His eyesight bothered him, and he slept badly, with nightmares of marching columns in the rain, of 'boots, boots, boots, boots, movin' up an' down again' to the tune of 'John Brown's Body'. The durbar is also the setting of the last story in *The Jungle Book*, 'Soldiers of the Queen.'

In the hot season of 1885 Kipling's father, Lockwood, the curator of the Lahore Museum, took his family once more to the hill-station of Simla. For six months of every year Simla was the home of the Viceroy's court, and in 1885 Kipling was able to join his parents and sister as special correspondent of his paper, commissioned to describe 'the annual spectacle of an Empire ruled from a remote and almost inaccessible village, seven thousand feet above the Indian Plains'.[13] The viceregal lodge was then an absurdly small house called 'Peterhoff' (the extant lodge was built during Dufferin's viceroyalty). There Lady Dufferin entertained 640 guests to dinner in the course of the season, and invited 250 people to each of her six evening receptions. Her initial impressions of Simla were not reassuring. She thought that it looked like Mount Ararat with the Ark balanced on top of it. 'Peterhoff' would have been suitable for any family desiring to lead a domestic and not an official life, but it was quite unfit for a Viceroy's establishment. 'Altogether it is the funniest place,' she wrote, 'At the back of the house you have about a yard to spare before you tumble down a precipice, and in front there is just room for one tennis court before you go over another. The A.D.C.s are all slipping off the hill in various little bungalows, and go through most perilous adventures to come to dinner. Walking, riding, driving, all seem to me to be indulged in at the risk of one's life, and even of unsafe roads there is a limited variety.'[14]

The Dufferins liked Lockwood Kipling and his attractive, witty wife, and the family soon found itself within a privileged circle in Simla society. The Viceroy's daughter, Lady Helen Blackwood, attended Lockwood's sketching class, and Dufferin would on occasion drop in to 'The Tendrils', the Kipling's Simla lodging, to chat with Lockwood about art and letters and listen with enjoyment to Mrs. Kipling's conversation. He said that dullness and Mrs. Kipling could not exist in the same room. Trix Kipling, Rudyard's sister, at seventeen wrote poems and stories, was an expert dancer, a gifted amateur actress, and a breaker of hearts. In 1886 she even captivated the Viceroy's son and aide-de-camp, Lord Clandeboye, who twice proposed to her and was twice rejected. Half a century later, she told Sir Ian Hamilton, the last of her

Simla dancing partners, that Lord Dufferin had approved her good sense, but that Lady Dufferin could not forgive her for turning down her 'splendid Arch'. 'His profile was an abiding joy to me,' she wrote, 'and I've always liked Irishmen, but I drew the line at marrying them somehow.' Of the Kipling family, Rudyard was the one who probably impressed the Dufferins least, but the Viceroy did notice one thing about him, his 'mysterious faculty for assimilating local colour without apparent effort'.[15]

In the autumn of 1885 Dufferin embarked on what was to prove the second great crisis of external policy during his viceroyalty, and it was one which exercised on the young Kipling an influence amounting to fascination, an influence which persisted for years and shaped much of his early writing. On Tuesday, 20 October 1885, the day before they left Simla, Lady Dufferin recorded precisely in her diary: 'We breakfasted at eight o'clock. At a quarter past the Viceroy signed the declaration of war with Burmah.'[16]

2

THE CONQUEST OF LOWER BURMA

The first Englishman known to have reached Burma was one Ralph
Fitch, an Elizabethan prospector, who in 1583 obtained a royal charter
to sail to the East Indies in search of trade. His account of his travels
begins thus: 'In the yeere of our Lord 1583, I Ralph Fitch of London
Merchant, being desirous to see the Countries of the East Indie, in the
companie of Master John Newberry Merchant . . . William Leedes
Jeweller, and James Storie Painter . . . did ship my selfe in a ship of
London called the *Tygre*, wherein wee went for Tripolis in Syrie; and
from thence we took way for Alepo which wee went in seven dayes with
the Carovan.'[1] The voyage is believed to be that darkly alluded to by the
witches in Act I Scene III of Shakespeare's *Macbeth*. Eventually the
party reached Goa in India, where the Portuguese arrested them as spies.
The Jesuits obtained Story's release so that he might paint their new
church. The others escaped and made their way to the court of the
Mogul Emperor Akbar at Fatehpur Sikri, where they decided to separate
and go each his own way. Newberry tried to return home by Afghanistan
and Persia, and died on the way, though not before securing for himself
a permanent place in the history of Tudor exploration. Leeds, the diamond expert, stayed in the Emperor's service. But Fitch resolutely
journeyed eastward to Bengal, where, towards the end of 1586, he joined
a Portuguese ship in the Hoogli River and set sail for Burma. He
landed at 'Cosmin' (which may have been Bassein), made his way
through the muddy creeks of the Irrawaddy delta to Syriam and the
kingdom of Pegu, and then travelled two hundred miles north to
Chiengmai. In January 1588 he sailed from Pegu to Malacca, the limit
of his eastward travels, before beginning the long journey home.

He arrived in England in 1591, to find, like many another early explorer, that his relatives had long since divided up his estate. When Hakluyt and others urged him to write his memoirs, Fitch, who had prudently kept no diaries, borrowed some of his more colourful descriptions from the journal of the Venetian, Caesar Fredericke, who had preceded him to Pegu in 1569. Nevertheless his own observations were full of interest. He had been much impressed with the great Shwe Dagon pagoda which still dominates the city of Rangoon. 'About two dayes journey from Pegu there is a Varelle, or pagode, which is the pilgrimage of the Pegues: it is called Dogoune and is of a woonderfulle bignesse, and all gilded from the foote to the toppe.'[2] He found the people well-disposed, 'the women white, round-faced with little eyes'. He noticed the royal white elephants which were fed from vessels of beaten silver and gold ('The king in his title is called the King of the White Elephants') and the Buddhist monks, the *pyongyis*, 'very strangely apparelled with one camboline or thinne cloth next to their body of a browne colour, another of yellow doubled many times upon their shoulder,' whom the people supported by placing rice, fish and herbs in their bowls, without being asked for anything.[3]

The East India Company made its first contact with Burma in 1617, six years after it had established a factory at Masulipatam on the Coromandel coast, when it sent Henry Forrest and John Staveley to recover the goods of a company servant who had died in Syriam. William Methwold, the Norfolk man who was in charge of the Masulipatam factory, was far from satisfied with his agents. He complained to the London headquarters of the Company that they were 'royotous, vitious and unfaithfull' and that Forrest was 'a vearie villane, debaucht, most audacious and dishonest'; they had consumed their capital, and 'taken up besides what their credit could supply, for which they could give no other account, but that most was lost at play, and the rest profusely spent'. In spite of their shortcomings, which included forging a complete set of false accounts, they returned from Pegu in 1620 with a letter from the king 'written upon a palmito leaf' signifying his desire to give 'free trade and entertainment to the English nation, if they would with their shipping repair unto his country'.[4] Forrest and Staveley were arrested and sent home in disgrace, and another twenty years elapsed before the Company succeeded in establishing a factory in Burma. Such was the uncertain beginning of the history of Britain's trade with Burma, to which rivalry with

C

the Dutch, the Portuguese and later the French was to provided a lively counterpoint.

Towards the end of the eighteenth century events had brought Britain and Burma into a closer, though not a friendlier, relationship. In the middle years of the century a new ruling dynasty had been founded by a Burmese warlord called Alaungpaya or Alompra (the name signified 'embryo Buddha'). He overcame the Mons of Lower Burma, who had captured and burnt the ancient city of Ava (from which the Burmese Kingdom took its name), and built a new capital around the Shwe Dagon pagoda, calling it Yandon or Rangoon—'the end of strife'.[5] In 1783 Alaungpaya's son Bodawpaya captured Akyab on the Bay of Bengal, and in 1785 annexed the whole province of Arakan, thus acquiring a common frontier with India. Thousands of Arakanese fled into British territory, and a long process of emigration began, which the British welcomed, since the Arakanese farmers settled in unpopulated areas and established thriving colonies. Rebellions in Arakan, the harshness of Burmese reprisals and the atmosphere of provocation and intrigue brought about a state of affairs which made a collision ultimately inevitable.

Britain had another obvious preoccupation in these years, the fear that France, with whom she was at war, would threaten the East India Company's possessions and interests by establishing her influence in neighbouring states. The kingdom of Burma was India's frontier on the south-east, and was 'regarded by the Supreme Government as part of the *glacis* encircling Indian lines of defence'.[6] The expansionist policy adopted by the Court of Ava led to clashes in Assam, Cachar, and Chittagong, and in 1824 Lord Amherst, the Governor-General of the East Indian Company, sent King Bagyidaw of Burma a stern note requesting him to disavow the Burmese action in seizing the island of Shapuri, and to punish those responsible. The island had meanwhile been reoccupied by British soldiers, though it was found to be so unhealthy that they were withdrawn shortly afterwards.

The Court of Ava very unwisely took the note to be a sign of weakness, and compounded its mistake by kidnapping two British naval officers and removing them to the interior. Curiously enough, their capture had arisen from Amherst's efforts to avoid a war, efforts which even included the setting up of an Anglo-Burmese commission to define the boundary. The Burmese delegates were so insolent that negotiations had to be broken off, and though Amherst probably miscalculated the true motives of the Burmese government, it is difficult to see what alternative was open to him but to make a formal declaration of war. This he did on 5 March 1824.

The conflict which followed was, in the words of one authority, 'the worst managed war in British military history',[7] which is saying a good deal. Not only did the military authorities in British India, in traditional fashion, underestimate the calibre of the enemy; they were almost totally ignorant of the climate and terrain of the theatre of war. In one respect, however, the military planning was original. For the first time it was proposed to use a naval force for river warfare in co-operation with the army. Rather than drain their resources by sending troops into the uncharted mountains and forests of Assam, the British planned boldly to strike in Lower Burma, and using the mobility provided by naval power to advance up the Irrawaddy towards Ava. This strategy was adhered to in each of the subsequent Anglo-Burmese wars.

The joint military and naval expedition assembled in May 1824 at Port Cornwallis in the Andaman Islands; it consisted of 63 ships and 8,500 British and Indian troops commanded by Sir Archibald Campbell, a veteran of the Peninsular War. The Admiralty had agreed to reinforce the Company's ships with vessels of the Royal Navy at the Company's expense, and the former included the steam vessel *Diana*, a 60 horse-power paddlewheeler with a funnel nearly as tall as a mast. She was the first steamer ever to be used by British forces, and the first to be seen in that part of the world. 'The very sight of her created more consternation than a herd of armed elephants.' The *Diana* was included in the expedition, against considerable official opposition, by the determined efforts of a young naval officer called Frederick Marryat, who was later to become famous as the novelist. Marryat fitted out the *Diana* and supervised her armament, including in it a Congreve rocket: later when she was run down by a transport, her engine thrown out of level, and the only engineer severely injured, it was Marryat who repaired her and kept her in action. One has only to remember the distrust of steam which naval officers were to preserve for decades to come, to realize how imaginative and foresighted such action was. In the course of the operation, when Commodore Grant fell ill, direct responsibility for the conduct of naval affairs devolved upon the thirty-two year old Marryat: 'it was he who organized drinking water for the fleet; he who led the column up the river to Rangoon; he who commanded the first blue-jackets to enter the city.'[8]

The combined force reached Rangoon on 11 May 1824. The arrival of the British fleet in the river threw the Burmese authorities into consternation, and the troops entered a deserted town. According to one officer, some of the soldiers discovered quantities of brandy in the cellar of a merchant's house and quickly became intoxicated; in this state 'they went rambling from house to house with lighted torches, and as may be fully anticipated, the town was set on fire and a great portion of it consumed in consequence.'[9] Another says nothing of the fire but writes vividly of the depression produced by the Burmese withdrawal. 'Deserted as we found ourselves by the people of the country, from whom alone we could expect supplies, unprovided with the means of moving either by land or water, and the rainy monsoon just setting in—no prospect remained to us but that of a long residence in the miserable and dirty hovels of Rangoon, trusting to the transports for provisions, with such partial supplies as our foraging parties might procure from time to time by distant and fatiguing marches into the interior of the country.'[10]

The British troops were soon to discover that their elusive enemy possessed both determination and considerable military skill. It took Campbell a month, after two unsuccessful attempts and very heavy losses, to capture the Kemmendine stockade and gain command of the river above Rangoon. The Burmese fought in their own way, which resembled in some respects the warfare of the twentieth century. They relied chiefly on infantry armed with flintlocks, long spears, and short swords: each man carried entrenching tools, and on taking up a position they would dig foxholes large enough to hold two men and a supply of food, water and brushwood. These holes were dug in such a way as to protect the occupants both from the weather and enemy fire. The Burmese were also experts in the construction of abatis and stockades of bamboo and teak beams, formidable obstacles which defied even light artillery. Above their trenches they built observation platforms in trees and even placed small guns in them.[11]

The general in command of the Burmese army was Maha Bandula. In 1824, when war with the British had seemed likely, King Bagidaw had sent him to Arakan where the bulk of the army was concentrated. The capture of Rangoon, however, which took the Burmese by surprise, caused a change of strategy. After the generals sent to the Rangoon front had failed to keep Campbell pinned down there, Bandula was recalled from Arakan and ordered to drive the British into the sea. At the height of the rainy season he brought his army of 60,000 men down the Arakan coast, then over mountains and through uninhabited jungles infested with leeches and the anopheles mosquito, into Burma proper, a feat comparable with Hannibal's crossing of the Alps. When the monsoon died out, he formed his army in a wide semi-circle from the Kemmendine to the Pazungdaung River, and from behind well-constructed earthworks prepared to attack the town. The British decision to invade the delta during the rainy season was now seen to have been a terrible mistake, for disease had reduced the original force of 11,000 to a mere 4,000 of whom 1,300 were European troops and the rest sepoys. The Burmese were expert at the war of attrition: highly mobile, they were well-accustomed to fighting in jungle and muddy creek. On the water they used fireboats, structures of timber and bamboo set ablaze with petroleum (of which the Burmese had a plentiful supply), and so cunningly designed that they wrapped themselves around the bows of the British ships. The Mons of the delta, whom Campbell had hoped would fight against the Burmese, proved to be disappointing allies.

Thrice Bandula's attacks on Kemmendine were repulsed, and then, on 5 December, Campbell struck hard at his right wing and routed his troops. He jubilantly reported 'the total defeat' of Bandula, but he was over-sanguine: ten days later Bandula was able to fire a quarter of Rangoon and put a vastly superior force into the field against him at Kokine. There, however, near the site of the modern university of Rangoon, the British and Indian infantry stormed the entrenched positions of the Burmese, while the marine destroyed some 200 of their fireboats.

The action was decisive. Bandula fell back on Danubyu, a key fortress on a raised area of the delta, commanding the water route to the north and the vital road from Rangoon to Bassein. Campbell now prepared two columns to advance northwards to take the Burmese capital of Ava: one, which he commanded himself, was to march into the interior by road, the other under General Cotton was to go up river, while a reserve of 4,000 troops remained in Rangoon. Cotton reached Danubyu first and called upon Bandula to surrender. The Burmese general's reply was dignified: 'We are each fighting for his country, and you will find me as steady in defending mine, as you in maintaining the honour of yours. If you wish to see Danabew come as friends and I will shew it to you. If you come as enemies, land.'[12]

General Cotton landed, and was repulsed by Bandula's 15,000 troops.

On 25 March Campbell joined him, and a general attack was launched on 1 April. In the course of the heavy fighting which followed, Bandula was killed by a shell, and when his death was known, the Burmese army broke up and fled in confusion. Campbell pressed on to Prome, but there active operations had to cease for the onset of the rains, and the British were obliged to spend a second rainy season in cantonments, menaced by disease and hunger.

The Burmese court used the time in a feverish effort to prepare new forces, but when the fighting began again in January 1826 these were steadily driven back. There followed negotiations for peace which dragged on for another month before Ava accepted the stringent British terms for a cessation of hostilities. By the treaty of Yandabo, signed on 24 February 1826, Arakan, Assam and Tenasserim were ceded to the East India Company, and the Burmese King undertook not to interfere in Manipur, Cachar and Jainta. He also agreed to receive a British Resident at the Court of Ava, to pay a crore of rupees in indemnity and to conclude a commercial treaty. The British undertook to retire to Rangoon on the payment of the first instalment of the indemnity, and on payment of the second to retire from the delta, which promises they kept, although it soon became clear that the arrangement was unwise.

For Britain the cost of the first Anglo-Burmese war was £13,000,000, of which £1,000,000 was recovered from the Burmese in indemnity. In lives it cost 15,000 of the total of 40,000 troops employed, and of the first expedition alone, 3,115 of the 3,586 troops who landed at Rangoon died in Burma, though only 150 of them in battle.[13]

The first British Resident to be appointed to the Court of Ava under the terms of the Treaty of Yandabo was John Crawfurd, a distinguished oriental scholar[14] who had been Raffles's successor as Governor of Singapore. Crawfurd with an escort of European soldiers was conveyed to Ava on board the *Diana* in September 1826. Unfortunately by that time the British armies had withdrawn to Rangoon. This hasty withdrawal, which was explained by fears for the health of the troops, made it virtually impossible for Crawfurd to make any progress in negotiations with the court. The difficulty was that the Burmese were totally incapable of believing that the treaty was binding on them, or even that it had been signed at all, once the odious foreign soldiers had disappeared. This combination of child-like innocence and tenacity, which refused to accept that anything unpleasant had happened, was much more difficult to deal with than the most intransigent national spirit; the British were opposed not with steel but with treacle. The Court of Ava at once began to evade its obligations by wrangling over the precise meaning of the provisions of Yandabo, and by regarding the imposition of a British Resident as an intolerable national humiliation. Upon the unfortunate Crawfurd the court heaped every form of ceremonial slight and personal discomfiture. At his first audience, arranged for an ordinary *Kodaw* or 'beg-pardon' day, Crawfurd was obliged to put down his umbrella as a mark of respect to the palace, and walk the full length of its eastern wall before he was admitted. Furious at such treatment, he refused to make the customary *shikho* to the palace or to remove his shoes when he entered the Council Chamber, whereupon he was left to cool his heels for two hours and a half. When finally he was allowed to present his official gifts to the King, an official read out an address of submission for him, begging forgiveness for his past offences.[15] It was hardly an auspicious beginning, and the situation did not improve thereafter. Not until November, after prolonged and tortuous haggling, was Crawfurd able to conclude the trade treaty provided for at Yandabo, for the Burmese persisted in the demand that it should not be signed while the British troops remained in Rangoon. In the end Crawfurd's original draft was reduced down to four clauses of little value, and even worse, the Burmese showed every disposition to re-negotiate the frontier stipulations of the treaty of Yandabo itself.

Crawfurd, 'rendered weary, hopeless and disgusted by the arrogance and impracticability of the Burmese ministers,'[16] at last returned to Calcutta and gave his opinion that it would not be practical to appoint a permanent Resident. This advice was not welcomed by the Supreme Government in Bengal, who had come to the opposite conclusion. In 1829 they decided to try again, and their choice fell upon a Major Burney of the 25th Bengal Native Infantry, a nephew of the novelist Fanny Burney. Burney, a tactful and intelligent man, was able to mollify some of the hostility and distrust of the King and his chief ministers, and by 1831 he had been given the unusual honour of elevation to the rank of *wundauk* or assistant *wungyi*. So friendly did the King become that he and Burney spent hours watching boat races and chatting about guns, painting and books. But Bagyidaw never forgot his humiliations at the hands of the British, and it was believed that they contributed largely to his mental breakdown after March 1831.

Burney, his usefulness now much diminished, wished to close down the uncomfortable Residency and carry on his work from Rangoon, but the Supreme Government would not hear of it. When, in July 1835, he returned to Ava after furlough, his position became very difficult, and much against his will, he was involved in the palace revolution whereby Bagyidaw's brother, the Tharrawaddy Prince, seized the throne.

It was an unpleasant Burmese custom to make the accession of a new king the occasion for a general massacre. Tharrawaddy imprisoned the former royal ministers, and eventually put five of them to death, but his record in this respect was merciful by comparison with the rest of his line, and it is clear that Burney's courageous protests deterred him from further bloodletting, though he was quite unable to understand the motives for such humanity. 'These hat-wearing people', he marvelled, 'cannot bear to see or hear of women being beaten or maltreated.' Thereafter relations between Tharrawaddy and the British Resident were strained, to say the least. In the end Burney withdrew from Ava and warned the Supreme Government that Tharrawaddy was listening to those of his ministers who believed that the territory lost at Yandabo might be recovered by force of arms.

Calcutta remained sceptical, and a successor to Burney was found in Colonel Richard Benson, another Bengal Army officer. Tharrawaddy, who had moved his court to Amarapura, was in no mood to receive another British Resident, and he simply arranged for his life to be made intolerable. After a few weeks Benson's health broke down; he reported thas his treatment was 'such as no English gentleman or more extensively no British subject ought to be exposed to' and he was allowed to return to Rangoon. Before he left Amarapura he handed over charge of the Residency to his assistant, Captain William McLeod, who with that fortitude which is sometimes vouchsafed to British subjects and English gentlemen in trying circumstances, clung on to the barely-habitable Residency until the monsoon broke and then, with the buildings in five feet of water, he too made for Rangoon. Thus ended, to Tharrawaddy's delight, the first attempt to establish a permanent British Resident at the Court of Burma.[17]

Tharrawaddy, like his brother and predecessor, eventually became insane, and in 1846 he died while being held prisoner by his sons. He was succeeded by his eldest son, Pagan Min, who celebrated his accession in the customary way by executing most of his relatives; thereafter his reign went from bad to worse. He spent most of his time in 'cock fighting, gambling and debauchery' and neglected royal business until the administration of the realm collapsed, while the local governors who owed him allegiance ruled as independent warlords.[18]

One such was Maung Ok, appointed Governor of the Province of Pegu in 1846, who determined to make his fortune at the expense of the merchants of Rangoon. In furtherance of this modest ambition he arrested the captains of two British merchant ships in 1851, a Mr. Sheppard, master of the barque *Monarch*, and a Mr. Lewis, master of the barque *Champion*. Both captains subsequently made complaints to Calcutta and submitted excessive claims for compensation. It was, as it happened, a particularly bad moment to choose to annoy the British, for Lord Dalhousie, the great Governor-General of India, had just brought the Sikh War to a satisfactory conclusion, and was ready to give Burma his full attention. The matter of the claims was in itself unimportant, but Dalhousie was convinced that to accept insults from the Burmese would reflect adversely on British prestige throughout the East. Therefore he decided to put the demand for reparation in such a form that the Burmese would treat it seriously.

Commodore Lambert, then in command of ships in the Hoogli River, was requested to steam to Rangoon in H.M.S. *Fox*, accompanied by the Company's vessels *Proserpine* and *Tenasserim*, and present a letter to the King demanding adequate compensation and the removal of the Governor of Pegu. Dalhousie did not want to provoke a war, and in what followed there was ample evidence of a similar disinclination on the part of the Burmese. Lambert's instructions were precise and limited: he was before all else to satisfy himself that the original depositions of Sheppard and Lewis were accurate. 'It is to be distinctly understood that no act of hostility is to be committed at present, though the reply of the Governor should be unfavourable, not until definite instructions regarding such hostilities shall be given by the Government of India.'[19]

At Rangoon, Lambert was treated with the studied insolence 'in which Burmese officials were so fatally expert',[20] but when his letter was sent directly to the King the reply was in the highest degree satisfactory: full redress was promised and a new Governor was appointed. Unfortunately, the new Governor disliked Europeans as heartily as his predecessor, and what then followed cannot be more succinctly recounted than in Dalhousie's own words. 'The Burmese continued their insolence and hostile tone, and finally the Commodore left Rangoon and established the blockade. This would have been all right; but before he went he thought proper, in disobedience of his orders, to make reprisals. He seized a ship belonging to the King which lay in the river. The Burmese manned the stockades and fired upon him. He anchored; sent the *Fox's* broadside into the stockade, where were 3,000 men, who disappeared to a man, and then destroyed their war boats and spiked and sank their guns. So all that fat is in the fire.'[21]

Years afterwards Dalhousie admitted an error of judgment in sending 'the combustible commodore' on so delicate a mission. 'It is easy to be wise after the fact. If I had the gift of prophecy I would not have employed Lambert to negotiate. But being only mortal, hearing of Lambert from everybody just what you say of him, recognizing the benefit of having negotiator and commander in one, if possible, and having to act through an officer of high rank not under my authority, I can't reproach myself with a fault in employing him though war did follow.'[22] Although the tedious negotiations which ensued showed plainly that neither the Government of India nor the Burmese court was eager to go to war for a trivial matter of compensation, Lambert's precipitate actions had created a situation to which Dalhousie believed he could not submit without risking irreparable damage to British prestige. For all his strictures on Lambert, carefully omitted from the documents in the subsequent Blue Book, Dalhousie took up a traditionally imperialist stance; in February an ultimatum was dispatched to the Burmese King, demanding compensation of ten lakhs of rupees 'to cover the cost already incurred by the Government of India in military preparations'.[23] By that time a pro-war party among the younger officials at the Burmese court had gained the upper hand. The ultimatum was allowed to expire on 1 April 1852 without a reply; on 12 April the main British expeditionary force sailed into Rangoon; a steamer flying the flag of truce went ahead to ask for an answer to Dalhousie's demands. The only reply was from the Burmese batteries on shore.

Dalhousie had studied the first Anglo-Burmese war in great detail, and he applied all his enormous administrative ability to avoid that war's mistakes. The task was complex. The organization of transport and supplies for a British expeditionary force was immensely difficult. The problem of command, where so many mutually jealous authorities were involved, was all but insuperable. But worse than these was the challenge of the climate and disease, and here Dalhousie's phenomenal diligence provided for the building of hospitals, the constant supply of fresh food and medical stores, and the allocation of steamers for the transport of casualties. No detail of preparation was overlooked that might minimize the cost of the war in lives or money.[24]

Yet from the beginning there were ominous signs of similarity to the first Anglo-Burmese war. To command the expedition Dalhousie had chosen Lieutenant-General Godwin, a veteran of the earlier campaign. The naval commander-in-chief was Rear-Admiral Austen, brother of Jane Austen. Both men were over seventy; Godwin was notoriously jealous of the Navy, and he was infuriated when Austen inconsiderately died at an early stage of the operations. His successor, Lambert, took precedence in rank, since he was commander-in-chief of H.M. Naval Forces in the Eastern Seas.

Godwin disapproved of Dalhousie's entire plan of campaign, and wished to conduct the war by exactly the same tactics that had been used in the first: 'nothing that was not done then can be done now—everything that was done then must be done over again.' With infinite tact and patience Dalhousie talked him round to his own ideas, but General Godwin was to remain difficult and erratic, and at critical moments was liable to revert to dilatory tactics without rational explanation, calling down upon himself not only the censure of the Governor-General but the derision of the press at home. *Punch* printed a cartoon of Godwin saying to a sailor who was knocking down a Burman, 'Oh dear, this is quite irregular, very irregular.'[25]

Nevertheless Dalhousie's plans were successful. Martaban, Rangoon and Bassein were taken without heavy losses and made defensible before the rainy season began. The hope was that these actions would induce King Pagan to accept the British terms, but months dragged on and no sign came from the Burmese court. Dalhousie came to the conclusion that the only way of arousing the Burmese would be to annex the whole province of Pegu. He submitted his plan of action, carefully documented and hedged about with alternatives, to the Government of Lord Aberdeen on 30 June 1852. The Government, of which Palmerston was a member, received it sympathetically. Godwin was now eager to move on to Amarapura, and the London press, which had been critical of the war to begin with, was now demanding that the Lord of the Universe should be humiliated by a peace dictated in his own capital.

Dalhousie knew that the Burmese would never agree to the formal cession of Pegu, and indeed history had shown that a treaty with the Burmese court was a decided liability since it was likely to involve the British Government in further disputes whenever its treaty rights were ignored. In August he went to Rangoon and recommended there that Pegu be annexed by unilateral proclamation. Godwin was given enough troops to continue the systematic occupation of the province; Prome was taken on 10 October and the town of Pegu on 22 November; on 20 December, by proclamation of the Governor-General, Pegu became a province of British Burma. It had at first been intended that the frontier should be established just north of Prome, but Prome proved to be very unhealthy for the troops. As it happened, the Irrawaddy valley to the north was renowned for its rich teak forests. The proclamation did not define the boundary, and in the absence of any reaction from the Burmese King, there was a strong temptation for the British to find healthier cantonments and include the rich Myédé forests within the annexed territory.

Meanwhile important developments had taken place at the Court of Ava. The King's half-brother Mindon Min, who was believed to be the leader of the peace party, fled to Shwebo, where his adherents began confused fighting with the royal forces. In February 1853 the senior *wungyi* of the Hlutdaw (the royal council) took Mindon's side and arrested the chief members of the government. Mindon, who had stayed aloof from the fighting, re-entered the capital and was hailed as king. One of his first acts was to release all the Europeans imprisoned at Amarapura, and to send two Italian priests as emissaries to the British to inform them of what had occurred.

Father Abbona and Father Domingo Tarolly, came down the Irrawaddy to find General Godwin and his forces halted at Myédé, some fifty miles north of Prome. Mindon Min had assumed that the British did not intend to occupy Pegu permanently, and when the emissaries returned with the news of the formal annexation of the province he was astounded. Two months later he sent a mission, led by the senior *wungyi*, to Prome to negotiate. The talks were fruitless. As a last resort, and to test the sincerity of the Burmese, Dalhousie authorized the British commissioners to give up the territory between Prome and Myédé if the Burmese would accept a treaty recognizing the annexation of Pegu. The *wungyi* refused, and the negotiations were broken off. The Myédé teak forests were retained by the British and, although no treaty was ever signed, hostilities were formally ended.[26]

'I am quite aware', wrote Dalhousie to a friend, 'that the annexation and occupation of Pegu without a treaty of peace is an anomalous policy in European eyes. I knew it would produce ridicule and outcry. But my duty is to do what is best for those I serve. . . . The war was an evil—any conquest was an evil; the occupation and halt in Pegu was an evil, but it was a less evil than going on to Ava, and therefore I adopted it. . . .'[27] *The Times* described the second Anglo-Burmese War as 'generally inglorious'. The campaign received relatively little attention in the press, and virtually none in Parliament. From one M.P., however, it received fervent condemnation. Richard Cobden, in curiously modern terms, attacked the whole concept of intervention in Indo-China on financial and strategic and, above all, on moral grounds. His pamphlet *How wars are got up in India: the origin of the Burmese war* was based on the published parliamentary papers, from which, he quite correctly alleged, important documents were omitted. And in letters to the Rev. H. Richards, secretary to the Peace Society, he described the bulletins of General Godwin as 'worthy of Bombastion Furiose himself—*when one compares the talk with the results.*' He had been assured by an East Indian director that the war was totally unnecessary: it had all been Lambert's fault. 'But nobody of any authority will publicly disavow the acts of those fighting men—*esprit de corps,* the spirit of nationality, and the great social sway of the military class all tend to sweep us more and more into the martial vortex. If God really rules this earth (as I solemnly believe he does) upon the principle of a self-acting retributive justice, then British doings in India and China will involve a serious reckoning with us on our children. And assuredly the day will come.'[28] But it had not come yet, and such views were then as out of fashion as today they would be in. The sober truth was that the war had cost the British tax-payer £1,000,000, and had been fought over a claim for less than £1,000.

3

THE GOLDEN DREAM

Mindon Min, the prince who now ascended the Burmese throne, was a man of exceptional character and ability. The son of one of Tharrawaddy's minor wives, he had been for many years a Buddhist monk, was devoutly religious, gentle in manner and opposed to bloodshed. Sir Henry Yule found him 'a man of conscience and principle' and thought that he had 'a good intelligent face'. 'There can be no doubt of his personal popularity,' Yule wrote, 'The people speak in terms of admiration of his good qualities and uniformly and with apparent sincerity, declare that they never had a king so just and so beneficent.'[1]

There was at first scant sign of a dramatic improvement in Anglo-Burmese relations. Mindon refused absolutely to recognize the British annexation of Pegu province, and he apparently continued to hope that the British might be persuaded to restore to him all his lost provinces. This hope was particularly strong when Britain was faced with the successive crises of the Crimean War in 1854–56, the Indian Mutiny in 1857 and the Anglo-French War with China in 1858–60. But he made no attempt to exploit Britain's difficulties other than by diplomatic means, and during the Mutiny he resisted the advice of anti-British courtiers to attack Pegu by remarking 'We do not strike a friend when he is in distress.' Mindon knew well enough that his army could scarcely invade Lower Burma with much hope of success, and that the result was more likely to be the total extinction of his kingdom. He therefore based his hopes on establishing generous and friendly relations with the British.

The resulting *détente* also owed much to the character of the British officials with whom Mindon had to deal. Chief among these was Captain

Arthur Phayre, whom Dalhousie had appointed as Commissioner of Pegu in 1852. Although he was born and educated in England, Arthur Purves Phayre came from an Irish family: his paternal grandfather was Colonel Phayre of Killoughram Forest, Co. Wexford. His father, Richard Phayre, after service in the East India Company, married a daughter of Matthew Ridgeway, the London publisher, and settled in Shrewsbury. Phayre entered the Bengal Army at sixteen. Details of his early career are few; he was said to be of excessively modest and retiring disposition, and his promotion was slow. But he was a most reliable and conscientious officer, with scholarly tastes and a talent for administration. At forty, after long serivce in Arakan, he was an authority on Burmese history and antiquities. Dalhousie was sufficiently impressed by his qualities to select him as commissioner over the head of his superior, Colonel Bogle, an experienced and well-qualified officer who was the obvious choice.[2]

Phayre's first duties had been to proclaim the annexation of Pegu, and to handle the subsequent unfruitful negotiations over Myédé. In dealing with Mindon, Dalhousie and Phayre now had a stroke of immense good fortune. The King was a man of humane instincts, who spared even the life of his rival Pagan Min, and, as we have already seen, one of his first actions had been to release all the European traders whom Pagan had imprisoned in Amarapura at the outset of the war. Among them was a Scottish trader in piece goods called Thomas Spears, who had arrived at Prome in June 1852 and impressed Godwin with his first-hand account of the situation in Amarapura. Spears, a native of Kirkcaldy, had spent many years in Burma and had a Burmese wife, Ma Cho. He made his livelihood by selling to the Burmese a special kind of silk which he imported from Europe. In January 1852 he had been arrested, placed in irons, and confined in jail with the other European residents of Amarapura. His merchandise was confiscated, and only the devotion of his servants had saved him from starvation. After Mindon's successful rebellion, however, he had been set free, and his goods had been restored to him. Mindon, on hearing that he intended to return to Calcutta, summoned him to Shwebo, and entrusted him with the terms of peace he wished to send to Phayre. Phayre rejected the proposals, but thought very well of Spears, and recommended to Dalhousie that he should be employed as an unofficial British agent in Amarapura. The Governor-General hesitated, foreseeing all manner of diplomatic complications, but finally agreed. Spears was to be paid 250 rupees per month; if he wrote two newsletters each month, and his intelligence was found to be 'early, full and correct', he was to receive 400 rupees. These instructions Spears carried out faithfully until he left for home in 1861.[3]

Spears returned to Amarapura in December 1853 and told Mindon of his new employment. Mindon was delighted to have a channel to convey his thoughts to the British, and he embarrassed Spears more than once by treating him as a properly accredited ambassador. Dalhousie was equally pleased: 'we have apparently found a very safe and sensible and judicious correspondent.'[4] Spears was much more than an intelligence agent; and ultimately the whole of the diplomatic correspondence between the Court of Ava and the Governor-General passed through his hands.

Through Spears it was possible to arrange for the exchange of missions between Calcutta and Amarapura. Dalhousie liberally entertained a party of Burmese ministers in 1854, and in the following year Phayre headed an embassy in the grand manner to Mindon's court. Each member of this mission was an expert on one or more fields of knowledge: the task of Dr. John Forsyth was to collect information on the climate and natural products of Upper Burma; Major Grant Allan was to concern himself with all military questions and 'the route to the capital'; Captain Rennie was to investigate changes in the course of the Irrawaddy since 1826; and Professor Oldham, of the Indian Geological Survey, was to assess the mineral resources of the area. The party also included an artist, Mr. Colesworthy Grant, and a pioneer photographer, with the improbable name of Linnaeus Tripe. The secretary, Sir Henry Yule, was a brilliant oriental scholar, and his account of the mission is a document of great historical interest.[5]

For two months the mission was lavishly entertained by Mindon. Elephants, richly caparisoned, carried Phayre and his companions to the palace for an audience of the King. Splendid in uniforms and epaulettes, but without their shoes, the envoys squatted on the floor until Mindon appeared high above them on a magnificent gilded throne, accompanied by his chief queen, and regarding them intently through opera-glasses. Phayre did not succeed in persuading Mindon to a treaty, but the mission brought back a rich harvest of information about Upper Burma, and Dalhousie considered it a success.

It was not a coincidence that a major objective of the 1855 mission was to gather technical information. Burma had become important to British commercial interests, not so much for its own natural resources, as yet

1. The first Marquis of Dufferin and Ava

2. Hariot, Lady Dufferin

3. General Sir George Stuart White, V.C.

4. Lord Randolph Churchill

not fully known, but as a possible means of opening up trade with Western China. The commercial potential of such a trade was thought to be vast, and this golden dream was to possess the thoughts of British chambers of commerce, and largely to influence British policy in Burma, for a very long time to come. The volume of trade between China and Burma had been considerable in the first half of the nineteenth century. By river and caravan route, Chinese silk, gold leaf and tea were traded for Burmese cotton, salt and rubies. This trade was abruptly halted in 1855, when the Panthays, a Sunni Moslem sect in Yunnan province, began a rebellion against Manchu authority and virtually established their own state. The new state was harassed by the hill tribes, principally Shans and Chinese encouraged by Peking, and the trade routes to Burma were closed.

The British knew remarkably little about Upper Burma, although earlier in the century intrepid individuals like Dr. Richardson and Lieutenant W. C. McLeod had made pioneer exploring journeys to the Chinese frontier.[6] The prospect of opening a 'back door' into Western China now provided a new incentive to exploration, and various routes for connecting Rangoon to China had been enthusiastically proposed. Their advocates, receiving insufficient encouragement in official circles, turned for support to the chambers of commerce in Britain, which in turn petitioned the India Office.

Phayre was not opposed to the principle of opening up trade with China, but he had a better knowledge of the obstacles, both geographical and diplomatic, to be encountered, and he tended to treat the commercial interests with some coolness. His Deputy Commissioner, Albert Fytche, however, was an enthusiast for trade with China. Fytche, who was a cousin of Lord Tennyson and a descendant of the Elizabethan Ralph Fitch, believed that the Panthay rebellion was an unrivalled opportunity for British merchants to intervene in Sino-Burmese trade.[7] Spears, far off in Amarapura, had his own scheme, which was to open up trade with Yunnan by caravan route through the town of Bhamo on the Burmese frontier. Spears had seen the Chinese caravans arriving in Bhamo, and he was a pioneer in drawing attention to its commercial importance.

In 1860 Dalhousie had sent a Mr. Temple and a Colonel Bruce to discuss with Phayre the administrative and commercial problems of British Burma, and their report, subsequently published by the House of Commons, became the basis of British commercial policy.[8] It strongly urged the use of the Irrawaddy as the main route to China, and the creation of a flotilla of steamships to provide transport for freight and passengers. This idea won the warm approval of Phayre, who suggested that an agreement between the Government and a private company would reduce running costs. Tenders were invited for the project, and the contract eventually went to the firm of Todd Finlay which had branches in Moulmein and Rangoon. A small company was formed to take over the Government's steamers in 1863, and in 1868 it was reorganized as the Irrawaddy Flotilla Company.[9]

King Mindon had meanwhile built for himself a new capital at Mandalay, a few miles north of Amarapura. In this, the *Shwemyo*, or Golden City, he had constructed a magnificent palace far enough from the river to escape the sound of the Flotilla Company steamers' whistles and 'their paddles chunkin' from Rangoon to Mandalay'. A great square was constructed to guard the inner city and the palace, with walls of red brick one and a quarter miles long and a surrounding moat seventy-five yards wide on which sailed the royal state barges. At its centre stood the palace, built in teak richly ornamented with vermilion and gold. Twelve years later Mindon had the text of the Buddhist scriptures engraved on 739 separate marble slabs and enshrined them in a forest of pagodas called the *Kuthodaw*, or Royal Merit. He achieved his dearest ambition by convening at Mandalay the Fifth Buddhist Council, at which it was decided to place a new *hti* (golden umbrella), set with jewels worth £62,000, on the spire of the Shwe Dagon Pagoda in Rangoon. The British allowed this ceremony, which had strong nationalist overtones, on the understanding that Mindon should not be present. The Sixth Buddhist Council was held in 1954.

It was to Mindon's new capital that Phayre travelled in November 1862 to sign a commercial treaty which allowed British traders to operate along the entire length of the Irrawaddy, and the Burmese to trade freely in Lower Burma. This concession was of the utmost importance, for it meant that the road to China was now open. Mindon also agreed that Phayre should send a joint survey-mission to explore the caravan route through Bhamo to Yunnan, and that he should appoint a British Resident at Mandalay. This step was made necessary when Spears, much to the regret of both Mindon and Phayre, decided to go to Europe on business in 1861, after settling his family in Rangoon.

In his place Phayre appointed as political agent, Dr. Clement Williams, an army surgeon, who was destined to add considerably to British knowledge of the upper reaches of the Irrawaddy beyond Mandalay. Williams was a man of many gifts, who while on leave in Mandalay in 1860 had acquired a phenomenal influence at the Burmese court by performing successful operations for cataract. The fact that he was also a student of Burmese literature and spoke Burmese well further enhanced Mindon's regard for him. He played an important part in the treaty negotiations of 1862.

Williams had made a special study of trade routes between Burma and China, and when rumours began to circulate in British Burma that the French had become interested in trade routes into Yunnan, Phayre agreed to his proposition for an expedition to Bhamo, and thence into China. Without Williams's special relationship to Mindon, the expedition would scarcely have been feasible, and, even so, it was necessary to proceed with caution. Williams suggested to Mindon that he should inspect the tea plantations in the Upper Myitnge area, and assess what they might contribute to the royal treasury. This ingenious proposal was accepted by Mindon although he was perfectly well aware of Williams's true objectives. He allowed the doctor to go to the tea plantations, but permission for an expedition to Bhamo was withheld until Phayre had left Mandalay.

Finally, on 24 January 1863 Williams set out for Bhamo with a royal licence and in one of the King's boats. At Bhamo the Burmese governor provided him with a house, but warned him that cross-frontier trade was impracticable for the present because of the activities of Kachin bandits. The Chinese merchants whom he interviewed were equally pessimistic on account of the Panthay rebellion still raging in China. Nevertheless, the longer Williams remained at Bhamo, the more convinced he became that the Irrawaddy route had a golden future. While Williams talked to merchants in the town, his Indian assistant Raj Singh explored the surrounding villages, talking to Kachins and Shans, and gathering valuable information which formed the basis for later maps of the region. Williams very much wanted to travel on overland, but Mindon's licence allowed him to go only as far as Bhamo. In vain he sent Raj Singh to plead for an extra pass; Mindon's son had just rebelled against him, in the traditional way, but had been forced to escape into British Burma, and the King wanted Williams at Mandalay. His reply was 'go and tell Williams I will give him permission to go anywhere next time, but now I want him here immediately. There is business and he must come down'.

So Williams returned to Mandalay, but without giving up his plans. He had made the important discovery that river steamers could go farther north than Bhamo, and he once more persuaded Mindon to allow him to go up to Bhamo to continue his explorations. But his licence expressly forbade him to travel outside Bhamo itself. He made several further attempts to obtain this permission in 1864, but each time he was told that it would not be convenient, and he never reached China. In January 1865 Williams was succeeded as political agent by Colonel Edward Sladen, and he was instructed to resume his Army duties. Rather than do so he left the Army, and, because of his special knowledge and experience, the Irrawaddy Flotilla Company immediately offered him a post as their Mandalay agent. In this capacity he was free to devote himself wholeheartedly to exploring the routes between Bhamo and Western China.[10]

Sladen, the official British representative, had barely time to establish himself in Mandalay when he was involved in a major crisis. On 2 August 1866, while a session of the Hlutdaw was being held in the summer palace at Mandalay, two of Mindon's sons broke in with thirty armed followers and slew the King's brother, the *Einshemin*, or heir apparent, who was presiding. One of the ministers and the two princes next in succession were also killed, but the rebels failed to capture Mindon who was three miles away in a summer residence. The King managed to reach the palace, where he withstood a night-long seige, and rallied the army which remained firmly loyal to him.

Sladen, who was present in the Hlutdaw when the murders took place, escaped from the building and managed to reach the British Residency, from which for the next seven days he worked to secure the safety of Mandalay's European residents. When Mindon warned him that he could not guarantee that they would not be harmed, Sladen assembled them, with such belongings as they could gather together, on board a British steamer lying in the river. Mindon's officers had commandeered the vessel to use against the rebels, and Sladen had the greatest difficulty in getting it safely away.

The rebellion was suppressed, and the rebel princes, seizing one of the King's steamers, also made their way down the Irrawaddy into British territory. Phayre promptly interned them in Rangoon, thereby earning Mindon's gratitude. Mindon was badly shaken by the insurrection, and for the rest of his reign he dared not take the risk of appointing another *Einshemin*, an omission which was to have unfortunate consequences.[11]

Phayre retired as Chief Commissioner in 1867 and was succeeded by Fytche, who negotiated a new, and much more effective, commercial treaty with Mindon. By its terms the Irrawaddy Flotilla Company's steamers began to ply regularly from Rangoon to Mandalay in 1868, and in the following year to Bhamo. The treaty also provided for a British political agent to be stationed at Bhamo. Fytche had now been entirely won over to the Irrawaddy route in preference to its chief rival, the 'Sprye' overland route to China. This was a plan, advocated by Captain Richard Sprye and his son, for a railway through the Shan States to Kengtung. Fytche gave permission for Williams's diary and Raj Singh's maps to be published in order to facilitate the establishment of permanent steam traffic on the Upper Irrawaddy, and supporters of the Sprye route now accused the authorities of preparing the way for the annexation of Upper Burma.

As soon as the 1867 treaty had been signed, Sladen set out for Bhamo with ambitious plans to survey the area to the north. Mindon's cooperation had been secured, but some of his ministers, and the Chinese merchants in Mandalay, were deeply suspicious of the venture. Sladen's expedition was partially financed by commercial interests in Rangoon, and he was really acting in a dual capacity, as the British political agent and as the unofficial representative of the businessmen in Lower Burma. The expedition left Mandalay on 13 January 1868 on board a steamer provided by the King, and in eight days reached Bhamo 'without any difficulty whatever'.[12]

On arrival, however, Sladen learned that the governor had been defeated and killed by Kachin bandits, and the headmen professed ignorance of any orders from Mandalay about the expedition. It was merely the beginning of many frustrations for Sladen. He was virtually immobilized for a month in Bhamo until a new governor was appointed and permission given for the expedition to continue its way. It was clear that the Burmese authorities were not anxious that Sladen should go farther north, while the Chinese merchants had tried to frighten him with stories of bandits, especially the exploits of one Li Hsieh-tai. Suspecting that the Chinese were in league with Li Hsieh-tai, Sladen sent scouts to the Moslem Panthay governor at Momein, and received most heartening news in return. The governor had taken the field against the bandits and defeated them. The Shans, who were independent of the King of Burma, were delighted to be freed of the attacks by the Chinese freebooters, and sent a deputation to rendezvous with Sladen, and conducted his party safely through the whole of the Shan country as far as the Chinese border, where a Panthay escort met them and led them (past the now ruined stronghold of Li Hsieh-tai) to Momein.

There the Panthay governor welcomed him with hospitality, and showed enthusiasm for his proposals to reopen trade with Burma. Although Sladen would have liked to have gone on to Talifu, the headquarters of the Panthay Government, his achievement in reaching Momein was considerable. The three possible routes between Bhamo and Momein were thoroughly surveyed, and a great amount of information about the whole area was collected. Sladen ran into difficulties on the return journey, but reached Bhamo safely on 5 September. He brought with him some thirty-one Kachin chiefs and their followers, who swore to provide safe-conduct for all traders crossing the hill ranges which they controlled.[13]

Sladen's mission to Momein established the importance of Bhamo in British thinking about Sino-Burmese trade, and the route received further support in books published by members of the expedition, the scientist Dr. Anderson and the commercial agent Captain Bowers. Control of Bhamo was now held to be essential for the development of the trade, and Sladen thus seemed to prepare the way for British intervention in Mindon's kingdom. Sladen himself admitted that 'what Burmah has always dreaded is that British interests would not be confined to British possessions but that contingencies might arise which would give the foreigner the right of extending his influence to Upper Burma, and to a point above and beyond the limits of the present Burmese capital.'[14]

Sladen's success in reaching Momein had depended on his winning over the Kachin and Shan chiefs, and he was prepared to advance his purpose by exploiting their traditional hostility to the Burmese. Thereafter Mindon regarded him with some suspicion, and on at least one occasion he compared him unfavourably to Phayre, of whom he declared that he had never heard anyone speak ill.[15] It was part of Sladen's plan that the British agent at Bhamo should have several engineers and surveyors on his staff, whose function would be to plan the road or railway which would eventually link the Irrawaddy with Momein or some point beyond it in Yunnan.

In March 1869, Captain G. A. Strover of the Madras Staff Corps was appointed as Sladen's assistant and sent to Bhamo. The enterprising Strover took with him some of the Rangoon traders and their wares, and dispatched missions to thirty-nine of the neighbouring chieftains. He also persuaded the Irrawaddy Flotilla Company to make a weekly run to Mandalay, and a monthly one to Bhamo, in return for a government subsidy. Secretly, Strover re-established contact with Momein, and even supplied the Panthays with arms. In this he was following the example of Sladen, who was sympathetic to the Panthay rebellion, but the policy was a dangerous one, for it conflicted with the wider aims of British policy toward China. In Momein Sladen had even gone so far as to suggest that Britain's friendly relations with Peking might be utilized in 'bringing about a reconciliation of contending interest in Yunnan', but Fytche, in exchanging courtesies with the Panthay governor, took care to explain that he could not help him either with arms or men in the Panthay war of independence.[16] Fytche's caution was vindicated when the Panthay state collapsed in 1873.

Only Mindon's steadfast determination to maintain good relations with the British prevented an open dispute over these manoeuvres, which the King could not regard as other than menacing the independence and sovereignty of his country. Increasingly, throughout the 1860s, the powerful commercial interests established in Rangoon and Calcutta, and their allies in London and Glasgow, were bringing political pressure to bear on the Government of India, advocating that it assume virtual control of Burma's foreign relations, and even hinting at the desirability of annexing Upper Burma, should a suitable pretext be presented. It was precisely because he appreciated this that Mindon patiently endeavoured to maintain good relations with the British officials. The Indian authorities were not disposed to take the same view as the chambers of commerce, but events outside Burma were not moving in Mindon's favour, for the British now had a colonial rival in Indo-China. Sladen's mission had been in part a response to the successful French Lagrée-Garnier expedition which had ascended the valley of the Mekong into Yunnan in 1867–68. Lagrée and Garnier found that the Mekong River was unnavigable, but that the Red River Valley leading into Yunnan through Tonkin (now North Vietnam) offered a much better prospect for trade. In the last years of the Second Empire, Louis Napoleon was too deeply involved elsewhere to pursue an active policy in Indo-China, but after the Franco-Prussian War, France turned increasingly to the East to seek compensation for the losses and humiliation suffered in Europe. The interest which she now began to take in trade with Yunnan aroused British suspicion, and a close watch was kept on French subjects travelling through Upper Burma.

The situation had ominous possibilities for the court in Mandalay. On the one hand, Mindon was anxious to keep on good terms with the British; on the other, he resented intensely the British refusal to allow him to communicate with London except through the Viceroy and Government of India, which implied that he was not regarded by the British as head of an equal sovereign state, and there was an obvious temptation for him to enter into negotiations with the French, Italians and even the Americans, all of whom were taking an interest in Upper Burma.

Mindon's first moves were designed to circumvent the Indian Government in communicating with London. He wrote to Queen Victoria and received a friendly, though unduly delayed, reply in which the Queen said that it would be a source of great satisfaction to her to receive tidings of the welfare of Mindon and his people. The letter ended:

'Hoping that you may long be spared to govern the country committed to your care by the Almighty Disposer of events.

I am, Your Majesty's sincere Friend,

VICTORIA R.'[17]

Encouraged by such greetings, Mindon now decided to send a mission to England, led by his most experienced minister, the Kinwun Mingyi, in order to establish direct relations with the British Crown. Anxious to observe protocol in every respect, he requested his ministers to consult Major McMahon, the political agent at Mandalay, on the correct form of address to the Queen. This apparently harmless approach brought down upon McMahon's head the wrath of Fytche, who accused him of having shown a 'strange ignorance and want of tact'. McMahon vigorously defended himself and absolved the Burmese of any intention to by-pass the Indian Viceroy, but Fytche was convinced that this was their motive, and he warned the Kinwun Mingyi that in England the mission might be confined to matters of ceremony and that no diplomatic discussions would be allowed to take place except through the channel of the Government of India.[18]

It was hardly surprising, therefore, that the Burmese ministers twisted the lion's tail a little by holding diplomatic discussions with other powers *en route*. The mission travelled by the new Suez Canal to Cairo, where they took time to look at the Pyramids, and then to Rome. The King of Italy received them with elaborate ceremony and they were lavishly entertained before leaving for Paris and London. In June 1872 they were received in London by the Queen, but cold-shouldered by the Foreign Office, and their entertainment was left to the chambers of commerce. In September they travelled to Scotland, and in October to Ireland, where they visited Dublin and were taken to Killarney. The speeches were much concerned with the great problem of the hour, how to link Burma to the El Dorado of Yunnan, but on 21 August 1872, in reply to the welcome extended by the Liverpool Chamber of Commerce, the Kinwun Mingyi overtly referred to the question of the mission's status.[19] 'Hitherto in affairs of state we have had to deal only with the Viceroy of India. Now the countries have become more close with the emergence of the telegraph, railways and steamers, the time, we consider, has come when our two countries should have more direct relations. Our relations with the Government of India have been cordial, but as you are doubtless aware there is a difference between dealing through agents and direct dealing between principals.'[20]

In Paris, to which they returned, the mission refused the offer of the British ambassador to present them to the French authorities. They sent Mindon reports of all the countries they had visited, and signed commercial treaties, of a fairly innocuous kind, with both Italy and France. Clearly Mindon was making a strong diplomatic effort to establish that independent Burma was more than a British protectorate; but 'the emergence of the telegraph, railways and steamers' to which the Kinwun Mingyi had alluded were daily increasing British influence in his kingdom. Then in 1873, two events occurred which helped to bring official thinking over to the side of the chambers of commerce. A French adventurer called Dupuis, who was interested in the Red River trade route to China, managed to persuade the Governor of Cochin-China to send a small French force into Tonkin and seize Hanoi. The French Government swiftly withdrew from this entanglement, but their interest in Tonkin did not cease. The implications of the incident were clear enough in British eyes.

Simultaneously, the Panthay rebellion was finally suppressed, and the authority of Peking re-established at Talifu. The Chinese were known to be favourable to reopening the trade routes to Burma. Chinese caravans soon began to reappear at Bhamo, and the Flotilla Company increased the frequency of its steamer service to one a fortnight. The businessmen now used the argument of potential French competition for the China trade to stimulate the authorities into some further action. The Chief Commissioner for British Burma urged the Viceroy to pay increased attention to the projects 'which have so long existed to reach the Western provinces of China through Burma' and suggested a joint British-Burmese mission to Yunnan.

In 1874 Lord Salisbury, who as Lord Cranborne had agreed to the Sladen mission in 1867, returned to the India Office, and authorized the sending of a similar but more ambitious survey expedition led by Colonel Horace Browne. Browne, who spoke Burmese well, had been with Phayre on the missions to Mandalay in 1859 and 1862, and had a deep interest in exploring the mountainous *terra incognita* to the north-east of Mandalay. Mindon, however, was not anxious to expose the feebleness of his authority over the Shan States and persuaded the British to agree to the much more accessible Bhamo route. In every other way Mindon was most co-operative, and the *Myowun* (town governor) of Bhamo levied a house tax to pay for the escort to the Chinese border. Before Mindon's support for the expedition had been sought, the Foreign Office had obtained the Chinese Government's agreement to allow A. J. Margary, a British consul at Shanghai, to make the journey westward across China to join up with Browne's party at the frontier. Margary achieved this spectacular feat, the first European since Marco Polo to do so, and met Browne just north of Bhamo. Then, over-confidently, he went ahead of the armed escort back towards China. On 21 February 1875, he was murdered by Chinese soldiers at a point just short of the frontier. Next day several thousand Chinese ambushed and tried to annihilate Browne's small force of sixteen Sikhs and their Burmese escort. They extricated themselves with the help of well-paid Kachins and struggled back to Bhamo. The mission had failed, but the murder of Margary elevated it to the status of a serious international incident, and gave it a renown which has overshadowed the earlier and more successful Sladen mission.[21]

In spite of Mandalay's co-operation in the Browne expedition, relations between Britain and Burma sharply deteriorated after 1875. It was hardly surprising, for commercial pressures and the fear of French rivalry led the British to negotiate with those subject or tributary peoples —the Shans, Kachins and Karens—who were only too prone to rebellion as it was. Mindon felt his authority being steadily eroded in what was left of his country: his candid assurance to the British authorities that he would never fight against them scarcely inhibited them from interfering in Upper Burma, and sooner or later he was bound to reach the point of balance between that pacific relationship and the national pride of his ministers and his people. His support to the Browne mission had given the Indian Government no cause for complaint, and he could truthfully say that he had set no-one against the British as Sladen had set Kachin and Karen against him.[22]

The diplomatic breaking point came over a matter of shoes. In 1875 Sir Douglas Forsyth, the Chief Commissioner for British Burma, went to Mandalay to discuss with Mindon the disputed question of Karenni independence, and, following the Burmese ceremonial custom which had been accepted by British envoys since the eighteenth century, removed his shoes before entering the palace. But this ordinary diplomatic courtesy suddenly was held by the Government of India and the Foreign Office to be no longer consonant with the dignity of British representatives. Mindon was informed that in future he would have to receive British officers in the same manner in which his officers were received by the Viceroy. Mindon not surprisingly refused to change Burmese ceremonial in response to such an ultimatum: Mr. Shaw, the British representative in Mandalay, was solemnly instructed not to remove his shoes when seeking an audience of the King, and consequently was barred henceforth from the palace. The official diplomatic links with Mandalay were broken, and there was now no Thomas Spears to repair them. This was the state of affairs when, in October 1878, King Mindon died.

4

THE LORD OF THE WHITE
ELEPHANTS

The events which followed Mindon's death might have been taken from
the grimmer kind of Eastern fairy tale. In theory the King chose his own
successor, for there was no rule of primogeniture, but since the murder
of the *Einshemin* in 1866 Mindon had not dared to appoint another, and
as he had forty-eight sons in all, the question of the succession was not
an easy one to resolve. On his deathbed Mindon had sent for the most
popular of his sons, the Nyaungyan Min, with the evident intention of
making him his heir, but before the prince arrived, Mindon's chief
queen, Sinpyumashin, who had borne him two daughters but no sons,
managed by an intrigue to seize control of the palace and its environs.
The Nyaungyan Min thought it prudent to stay out of her reach, and
with his younger brother, Nyaung Ok, sought refuge in the British Residency. They were then smuggled on board a British steamer and taken
to Rangoon; subsequently, for fear of assassination, they were removed
to Calcutta.

It was the custom for Burmese kings to marry their half-sisters, and
Sinpyumashin now proceeded to marry her second daughter Supayalat
to the Thibaw Min, who, in contrast to his older half-brothers, was almost unknown, and had no political support in the country. His mother
was a Shan princess whom Mindon had divorced for immorality: she
had become a nun, and Thibaw himself, from the age of seven, had lived
as a monk in a monastery within the palace grounds, gaining a reputation as a promising scholar, with kindly and gracious manners. He had
also been for a time the pupil of the Rev. Dr. Marks, the representative
of the Society for the Propagation of the Gospel, whom Mindon had
allowed to build a church in Mandalay. Sinpyumashin had shown kind-

ness to the disgraced wife, and she now had Thibaw placed upon the throne. The new King was therefore from the outset completely under the domination of his wife and mother-in-law, both of whom had strong personalities.

The experienced Kinwun Mingyi, who apparently supported the plot because he hoped that the accession of a weak king would enable him to introduce much-needed reforms, was soon pushed into the background, though he managed to stay in office and exercised considerable influence throughout Thibaw's reign and after it. The virtual ruler of Burma was the rapacious Queen Supayalat, assisted by one Taingda, the chief of the palace guard, and by the Hlethin Atwinwun, the master of the royal barges, who was married to Taingda's daughter.[1]

One of the conspirators' first moves was to arrest several hundred of the King's relatives, and in February 1879 Thibaw was persuaded to sanction the execution of four score of them, including eight of his prince-brothers. Such executions, which until Mindon's time had been almost a tradition at the accession of a new monarch, were carried out with gruesome ritual. Since it was taboo to shed royal blood, the victims were blindfolded and strangled or clubbed to death by criminals released from jail, and fortified with alcohol for the purpose. Then the bodies, alive or dead, were thrown into a large trench and the earth trampled down by elephants.[2]

Mr. Shaw, the British Resident, with great courage managed to prevent further slaughter by threatening to haul down the flag and break off relations with the Burmese court. When news of the massacre reached Rangoon, it produced a revulsion of horror. The businessmen urged the Secretary of State to settle pending differences with Mandalay and make Upper Burma a British protectorate. The time was not propitious, however, for the Viceroy, Lord Lytton, was preoccupied with Afghanistan, where things were going badly, and it would have been foolish to commit the resources of the Indian Empire on two fronts simultaneously. The India Office replied that procedure by ultimatum was inadvisable; and the Nyaungyan Min, who had returned to Rangoon in expectation of British intervention, was sent back to Calcutta.

The palace clique now became very alarmed at the British reaction, and fearing an immediate march on Mandalay, called up troops and sent them to the frontier. On the British side an armed steamer was kept in readiness to go to the aid of the Residency, though Shaw knew how vain such a gesture would be. Years later, Sir Charles Aitchison wrote to the

Viceroy's secretary: 'The correspondence with poor Mr Shaw in 1879 is very humiliating reading. He was regularly in the lion's den, and he used to beg that not a man should be sent to his help, as the first sight of a British uniform across the frontier would be the signal for his decapitation.'[3]

Shaw, who was ill with heart disease, died in June 1879, and was replaced by Colonel Browne, who reported encouragingly that the Kinwun Mingyi was ready to declare for the Nyaungyan Prince if he could do so safely, and the Queen Mother was contemplating an increase in personal insurance by marrying Supayalat's elder sister to Nyaungyan. Thibaw had sought escape from his remorse in alcohol; telegrams from Mandalay during the crisis reported that the King was 'still drinking' and he was henceforth portrayed in the British press as a hopeless gin-addict.[4]

That was not the impression he made on a German traveller, Dr. Joest, one of the few Europeans to be granted an audience at that time. He found the King a handsome youth, 'somewhat stout for his age, being only twenty-one', but otherwise the best-looking Burmese he had seen. 'According to the custom of the country, his hair was arranged in a big top-knot on the top of his head, surrounded by a narrow band of white muslin; his round face, which was almost white, made a very pleasant impression; his eyes are small and slightly almond-shaped; and with his full lips and small moustache he makes the impression of an indolent, blasé, perhaps rather sensual young man. Cruelty is stamped upon his features, but not intemperance.... He wore a close-fitting jacket of white satin, with long tight sleeves, two rows of diamond buttons, and his insignia, also in diamonds. In his ears and on his hands I perceived the glitter of precious stones. A silken *putso* in green and yellow stripes completed his apparel; his feet and legs were bare.... He neither smoked nor chewed tobacco, and I must repeat he impressed me sympathetically.'[5]

Britain's 'forbearance' with Thibaw in 1879 was largely dictated by the fact that she already had two wars on her hands, one against the Afghans and the other in Africa against Cetewayo and the Zulus. Both were going badly, and there was in addition a strong likelihood of trouble with the Boers. But relations between the Residency and the Burmese court remained very strained, for Thibaw adamantly refused to receive any Briton who came to the palace wearing shoes. In August Browne withdrew to Rangoon with some of his staff, leaving the Residency in the care of a *chargé d'affaires*, Mr. St. Barbe, who lived in a state of virtual siege. No one dared enter or leave the Residency and it was rumoured that Thibaw intended to massacre its inmates. On 7 September news came from Afghanistan of the murder of Sir Louis Cavagnari, the British Resident in Kabul, and his entire staff. St. Barbe was at once instructed to close down the Residency, and soon afterwards he and his colleagues left Mandalay without interference from the Burmese.

Thibaw indeed reacted with surprise and dismay. Why, he politely enquired, at a time of peace between 'these two great dominions' had the English political officer 'suddenly and precipitately quitted the Royal Gem City'? He sent envoys with gifts for the Viceroy and appealed to him to preserve the 'grand friendship'.[6] When the envoys reached the British frontier at Thayetmyo, however, they were detained there. The Commissioner asked them if they had authority to negotiate a new treaty, or express a desire for the return of the Resident. They replied that their purpose was simply to allay the uneasiness caused by the closing of the Residency, whereupon the Commissioner advised the Government of India that nothing was to be gained from negotiating with an embassy which had such vague instructions, and that to receive them would be regarded throughout Burma as a diplomatic victory for Thibaw.

The mission remained hopefully at Thayetmyo, but every pretext was found to prevent it travelling on to Calcutta. In vain did Thibaw invest it with power to negotiate a new treaty for trade, extradition and the exchange of diplomatic representatives. The Commissioner insisted upon the settlement of outstanding differences and the reception of a Resident at Mandalay with proper ceremonial. Neither side would yield on principle, and in May 1880 the embassy returned home. Lord Hartington, the Secretary of State, was doubtful of the wisdom of rejecting the Burmese overtures outright, but he accepted the advice of the Commissioner and the Viceroy.[7]

In 1880 Gladstone was returned to office at the head of a Liberal Government sternly resolved to avoid new imperialist entanglements, and the Burma question fell into the background, at least as far as London was concerned. The chief aim of official British policy now was to negotiate new commercial treaties with Upper Burma to supersede those of 1862 and 1867, which had never worked satisfactorily, and which, in any case, Thibaw showed little inclination to honour. Signs that he intended to renew the traditional policy of granting monopolies made a new treaty the more desirable. In 1882 Thibaw sent envoys to Calcutta, and the Viceroy, Lord Ripon, had high hopes of a friendly settlement.

Negotiations dragged on for months, and both sides made significant concessions, but in the end the ambassadors were suddenly recalled to Mandalay, at the behest, it was afterwards said, of the Queen's adviser, Taingda, an inveterate enemy of foreigners. 'We fear', wrote Ripon, 'that whilst the Burmese court remain in their present disposition there is little prospect of improving our treaty relations with them, and for the present our efforts must, in all probability, be limited to securing observance of existing treaties, and to the protection of British subjects visiting Upper Burmah.'[8]

Burma, with its congeries of races, had never been easy to govern and, once Mindon's strong hand had been removed, the authority of the central government rapidly declined. Corruption invaded the whole system of administration. Queen Supayalat and Taingda, promoted to the rank of *mingyi* in 1883, were greedy and ruthless. The latter often acted hand in hand with the lawless dacoits who roamed the King's territories looting the villages and killing and terrorizing the *myowuns*, or headmen. The dacoit leaders, self-styled *bos* ('colonels'), were sometimes popular figures, Robin Hoods who defended villagers' rights against oppressive royal officials, but often, too, they were hated and feared. Gradually the administrative system of Upper Burma was breaking down, despite the efforts of the Kinwun Mingyi to introduce progressive reforms. Much of the King's authority was passing into the hands of local warlords. A serious rebellion broke out in the Shan States in 1883; the Kachins invaded Burma in 1884, while Chinese freebooters first helped the Burmese to repulse them from Bhamo, and then sacked and burned the city themselves.

Queen Supayalat was universally considered to be the real culprit. Mr. Peter Camaratta, a Portuguese in the service of the Burmese court, secretly informed the British that since 1882 Supayalat had assumed absolute power and that the authority of the ministers was nominal. She even acted as the royal treasurer. 'Not a single payment, however small, can be paid without her order, not even an item of 20 rupees for repairs of a bridge or any public works. Repeated applications have been made by the ministers to the King and Queen for wages due to troops and foreigners in the royal service with no effect whatever, and hence the country is infested with dacoits and robbers, being unpaid soldiers of the Burmese Government, and most of the dacoits, when caught, declare that they have to share their spoil with the ministers.'

After the fall of Mandalay, some French nuns settled in the city gave

5. King Thibaw of Burma with Queen Supayalat and her sister. From a negative found in the palace at Mandalay.

6. Burmese dead at Minhla. The trees had been set on fire by the shells of the *Kathleen* and the *Irrawaddy*.

7. The Flotilla
advancing up
the Irrawaddy

Lady Dufferin a vivid description of Supayalat's domination of the King. 'They both lived in small back rooms, sitting all day side by side on the ground, and if he moved away she used to tell him to come back quickly. They seldom went about the Palace, and only appeared on state occasions in the large apartments. She was a very violent and passionate woman, governed entirely by impulse and caprice, thinking herself the very greatest person in all the world, and unable to conceive the possibility of misfortune or retribution falling upon her.' She had been surrounded by maids and eunuchs, and had a wonderful talent for keeping them employed, so that they were like ants always fetching or carrying, or in some way fulfilling her behests. Thibaw had a guard of women, who were relieved at stated hours like soldiers, but Supayalat 'took good care of him, and if he looked at another woman, woe betide that unfortunate creature'.

She had been cruel as well as capricious, and the nuns told Lady Dufferin that they had sat with her in one room while women were being beaten in the next, and that she and her Court were highly amused at their cries, and treated it all as an enjoyable fête. Supayalat liked the sisters and used to send constantly for them. 'Some days she made them translate to her all the French novels that could be found; other days she displayed her jewels—such diamonds and rubies! The nuns described dazzling heaps of them covering the floor. Other times she gave them commissions: they were to send to Paris, to Calcutta, to Rangoon, to get jewels and every other sort of thing that came into her head—watches without end, photograph albums, frames, and stuffs.' At first they were paid, but for the last two years Supayalat had given them nothing, and Lady Dufferin thought that the nuns had got themselves into rather a mess, as they had some large business transactions with her. They had also done a good deal of needlework for her, and once, when she decided that trousers made a good dress for women, they had set to work and trousered the whole Court. She had given great quantities of presents to people she liked, and one of her amusements on state occasions or fête days was to sit on the dais, with a great pile of money before her, and to call people up to take as much as they could carry in their two hands. She was fond of music, and would send for European ladies to come and play the piano to her, but they had to do so kneeling. A photographer was sent for sometimes, and was kept photographing the ladies of the Court all day long.[9]

Even more alarming in British eyes than the weakness and

incompetence of Thibaw's government was the reappearance after 1881 of French imperialism in Indo-China. From their first colony of Cochin-China, the area around Saigon, the French had gradually extended their influence to the kingdom of Annam, and then to Tonkin, which now forms the larger part of North Vietnam. Control of the land on either side of the Red River, which pointed like an arrow into China, promised them access to the coveted Yunnan trade. This in itself was enough to arouse suspicion, but the British Government was also concerned with the strategic implications of French colonial expansion. The French were establishing themselves in an area where Britain already had a considerable territorial interest, and the probable extension of French authority along the upper reaches of the Meking posed a threat, admittedly a distant one, to the safety of the Indian Empire.[10]

It has been argued that commercial greed was the cause of the third Anglo-Burmese War, and that the fear of France's gaining control of Upper Burma was merely the pretext, and not the motive, for intervention.[11] But, apart from the fact that it is not easy to distinguish between economic motives and the needs of imperial strategy—they were interdependent—the interests of the parties concerned were not completely coincident. The Government of India was sensitive to the prospect of French commercial gains in Upper Burma and to a lesser extent with the threat to India's security, but whereas the chambers of commerce wanted official backing for overland trade-routes into China, the authorities in Calcutta throughout favoured the Irrawaddy-Bhamo approach for military and strategic reasons, and had indeed prepared plans for sending troops up the Irrawaddy if war with Burma should come. The Foreign Office, on the other hand, thought of French expansion in Indo-China in terms of an increase in territorial and economic might by a European rival. And whereas Burma was considered the sphere of influence of the Government of India, the Foreign Office made it clear that relations with France and China were very much its concern. These differences were to become important later.

Suspicion of French intrigues in Upper Burma went back at least to the beginning of Mindon's reign, when the activities of a mysterious 'General D'Orgoni'* had aroused the anger of Dalhousie.[12] In 1873 the Count de Rochechouart had ratified in Mandalay the commercial treaty signed by the Kinwun Mingyi in Paris, but two secret proposals, that France proffer its good offices in any dispute between Burma and a third

* An anagram of his real name, which was apparently Girodon.

party, and that she provide officers to train Mindon's army, were subsequently repudiated in Paris.[13]

In 1882 France was involved in a small-scale war in Tonkin and Hanoi was once again taken. In Paris, however, the government was more cautious than the commanders in the field, and began treaty negotiations not only with the Emperor of Annam but with the Chinese, who claimed suzerainty of Tonkin. While these negotiations were going on, the French naval commander Henri Rivière renewed the offensive and was defeated and killed by Chinese and Annamite forces fighting alongside Chinese irregulars known as the 'Black Flags'. The popular demand that Rivière should be avenged led Jules Ferry, who became Prime Minister in February 1883, to pursue a forward policy in Tonkin and wage a full-scale war against China which lasted for two years. As the war continued, Ferry became convinced of the virtue of an active colonial policy, which he had not at first favoured, leading to the conquest of Indo-China, and its momentous consequences for France in the twentieth century.[14] Against this background, the intrigues of French agents in Upper Burma became a matter of urgent concern for the British authorities in Rangoon and Calcutta.

To make matters more acute, Thibaw in 1883 dispatched a mission to Europe, ostensibly for the purpose of assembling information about the industrial arts and sciences, but really in order to conclude a commercial treaty or alliance which would offset British influence in his kingdom. The mission was led by an *atwinwun*, an officer of the royal household; his companions, all of whom had been educated in Europe during Mindon's reign, spoke French and English. Accompanied by a M. de Trévelec they made straight for Paris and the Quai d'Orsay. At the time of the treaty negotiations in 1873 the French had refused to enter into an undertaking to supply arms to Burma; it was now suspected that the Burmese ministers would renew the request, and as a consequence the British ambassador, Lord Lyons, at once began diplomatic conversations on the subject with Ferry, who was Foreign Minister as well as *président du conseil*. 'I begged M. Jules Ferry', he reported, 'to bear in mind the very special importance of Burmah to Britain, and I added that I should be very particularly obliged if he would frankly make known to me anything further which might take place between the French Government and that country.'[15] Despite this request, Lyons was obliged to rely very much on second-hand sources for information about the mission in the months which followed, but he took every occasion to impress upon successive Foreign Ministers 'the peculiar relations between Burmah and British India and the strong objections of Her Majesty's Government to the conclusion of any agreement between Burmah and a Foreign Government containing stipulations beyond those of a purely commercial character.'[16]

From the beginning Ferry's replies were evasive. He assured Lyons that no agreement with Burma would be made at Paris, but when Lyons persisted, he gradually admitted that a treaty was being discussed for the exchange of diplomatic agents between the two countries. He pointed out that as Tonkin was in a very disturbed state, his government was not disposed to take any step which might facilitate the introduction of arms into that area. In July 1884 Lyons formally presented the British position in writing, and at this Ferry stated that it was intended to appoint a French Consul-General at Mandalay, and that it was very difficult to draw a clear line between what was political and what was commercial. He finally revealed that the Burmese wanted a full political alliance and facilities to purchase arms, and he gave Lyons a specific assurance that no such treaty would be signed.

Lyons was convinced that the Burmese 'with the astuteness of an oriental people' would deliberately try to introduce into their treaty some stipulation more or less incompatible with their relationship to India, but he also judged that France would hesitate to put herself in a position where the Burmese could appeal to her for help if they were in dispute with England. The Foreign Office therefore cautiously accepted Ferry's assurances as sincere. Again there was a discernible difference in outlook between the Foreign and India Offices, for Lord Kimberley, the Secretary of State for India, believed that the real danger lay in the establishment of French influence at Mandalay and the consequent prejudice to British commercial interests.[17]

Meanwhile rumours began to circulate in Paris, and soon found their way back to Calcutta and Rangoon. It was said that Thibaw had ceded to France the ruby mines of Mogok, and even the Shan States, and that a contract had been signed with an unknown Frenchman, granting him the right to work all the mines of Burma except two coalmines. Lyons did not take such rumours very seriously, but it later appeared that they contained some truth.[18]

While this was happening in Paris, there was a further deterioration in

Anglo-Burmese relations. Ever since 1881 an argument had been going on with the Court of Ava over the exact definition of the border with the British protected State of Manipur. The Burmese had declined to co-operate in a boundary commission appointed by Calcutta, and in 1884 they formally objected to the new boundary, and threatened to attack the Indian stations and pull down the boundary posts. The Chief Commissioner of Assam instructed the Maharaja of Manipur to resist any Burmese attack and promised him reinforcements. No attack was made, but the increasing anarchy in Upper Burma created a good deal of friction along the borders.

These events coincided with a renewed slaughter in Mandalay, this time of followers of the exiled princes. In Rangoon indignation boiled over. From the pulpit of the Anglican Cathedral Dr. Marks inveighed against the crimes of his former pupil. Money was collected and sent to the Mingyan Prince (Nyaung Ok), who was now living in French Pondicherry, and he was urged to lead a rebellion in Upper Burma. The French, however, regarding him as a useful card in their hand, kept a tight grasp on him.

On 11 October 1884, a meeting of nearly a thousand people, representing British, Indian and Chinese business interests, assembled in Rangoon Town Hall and passed the following resolutions:

'1. That the misgovernment in Upper Burma under King Theebaw, culminating in the recent massacres, entailed misery and distress on the inhabitants of the country.
2. That the immediate interference of H.M.G. was absolutely necessary, as the tranquillity and prosperity of British Burma and Upper Burma were intimately associated and bound up with each other.
3. That Upper Burma should be annexed, or failing that, that a protectorate should be established, with a Prince other than the present Ruler on the throne.'

Charles Bernard, the Chief Commissioner, forwarded the resolutions to the Government of India, but expressed his own clear dissent from the third. Bernard, a nephew of John Lawrence, was a humane and intelligent administrator, conscientious to a fault, and as knowledgeable about the Burmese as any European was likely to be. His view was that Britain had not the right, nor even at that moment a pretext, for annexing Upper Burma, and he adhered to this opinion through the months ahead. In a long and careful dispatch to the Viceroy he declared that if

Thibaw's Government 'transgressed British frontiers, invaded British allies, maltreated British subjects, broke treaties, continued to commit massacres, rejected British projects and refused redress, matters would be different'.[19] But things had not come to that pass. For the time being, the Government of India was disposed to take his advice. 'We have been urged', wrote Dufferin to Kimberley in March 1885, 'to annex Upper Burma or to dethrone the present King, and establish another ruler protected by us. These measures, however, do not appear to us to be justified by the existing state of affairs, and the commercial community have been so informed.'[20]

The situation changed with the arrival in Mandalay on 1 June 1885 of a French consul, M. Haas. Haas was a restless, ambitious man anxious to achieve results in a short time. Within a few weeks he had obtained from the Burmese a concession to build a railway from Mandalay to Toungoo to join up with the British line from Rangoon, then nearing completion. France would lend two and a half million pounds for this project, and a similar sum for the setting up of a currency-issuing National Bank; in return for these loans the French would assume management of the royal monopolies and take $7\frac{1}{2}$ per cent interest from river dues and oil royalties. To cover his activities, Haas urged Thibaw to improve relations with the British by agreeing to the return of a Resident, and to negotiate treaties with France, Germany and Italy. It was not bad advice, but Thibaw rejected it, while accepting the commercial agreements without hesitation.[21]

Even before Haas had obtained his concessions, however, the state of the diplomatic game had been altered by the vagaries of the democratic process in both France and Britain. By 1885 the French naval blockade had forced China to accept French terms for peace in Tonkin, but in March the French troops were thrown back from Lang-son, and the news caused a revulsion of public opinion against the costly adventures in Indo-China. Ferry's government was defeated, the Chamber of Deputies deciding by a majority of only one vote to hold on to Tonkin. In England in June Gladstone was defeated by a coalition of Conservatives and Irish Nationalists, and Lord Salisbury formed a caretaker government to hold office until an election could be held on the new household franchise enacted in 1884. Thus it happened that Britain acquired a government that was likely to pursue a 'forward' policy in imperial affairs at the very moment when France had decided to abandon such a policy. Salisbury gave the India Office to Lord Randolph Churchill, the son of the Duke of Marlborough, an able and extremely ambitious young politician who deeply distrusted French activities in Indo-China and turned a ready ear to the complaints of the chambers of commerce.

The full facts concerning the negotiations between Haas and the Burmese court, along with rumours of further French designs upon the teak forests and the Irrawaddy navigation, were communicated to Bernard by Mr. Andreino, the Italian consul at Mandalay and agent for the Irrawaddy Flotilla Company, a brave and resourceful man who disliked Haas and was jealous of his influence. It was perhaps from the same source that Bernard received a startling piece of intelligence in July 1885. A letter from Ferry to the Burmese Minister of Foreign Affairs, dated 15 January (a few days before the signing of the Franco-Burmese treaty) was seen and copied by a servant in the palace at Mandalay. One paragraph of the letter started: 'With respect to transport through the province of Tonquin to Burma of arms of various kinds, ammunition and military stores generally, amicable arrangements will be come to with the Burmese Government for the passage of the same when peace and order prevail in Tonquin, and the officers stationed there are satisfied that it is proper, and that there is no danger.' Bernard at once sent the copy to Dufferin, who telegraphed London that Bernard had received it 'from trustworthy sources' and was 'inclined to regard it as genuine'.[22]

On the face of it, this seemed to indicate that Ferry had deliberately misled the British ambassador in Paris, but as evidence it was tenuous. The British Government nevertheless made up its mind to warn France away from any thought of setting up a French protectorate in Upper Burma. Salisbury showed the letter to the French ambassador, M. Waddington, on 7 August. Waddington denied all knowledge of the concession and said he would discuss the matter with M. de Freycinet, Ferry's successor as Prime Minister. To the British ambassador in Paris, Salisbury wrote that H.M.G. could not 'acquiesce in the transfer to any person who was not a British subject, of control over any portion of the Burmese revenue, or of the prerogatives which . . . are usually vested in the Ruler of the country'. He was sure that the French Government was fully aware of the precautions necessary to prevent 'confusion arising in the affairs of semi-civilized dependent states', and Lyons was to take the first opportunity of speaking to M. de Freycinet in this sense. As a result of this diplomatic pressure the Freycinet Government eventually repudiated the activities of Haas in Mandalay, and he was recalled for having acted without authority.[23]

A year later, the French Consul-General in Indo-China told Dufferin at Simla that Ferry had had no intention of annexing Upper Burma, but that his plan had been 'to establish large French commercial interests at Mandalay, and to secure the political ascendency of France in the upper valley of the Irrawaddy, with a view to acquiring a position which would enable him to put pressure upon England, and thus obtain whatever advantages such a condition of things might procure'.[24] This was exactly what Britain desired to obviate, and the only safe way of doing so was to make Upper Burma a British protectorate. Sir Owen Burne, Lord Randolph's secretary, wrote to his opposite number in the Foreign Office: 'I consider all our diplomatic correspondence with France as so much waste paper. It does not put *any real* stop to a growing mischief, which ere long may get quite beyond our control. . . . I say unhesitatingly that we should now get any pretext to annex or make Burma into a protected State. King Theebaw's sins are many and great and I feel quite sure your able pen, aided by a few snarls from myself, could formulate a Bill of indictment against him that would make every old woman in London weep!'[25]

Thibaw himself was all too willing to provide the pretext. In August 1885 the Hlutdaw suddenly alleged that the Bombay-Burma Trading Corporation had fraudulently exported timber from Upper Burma without paying agreed royalties. The Corporation, whose headquarters were in Rangoon, had for years worked the Ningyan teak forests north of Toungoo by contract with the Burmese Government. The Hlutdaw gave an *ex parte* judgment that the Corporation had defrauded Thibaw of £73,333 and the foresters of £33,333. It fined the Corporation double the first amount, and ordered it to pay the second to the foresters; if the fine were not paid, in four monthly instalments, then the Corporation's timber would be seized.

The Corporation at once offered to produce its books and the foresters' acquittances, but the Hlutdaw refused to alter its decision. The British Government was informed, and Bernard was asked for his advice. He replied honestly that he had not sufficient information to give a definite opinion on whether or not money was owed to the Mandalay authorities. He had at once suggested arbitration, but the Hlutdaw refused absolutely to consider it, and he considered that, in any case, the fine was exorbitant and unjust. Subsequently he was able to make a full examination of the Corporation's accounts, and he found that the Hlut-daw's allegations were false, a conclusion which historians have since vindicated.[26] The charge seems to have originated partly from the corrupt dealings of one of Thibaw's local officials, and partly from the Hlut-daw's desire to clear the way for further concessions to the French. But in view of what the Burmese ministers must have known about the British attitude, the action was ill-timed and imprudent.

The chambers of commerce at once renewed their pressure. There was no disagreement about the necessity to take advantage of the Hlut-daw's demands, only about the nature of the action to be taken. The London Chamber of Commerce, supported by many others in the United Kingdom, petitioned Lord Randolph Churchill urging him to instruct the Government of India either to annex Upper Burma or to make it a protectorate with a sovereign under British control. They were soon able to congratulate him on his prompt and decisive action. On 22 October an ultimatum was sent by steamer to Mandalay, and a reply demanded by 10 November at the latest to the following requests: that Burma should allow the fine on the Bombay-Burma Trading Corporation to go to arbitration, that a British Resident should be received at Mandalay 'with proper guard (of honour) and a steamer for his personal protection', that he should have access to the King 'without submitting to any humiliating ceremony' and that Burma should in future regulate its external relations 'in accordance with the advice of the Government of India as is now done by the Amir of Afghanistan'. Significantly, the ultimatum also included a clause about the opening up of trade with China via Bhamo.[27]

At Mandalay, only the Kinwun Mingyi gave the ultimatum any serious consideration. He urged that a conciliatory reply should be drafted, and tried to reduce the Bombay-Burma fine, but Queen Supayalat and the Taingda Mingyi overruled him. At the eleventh hour, however, the Burmese did try to avert war. On 3 November Tann Giet, Thibaw's minister plenipotentiary in Paris, wrote to Lord Lyons:

'*M. l'ambassadeur,*

Je suis profondément convaincu que la situation critique qui existe actuellement entre l'Angleterre et la Birmanie n'est que le résultat d'un malentendu. . . .'

This misunderstanding he would be happy to try to remove by employing every means to find a solution satisfactory to both governments. To this end he was prepared to seek authorization to come to London and negotiate on the differences '*et éviter ainsi l'afflusion du sang*'.[28]

Two days later the Burmese Government replied formally to the ultimatum, accepting two of the major conditions. The Bombay-Burma Corporation could petition the King and he would see that foreign traders and merchants did not suffer hardship; and a British agent would be allowed to reside in Mandalay and come and go 'as in former times'. But the Court of Ava refused absolutely to give up its sovereignty by allowing the Government of India to regulate its external relations. 'Friendly relations with France, Italy and other States have been, are being, and will be maintained.'[29] It was a dignified and reasonable reply, but it was very definitely a rejection of the ultimatum. Thibaw had decided to fight.

5

THE OLD FLOTILLA

Long before the reply to the ultimatum was received, the Burma Field Force had been assembled and fully equipped, and was simply waiting for the signal to cross the frontier. On 22 October Dufferin wrote to M. E. Grant Duff, the Governor of Madras: 'At last the cup of Theebaw is full, and it looks very much as if we should have to go to war with him. Although I was aware that both the late and present Governments would not regard the establishment of our supreme influence in Burmah with disfavour, I had fully determined not to move in that direction unless compelled by circumstances, not only because I have already as much trouble on my hands as is sufficient for one man's attention, but I am naturally an enemy of annexation, war, and everything that can result in the loss of human life. . . .' The Mandalay authorities, however, had forced his hand. 'This being the case, we must bring them to reason; and as when once one has to move, half measures too often lead to bad results; with the consent of the Secretary of State, I have taken the bull by the horns, and have dispatched an ultimatum which, if not replied to in a proper manner, will be supported by the dispatch of ten thousand men up the Irrawaddy. We have thought it proper to give the Madras Army a chance, and with this view have chosen one of your officers to command the expedition, and the bulk of the troops will also be drawn from your kingdom. I am sure this will please you, and I have no doubt they will do credit to their Province.'[1]

There was, as it happened, an eminently suitable senior officer of the Madras Army who had recently commanded the Burma division, and had devoted a good deal of time to reconnaissance of the Upper Burma frontier. Major-General Sir Harry Prendergast, V.C., on whom the

Viceroy's choice fell, was, like so many of his fellow officers, of Anglo-Irish stock. His grandfather, Sir Jeffrey Prendergast, born at Clonmel in 1769, had entered the service of the East India Company and become a distinguished soldier; he was knighted in 1838 and died a general in 1856. Thomas Prendergast, Sir Jeffrey's son, also made his career in the Company, as a collector and magistrate in the Madras Presidency, but he was destined to find a more lasting fame in a quite different sphere of activity. When he retired on the annuity fund in 1859 he settled in Cheltenham, where, despite the affliction of total blindness, he worked to perfect what he called the 'mastery' system of acquiring foreign languages. This system was based on the way in which children learn to speak, by repeating words and phrases heard but not understood, until they are able to construct intelligible sentences. By this means Prendergast had himself learned the Madras vernacular, Tamil and Telugu, and he now expounded the method in a book, *The Mastery of Languages*, published in 1864. He subsequently produced manuals of French, Spanish, German, Hebrew and Latin which enjoyed a considerable vogue and went through many editions.[2]

Harry North Dalrymple Prendergast was the linguist's second son, born in India in 1834, and educated at Cheam School and Brighton College. Two years at Addiscombe Military College followed, then service in the Persian War of 1856–7. It was with the Malwa Field Force, after the outbreak of the Indian Mutiny, that the young soldier was to prove his extraordinary valour, being recommended twice for the Victoria Cross. On 21 November 1857, at Mundisore, he saved the life of Lieutenant Dew of the 14th Light Dragoons by riding down a rebel who was about to shoot Dew at point blank range. The bullet passed through Prendergast's chest just to the left of his heart, but he survived to be in action again, to be severely wounded twice more, and to have a horse shot under him, before the end of the campaign. The full story was even more remarkable than in the citation, for, at Mundisore, in order to allow the infantry time to fall in, the three young officers had led a cavalry charge right into the heart of the enemy host, Prendergast finding himself between their standard bearers when he reined in.

In 1867, by now a Major in the Madras Sappers, he took part in the invasion of Abyssinia and was present at the fall of Magdala, and in 1878 he was in the Indian Army force which Disraeli dispatched to Malta and Cyprus. He became a Brigadier-General in 1880 and a Major-General in 1882; soon afterwards he was given command of the Burma division, and was so convinced that the invasion of Upper Burma was imminent that he turned down an important command in India. Finally in 1884, when the chance of a Burma campaign seemed to be fading, he accepted command of the Hyderabad Subsidiary Force.[3]

When he was selected to command the Burma expedition, Dufferin wrote to him: 'Of course it is not yet certain whether or no the Government of Mandalay will yield to our demands, but we must be prepared to strike at once in case they do not. Celerity and decision economise both human life and money. I do not imagine that you will meet with any serious resistance if you should be required to advance. Still we must be careful not to despise our enemy too much. Of late years we have suffered terribly from our imprudence in this respect. It is with this view that I have furnished you with a larger force than may perhaps be absolutely required.'[4] A few days later Dufferin wrote again to say that the Foreign Department had drawn up his instructions. He hoped that he would be able to make his way to Mandalay without suffering much loss, or inflicting any severe punishment upon the enemy. 'If your occupation of the capital of Upper Burma could be effected in a bloodless manner, it would be extremely creditable to you, and far more advantageous to the ultimate objects of the Government than any number of victorious encounters in the field.'[5]

Part of the text of Prendergast's official instructions from the Foreign Department read as follows: 'From the time you enter the enemy's territory you will be vested with supreme political as well as military authority. Colonel Sladen will be placed under your orders as political officer. . . . With regard to political matters, you should correspond direct with the Government of India in the Foreign Department, repeating all telegrams immediately to the Chief Commissioner, and send him a copy of all letters simultaneously with the original dispatches. You will understand that after you cross the frontier no offer of submission can be accepted or can affect the movement of the troops; Mandalay must be occupied and Theebaw dethroned. You should announce this definitely to the Burmese authorities and population. You will be informed hereafter whether Burma (Upper) is to be annexed. If so, the Chief Commissioner will go to Mandalay and assume civil control meanwhile.' Prendergast was enjoined to leave political officers at strongholds or important places garrisoned by him after their surrender, to make full use of Sladen's exceptional experience and knowledge of Burmese affairs, and to meet Bernard's wishes where possible. 'The immediate objects of the expedition are the occupation of Mandalay and the dethronement of King Theebaw, and it is extremely desirable that these objects should be attained rather by the display than by the use of force.'[6]

The Burma Field Force was to consist of about 10,000 troops, organized in three infantry brigades. One brigade was from the Bengal Army, the other two from the Army of the Madras Presidency. The first brigade consisted of the 2nd Battalion of the Liverpool Regiment, the 2nd Queen's Own Bengal Infantry and the 11th Bengal Infantry; the second of the 1st Battalion Royal Welch Fusiliers, and the 21st and 25th Madras Infantry; the third of the 2nd Battalion of the Hampshire (67th) Regiment, and the 12th and 23rd Madras Infantry. There were in addition six companies of sappers and miners, three batteries of the Royal Artillery, and three mountain batteries from India. Colonel F. B. Norman, a brother of Field-Marshal Sir Henry Norman, commanded the Bengal Brigade. The second and third brigades were commanded by Colonel H. H. Foord and Colonel G. S. White of the Madras Army.[7] All three became acting Brigadier-Generals for the duration of the campaign.

George Stuart White was, like the Viceroy, an Ulsterman, whose family home was Whitehall, near Broughshane in Co. Antrim. He entered the army in 1853, after Sandhurst, and served through the Indian Mutiny and the Afghan War of 1878–80 with the Gordon Highlanders, whose colonel he became in 1881. He had won the V.C. at Charasia, and had been with Roberts on the march from Kabul to Kandahar. For a brief spell he had been Military Secretary to the previous Viceroy, Lord Ripon. White eagerly looked forward to the Burma campaign as an opportunity of promotion, and his correspondence provides much detailed information about it.[8]

General Prendergast arrived in Madras on 29 October, just as the troops from the selected regiments were being assembled on the *glacis* of Fort St. George. Heavy rain, which had begun on the previous day, continued incessantly until the night of Monday, 2 November, when it culminated in a severe storm. The tents were flooded, and the troops suffered great discomfort. The rain also made the task of collecting the stores and putting them on board the transports exceedingly difficult, and delayed the embarkation of the Force for twenty-four hours.[9] White, who reached Madras on the last day of October, wrote in his pocket diary, 'Moved into camp on the *glacis*. Rain, rain, rain.' On 2 November the Governor of Madras, M. E. Grant Duff, entertained Prendergast and his officers at dinner. The evening was an interesting one, for as Grant Duff, a former M.P. with literary tastes, set the table in a roar with his witty comments on European politics and politicians, a gigantic thunderstorm was breaking over the Fort. White went 'home early in a downpour to a wet tent'.[10]

The next day dawned fine and clear, and the misery of the troops ended with orders for immediate embarkation in steamers of the British India Company. At nightfall they sailed for Rangoon. The weather continued fine and the sea calm, but many of the sepoys were nevertheless 'very sick and helpless'. White passed the time at sea by studying a gazetteer of Burma and the secret memorandum on the plan of operations. 'I cannot think that anything will now turn us from Mandalay,' he wrote to his wife, 'but I hope that Theebaw's answer may be defiant, so that we may have a soldier's and not a policeman's duty to perform....'[11] On the night of 6 November, the ships anchored off the Mouths of the Irrawaddy, and next afternoon General Prendergast and his headquarters staff had disembarked from the Indian Marine troopship *Clive* and were in consultation with the Chief Commissioner.

From Rangoon the troops were moved up to Thayetmyo on the frontier with Upper Burma, where on 11 November they were joined by Brigadier-General Norman and the Bengal Brigade. The road to Mandalay stretched northwards along the shining waters of the Irrawaddy. The upper part of the river was now well charted and the Flotilla Company's captains were acquainted with its hazards and peculiarities, but the shifting sand bars and strong currents made navigation a continuous challenge. The Field Force was to be carried upstream (it was hoped swiftly) in steamers and flats hired from the Irrawaddy Flotilla Company. The steamers had rapidly been refitted with arms racks, accoutrement pegs, water tanks and latrines, and the flats (large barges which could be towed by the steamers) equipped to carry the artillery. The Military Department of the Government of India had been 'rather taken aback' by the very high rates at which, under a contract of 1879, they had to pay, Rs 45 a ton (including coal) for the steamers, and Rs 15 a ton for flats per month. For this reason the vessels were not taken up until the troops had left India. The steamers and flats were now joined at Thayetmyo by small steam launches fitted with machine-guns to sweep the thick jungle on either bank of the river, and by two gun boats of the Indian Marine, the *Irrawaddy* and the *Kathleen*. 'On this expedition,' Bernard reported with pride to Mackenzie Wallace, 'we have more machine-guns than were ever together in India before.' When assembled, these ships formed a large flotilla which, steaming up river in line astern, extended for some four or five miles.[12]

The military plans had been carefully prepared many years before. Intelligence had revealed that the Burmese had strengthened some of the small forts and stockades along the river banks, but these dispositions had been carefully mapped and drawn and, as far as was known, the Burmese possessed no heavy artillery or knowledge of mines. Stockades exactly similar to those which might be encountered were carefully constructed at Dum-Dum in India, and experiments made to find the best way of breaching them. Very elaborate medical arrangements were made to deal with casualties or epidemics, and the flotilla carried a large supply of antiscorbutics—one ounce of lime juice and one ounce of sugar per week for each man. Since no fresh meat was procurable at Rangoon, some 800 sheep and goats were to be sent each week by steamer from Calcutta. Rations for the troops were based on those required during the Afghan campaign of 1878–80.[13]

The Government of India had taken other kinds of precautions also. Bernard prevailed upon Dr. Forchhammer, a brilliant young Swiss professor of oriental languages in Rangoon, to draw up a list of the chief monasteries in Mandalay which had valuable libraries. This was done, Forchhammer providing an exhaustive *catalogue raisonée* of the rarest Pali manuscripts and their exact location, together with a note on Upper Burma antiquities in general. It was promptly communicated to General Prendergast by Mackenzie Wallace, who expressed a hope that when Mandalay was taken it might be possible to avoid occupying, burning or injuring any of the monasteries, 'unless they be made rallying places for armed resistance'.[14]

Bernard was worried about the problem of keeping peace in Lower Burma, especially in Rangoon itself. On 10 November he reported that one military picket had been stationed on the outskirts of the town for the previous four nights, and that from 14 November there would be the full number of infantry and volunteer pickets to 'prevent bad characters raising their heads'. About 300 Burmese elders were patrolling the streets at night 'in the most praiseworthy manner'. After the town had been denuded of troops for the Toungoo column he expected still to have 'one wing of British infantry, seven companies of Madras infantry, a battery of artillery, and four men-of-war, with reduced crews, in the river'.[15] At Bernard's request a force had been assembled at the railway terminus of Toungoo, where many employees of the Bombay-Burma Trading Corporation had gathered. On 24 November it began to advance towards Ningyan in support of the main operation on the Irrawaddy.

6

AT THE MINHLA REDOUBT

The G.O.C. and his headquarters staff arrived at Thayetmyo on board a small river steamer, the *Thambyadine*, on the afternoon of Friday 13. Some useful intelligence had come down the river just before his arrival. The Flotilla Company's steamer *Talifu* had reached the frontier from Mandalay on Wednesday evening, and her captain reported great excitement in the city. The foreigners who were unable to leave were barricading themselves in Dr. Williams's old house, under the direction of the redoubtable Andreino. The *Talifu* had got away only with difficulty, an attempt having been made to detain her at Minhla until a steamer with Burmese troops arrived, but the captain had cut his moorings and steamed down the river. He reported that two Italian officers had volunteered to block the river, and that some 8,000 Burmese troops were encamped at the Gue Goun Kamyo Fort across the river from Minhla. He had no news of the *Dowoon*, another Flotilla Company steamer still in Burmese waters.[1]

Also waiting for Prendergast was the Foreign Office telegram informing him that the Burmese reply to the British ultimatum had been unsatisfactory, and that he should at once advance on Mandalay. At first light on the 14th, therefore, the *Irrawaddy* (Commander Clutterbuck, R.N.) and the *Kathleen* (Lieutenant French, R.N.) crossed the frontier to reconnoitre and to bring in some Burmese vessels which were known to be nearby. The ships were found and captured after some sharp fire. The action was only just in time, for the Burmese had intended to use them to block the channel either at Sinboungweh or at Minhla. The operation had been entrusted to two Italian engineers, Captain Camotto and Captain Molinari. One of the flats had been prepared for sinking in the river, and had rows of teak posts, six inches square and ten feet long with sharpened points to destroy any steamer which might run against them. Camotto jumped off the flat and swam to the bank, leaving his clothes and all his papers, including letters and a journal, and detailed drawings which revealed the extent of Thibaw's military preparations.

Camotto's diary and letters were translated by Captain Speed of the Royal Engineers, and they yielded some interesting information. In a letter to relatives in Italy, dated 7 November, he had written: 'The English have, through fear of France, imposed conditions unacceptable to Burma and war is imminent. I have been re-employed on only Rs 400. The defence of the frontier was confided to me and to Captain Molinari (of Genoa) by the King and his ministers. To me is entrusted the great and arduous task of closing the River Irrawaddy, the great and only communication of the country. Molinari is charged with the fortresses, etc. Tomorrow we both start in a steamer in haste. If the English approach they will find a hard nut.' He added reassuringly, 'Be certain that in doing my duty I shall not expose myself more than actually necessary. The worst can be a *ralla* lost, and become a prisoner of the English, who will respect me.'[2]

The *Irrawaddy* also found the *Dowoon*, with four flats in tow, and almost opened fire on her before she was identified. Her master, Captain Matthews, had a dramatic story to tell. He had managed to get away from Mandalay on the 12th, but at a village further down the river the headman had tried to detain him by force, and had led an attack on the steamer. The captain resisted, and the Burmese shouted to spear him, whereupon the pilot, an American named Batteley, shot the headman. 'This staggered the Burmans, who fell back, and I slipped my cable and decamped.' He then went to Minhla, where again an effort was made to detain him, and in escaping he came under fire from Gue Gyoun Kamyo.[3]

The action of the next day may be described in Prendergast's own words. 'On the 16th, a brigade was landed on each bank of the river two or three miles below Sinboungweh, with the object of turning the enemy's works, while the *Irrawaddy* shelled the batteries on the right bank at long ranges. The manoeuvres were well conducted, and nothing could be prettier than the skirmishing of the infantry over the hills, but on both banks the Burmans evacuated before the troops could get in rear of them. The stockades were burnt, and eleven guns were destroyed, as it would have caused delay to carry them away. The day was hot, and there were several cases of sunstroke.'[4]

There were only two really formidable clusters of forts commanding the river between the British forces and Mandalay. The first of these was at Minhla, some sixty miles from the frontier, and it consisted of two large forts, one on either bank, and a number of smaller works. The Minhla Fort, on the western bank, was thought not to be in use, as it had been much damaged by floodwaters. High up on the other side of the river was situated the great brick fort of Gue Gyoun Kamyo, designed by Italian engineers and one of the strongest in Burma. It commanded the river for two miles, the military experts said that it must be taken to clear to road to Mandalay. The garrison of some 1,700 men was commanded by a son-in-law of the Taingda Mingyi, and the reports of the Flotilla Company's captains indicated that it had been strongly reinforced during the previous few days.

Prendergast had decided to attack Gue Gyoun Kamyo and Minhla simultaneously, and not surprisingly to send the pick of his force against the former. He issued orders that General Foord's brigade was to land on the left bank at Patanago and take Gue Gyoun Kamyo by assault. General White's brigade, still on board the steamers coming up river, was to follow them as reserve. General Norman's brigade was to land on the right bank at Maloon, march to the Governor's palace at Minhla, and take prisoner the Governor and other high officials if possible. Meanwhile the *Irrawaddy* was to engage Gue Gyoun Kamyo at long ranges and to try to breach the loop-holed walls of the fort, especially on the western side. Fire from the gunboats was to cease two hours after landing of the troops, or when a white flag was hoisted on the white pagoda to the east of the fort.

Accordingly, early on the 17th, General Foord landed at Patanago with the Liverpool Regiment, the 21st and 25th Madras Infantry, and the Madras Pioneers with scaling parties carrying bamboo ladders. A good cart road ran northwards from the village, and they were able to proceed quickly in column of route. After marching some seven or eight miles through thickly-wooded terrain they reached the high ground just to the east of the fortifications. Burmese soldiers in uniform were plainly visible on the ramparts of the fort and many flags were flying above the walls.

The land advance, however, seemed to take the Burmese completely by surprise. Their attention was directed to the river below, where the

Irrawaddy and the *Kathleen*, steaming to within 1,800 yards of the fort, shelled it with twenty-pounders and nine-pounders and swept the ramparts with Nordenfeldt and Gardner machine-guns. When the troops arrived every Burmese gun was still pointed towards the river, and at the sight of the British soldiers in their rear the garrison hurriedly evacuated the fort. The east face was stormed, and a party led by Sladen burst open the north-east gate and got inside. By 1 o'clock Gue Gyoun Kamyo was in British hands.[5]

On the other side of the river it was a different story. Expecting the occupation of the Minhla forts to be a mere formality, Prendergast had detailed a smaller force for the right bank, and it was further weakened by the fact that the steamer carrying General Norman and the Royal Welch Fusiliers did not reached the landing point in time for them to take part. The force landed therefore consisted of the 2nd Battalion of the Queen's Own Bengal Infantry, the 11th Bengal Infantry and the 12th Madras Infantry, under the command of Colonel Baker of the Queen's Own. Major MacNeill of the Intelligence Department accompanied the force as Staff Officer. From the moment of landing they were in difficulties: the jungle, though not high, was unexpectedly dense, and they had to advance very slowly along narrow and twisting tracks. Occasionally they had to hew their way through the thickets, and at noon they were suddenly fired upon at close quarters from the cover of the jungle.

Shortly after starting, a Burmese villager had told them that considerable numbers of royal troops had landed from a steamer on the previous day and that they were dug in and stockaded ahead of them. When the ambush took place, the 12th Madras Infantry were leading, and perceiving that it would be useless to return the fire while the enemy were so well concealed, the officers ran to the front and called on the men to advance. There was some hesitation and confusion, but eventually a handful of Madras and Bengal troops followed the officers, under heavy fire, through the thick thorn hedge, and over hastily-constructed entrenchments and breastworks of carts and bamboos, into the stockaded village. At this point MacNeill, who was in front directing the advance, and another officer, Lieutenant Sillery of the 12th Madras, were badly wounded. MacNeill had been hit twice in the leg, but he had his wounds tied up and went on.

The Burmese also made a determined stand at the Governor's palace and worked their guns vigorously. The 11th Bengal, now leading the advance, found themselves under hot fire in very cramped country, but gradually they drove the enemy from point to point. Lieutenant R. A. T. Dury, a young officer who had been seconded to the regiment from the South Wales Borderers, was mortally wounded leading his men in the attack. After the storming of the stockade, the Governor's palace was taken and set on fire. The troops then reformed and wheeled to the right, advancing eastward on the town of Minhla. About a thousand yards away they could see, above the surrounding thickets, the great masonry redoubt of the Minhla fort, and almost at once they found themselves again in close contact with the enemy, who, well-concealed and well-armed, disputed every inch of cover up to the redoubt.

Concerted action was impossible on the narrow sinuous tracks, and once again the sepoys were pinned down, in whatever cover they could find, by heavy and accurate Burmese fire. It was decided to try to take the redoubt by rushing it. Colonel Simpson, Major Hill and Lieutenant Wilkinson with thirty sepoys raced across sixty yards of open ground to shelter under the huge ramp, on the west side of the redoubt, which the Burmese used for dragging up their artillery. There they found Lieutenant Downes, of the 11th Bengal, with a dozen of his men, and planned the assault. The ramp consisted of a double slope leading from the ground to the parapet, where the slopes met. It was steep, and out of repair for the first six or eight feet from the ground, but 'fairly practicable for infantry'. Lieutenants Wilkinson and Downes led the assault with three or four sepoys. Wilkinson was first to reach the parapet, and as he did so, he slipped and fell, and was immediately set upon by the Burmese, receiving a terrible cut across the head from a *dah*, and four other wounds besides. Only the rush of the sepoys coming behind saved his life.[6]

Meanwhile the Queen's Own Bengal Infantry, swinging round and deploying on the river bank, trapped the Burmese soldiers fleeing from the redoubt, and many were shot or driven into the river and drowned. Some 270 were taken prisoner. The masonry redoubt was the central point in the defence of Minhla, and after its fall resistance was slight. High up on the opposite bank General Prendergast and his officers, who had plenty of time on their hands, had a grandstand view of the whole action, but felt acutely helpless. White had landed the Hampshires and Cinque Ports Royal Artillery and climbed up to Gue Gyoun Kamyo, only to find that there was nothing for them to do. He was not surprised that the Burmese had abandoned the fort, for it was commanded by higher ground where the advancing troops had found a house, empty and deserted, in which Camotto had been living. He thought Gue Gyoun Kamyo 'a most indefensible position, quite untenable'.

Hundreds of feet below, the *Irrawaddy* and the *Kathleen* were firing at the Minhla fort. They had turned their attention to it as soon as the agreed flag had gone up on the white pagoda, but without much success in knocking out the Burmese guns. Several wooden houses in Minhla, however, had been set alight by the shells, and a large part of the town was now in flames. White could see Baker's troops sweeping over the stockades and attacking the redoubt. 'While I had my glasses up our sepoys drove a crowd of Burmans out of the fort to the edge of the river and they were verily between the devil and the deep blue sea. Many of them took to the river and swam, and the sepoys fired volleys at their heads. I think all were shot or drowned.'[7]

Some thirty or forty wounded Burmese were, in fact, received into the field hospitals, and about one hundred Burmese dead were found. On the British side three sepoys were killed and twenty-four wounded. The casualty rate among the European officers was high, Lieutenant Dury having been killed, and three other subalterns wounded, two of them dangerously. Major MacNeill had also been wounded. After the fall of the redoubt, the *Kathleen* took on board from the *Irrawaddy* a medical officer and some stretchers and steamed alongside a flat moored directly under walls in order to bring assistance quickly to the wounded. The bluejackets got on board, and Colonel Sanford of the Royal Engineers and a naval officer called Trench were about to follow them when two mines exploded in the sternhold. The *Kathleen* was undamaged, and no one was injured, but the flat was set ablaze and burned to the water's edge. It was subsequently discovered that the mines had been detonated from the shore by the Italians.[8]

Minhla was to be the only action of any consequence during the campaign. There was no doubt that the Burmese had made a determined stand there, and fought very bravely. They had also, either by design or accident, outmanoeuvred Prendergast by luring him and the bulk of his force to Gue Gyoun Kamyo. Had Prendergast been delayed for one more day, and the river blocked by the Italian engineers, it might well have taken some very stiff fighting and heavy casualties to secure the forts, and Thibaw's officers would have been given more time to prepare the defences of Mandalay.

White was disposed to be very critical. To his wife he wrote: 'The General was (between you and me) in too great a hurry. Half the force had not come up. . . . There were no hospital ships up, and a great want of medical arrangements on the field.' (Against this it may be said that Prendergast was obeying Dufferin's instructions on the necessity for speed, and his swift attack was justified by later events. It was for his excessive caution at Ladysmith that White was to be criticized fifteen years later.) White had another reason to be dissatisfied with the engagement: '. . . one of the regiments of my brigade, the 12th Madras Infantry, were given more to do than the Madrassee cared very much about. They accordingly lost heavily in officers. The other regiment (Bengal 11th Native Infantry) behaved much better.' His summing up was that they had 'a heavy day instead of a very light one. There would have been much for the newspaper critics to carp at'.[9]

'Does anyone remember the affair at Minhla?' inquired Kipling only four years later. He remembered it for two reasons. The first was that he wanted to be there, and had unsuccessfully tried to persuade the editor of the *Civil and Military Gazette* to send him to Burma to cover the campaign. The second was that when he read the casualty list he remembered that Lieutenant Dury had been his school-fellow at the United Services College. In a letter to Lionel Dunsterville, Kipling wrote: 'I tried to go to Burma for the paper but I couldn't be spared. By the way, did you see that poor Durey [*sic*] was killed by those swine? There's £1,800 worth of education gone to smash and a good fellow with it.'*[10]

When he made his brief visit to Rangoon in 1890 Kipling still preserved the freshest recollection of Dury's death, and he introduced it into his account of the conversation in the Pegu Club. 'Then they told me of the death of an old school-fellow under the ramp of the Minhla redoubt—does anyone remember the affair at Minhla that opened the third Burmese ball?'

' "I was close to him," said a voice. "He died in A's arms, I fancy, but

---

* Cf. 'Arithmetic on the Frontier,' which appeared in June 1886.
> *Two thousand pounds of education*
> *Drops to a ten-rupee jezail—*
> *The Crammer's boast, the Squadron's pride,*
> *Shot like a rabbit in a ride!*

Another reference to Dury's death appears in *Stalky and Co.*, Macmillan, Uniform Edition, p. 196. ' ". . . what about marching in public," said Hogan, not foreseeing that three years later he should die in the Burmese sunlight outside Minhla Fort.'

I'm not quite sure. Anyhow, I know he died easily. He was a good fellow" . . . I went out into the steamy night, my head ringing with stories of battle, murder, and sudden death. I had reached the fringe of the veil that hides Upper Burma, and I would have given much to have gone up the river and seen a score of old friends, now jungle-worn men of war. All that night I dreamed of interminable staircases down which swept thousands of pretty girls, so brilliantly robed that my eyes ached at the sight. There was a great golden bell at the top of the stairs, and at the bottom, his face turned to the sky, lay poor old D—— dead at Minhla, and a host of unshaven ragamuffins in khaki were keeping guard over him.'

If White was correct in alleging that Prendergast had attacked before the hospital ships were up, the delay in attending to the wounded was mercifully short. In his formal report the chief medical officer to the expedition, Deputy Surgeon-General J. McN. Donnelly, describes how the hospital ship was moored at the bank below Minhla smoothly and without fuss, and how the arrangements for dealing with casualties were put into operation. They had been most carefully planned. Two large base hospitals had been established at Thayetmyo, one for British and one for Indian soldiers, to receive wounded who might be sent down-river. One of the more commodious transports had been fitted out as a floating hospital with the flotilla; she towed two flats and if a sudden outbreak of disease should render her useless for accommodating casualties, a tender was standing by to transfer the sick rapidly to Thayetmyo. In addition the flotilla carried six fully-equipped field hospitals which could be put ashore entire or in sections within a short time to operate as close to the fighting as possible.

The recovery of the wounded began as soon as the hospital ship tied up, and the most thorough search continued by lamplight until 1 o'clock in the morning. By that time Donnelly was certain that no man who was still breathing had not been found. The Burmese wounded were treated in exactly the same way as British, and every man had an iron bedstead, a mattress, soft pillows and warm blankets. Some of the Burmese had very serious wounds requiring surgery that went on until 4 a.m. The surgical care, it was claimed, was up to the standard of a London hospital. In all, some forty-one patients were treated.[12]

At Minhla, however, an enemy appeared far more formidable than the Burmese, 'a source of disaster more potent than any human agency could inflict.' On the day following the battle it began to rain heavily just before dawn, and the weather, which had hitherto been bright and warm became suddenly cold, damp and misty. Such weather was rarely experienced on the Irrawaddy at that season of the year. As the temperature dropped, the *Irrawaddy* suddenly reported that she had three cases of cholera on board. Cholera, endemic in India and south-east Asia, was highly erratic in its manifestations; it could, as Kipling said, kill every soldier on one side of a barrack room and spare the other. More than one focus of infection sprang up at the same time, yet the disease could die away as quickly as it appeared. It attacked impartially officer and ranker, European and Indian. The epidemic which broke out on the flotilla followed this pattern; apparently isolated cases appeared on several of the steamers, both in the 67th Regiment and in the Madras Regiments.[13] The surgeon-general decided that the only judicious course was to establish a special cholera hospital at Minhla, to isolate the sick from both the flotilla hospital and Thayetmyo. He therefore went ashore and selected a large airy *zayat*, or rest-house, about 300 yards from the Minhla fort, and the cholera patients were transferred to it. A flat vacated by the troops left to garrison Minhla was attached to the hospital ship for the isolation of cholera cases, and it was fitted with large awnings to shield them from the heat of the sun.* During the day the occurrence of a case of the disease in any vessel was notified by signal, and as soon as the flotilla anchored for the night, the patient was transferred to the cholera flat by steam launch.

From that time cholera never left the force. More sepoys and followers caught the disease than British soldiers, but they had a greater resistance to it, and more of them recovered. The figures for the period from 17 November until 20 December, when the cholera died out, were 35 British, 28 died; 115 Indian, 49 died; and 121 followers, 77 died.[14] The disease also took its toll of the Toungoo column, which crossed into Upper Burma on 24 November, and after meeting some Burmese resistance reached Eylah on the 30th. There they were ordered to stand fast, but cholera broke out, the result probably of the soldiers drinking from the marshes and swamps, and the column had to break camp and push on to take Ningyan, which the Burmese had abandoned.[15]

* Cf. Kipling, '*With our sick beneath the awnings as we went to Mandalay.*'

7

THE ROYAL GEM CITY

The next day was spent in reorganizing the flotilla and carrying out a reconnaissance ahead. At first light the *Irrawaddy* and *Kathleen* with two of the steamers began to move upstream. Some distance above Minhla two Europeans came down to the bank and waved their hats to attract attention. Commander Carpenter took them on board in a steam launch; they proved to be Camotto and Molinari, who were 'in miserable plight' and very anxious to give themselves up as they 'would have been murdered by the Burmans on account of their ill success'. They handed over their papers, a loaded revolver and a small bag of rupees. A pocket-book which Camotto tried to hide in the cabin of the steamer was found to contain plans of vessels and river defences. Prendergast ordered that they were to be clothed and well treated but not allowed to escape.[1]

Towards evening it began to rain, and it rained heavily throughout the night and all of the following day. The flotilla crept forward for about twenty miles, but the going was difficult. The line of steamers, strung out at squadron sailing intervals, extended for more than four miles. The heavy rain, poor visibility and the strength of the currents made navigation difficult, and much depended on the efficiency of the signalling between the ships which went on incessantly night and day. To make matters worse, one of the barges carrying two 6.3 inch howitzers foundered without warning.[2]

On the 22nd the *Irrawaddy* reported that a Burmese land force and two of the King's steamers were at a point two miles beyond Pagan. The steamers towing the barges with heavy guns went forward and drove the Burmese from their batteries by long range fire. Eleven small guns were taken and destroyed, and the royal ships were scuttled by their crews

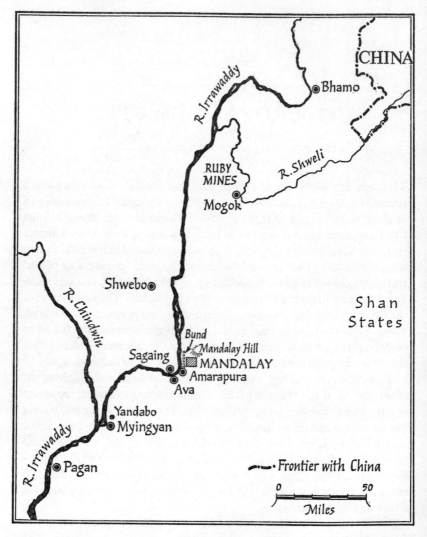

2. The Mandalay Area

On the 23rd, amid torrents of rain, two companies of the Liverpool
Regiment, four companies of the 13th Bengal Infantry, and a company of
Sappers with two mountain guns landed at Pagan, to find that all the
Burmese troops and local officials had fled. The townsfolk, however,
appeared to be friendly. The villages in the surrounding area had been
thoroughly plundered by Thibaw's soldiers on the previous day and
were for the most part deserted.[3]

On the evening of the 24th, while the guns were engaging the enemy
some miles farther upstream at Mingyan, his troops appeared in considerable numbers. A large body of Burmese soldiers, dressed brilliantly
in red, white and magenta coats, the officers with gold umbrellas held
above them, had collected on rising ground about three miles inland.
This seemed to be the Burmese reserve and headquarters, 'as the men
composing it took no part in the fighting'. The steamers and barges engaged and silenced the Burmese batteries, and the richly-clad host
retired unscathed and in good order. Considerable quantities of guns
were found in the shore batteries, which were 'ingeniously constructed'.
It was subsequently discovered that the Burmese commander at
Mingyan was the Hlethin Atwinwun, the best of Thibaw's generals,
who after prudently observing the action from his hilltop, telegraphed
Mandalay to report that he had gained a great victory over the English.
Thibaw at once dispatched to him 270 gold medals for distribution
to his troops and a number of gold cups and bowls. The flotilla left
Mingyan at 3.45 p.m. on the 25th, leaving a garrison of 500 men
('none too large' in White's opinion), and came to anchor at Yandabo,
not far from the tree under which the treaty of 1825 had been signed.[4]

Next morning the river was shrouded with a thick white mist, which
did not clear until some time after sunrise. The flotilla was now nearing
Ava, and the second most formidable group of fortifications guarding the
approaches to Mandalay. It was here, if anywhere, that Thibaw's troops
would make their stand in defence of the capital. Large bodies of Burmese troops were stationed in the fort at Ava; at Sagaing, on the opposite
bank, there was a strong fort and two smaller earthworks also occupied
by considerable numbers of soldiers. In all it was estimated that some
8,000 Burmese were opposing the British advance.

White was to lead the attack on Ava with his brigade, and, too busy
drawing up his plans to be able to write home, he took the precaution of
jotting down in his diary his last wishes to his wife and family. 'Have
issued orders for the attack by my brigade. Hope all will go well and that

I may get through with safety and credit. My last wishes to you dear Amy and teach my children to love their father's memory.'⁵ Whatever premonition troubled him was not fulfilled. No action took place, and White was to be spared for many another encounter, but he was conscious of a feeling of anti-climax and even of grievance. It was nearly a fortnight before he was able to snatch the time to write a full account of that day's events, and how 'as the sun was pouring a flood of golden light upon the last hours of Burman independence' the smooth waters of the Irrawaddy were 'suddenly broken by flashing of many oars and the richly gilded state barge of the King. The white flag told us too surely, from a soldier's point of view, what the mission of the white-robed ministers was. They were, however, promptly dismissed with a message that unconditional surrender of the King and the country was the only term. This they hesitated about, and we thought we might have a chance of having to take the place. It was, of course, uncivilized to be disappointed, but, on the other hand, think that I had been given the hard work, and had all my plans written out and prepared.'⁶

The official account states that in the late afternoon a state barge flying Thibaw's flag at the stern and a flag of truce at the bow was taken in tow and brought alongside the steamer *Dowoon*. The crew consisted of a helmsman and forty-four rowers, and the barge and the oars were richly gilded. Seated in the bows, under enormous hat umbrellas, were two envoys, who removed their shoes and came on board the *Dowoon* for a long interview with Prendergast and Sladen. The chief envoy, who was described as the Minister of the Interior, bore a letter from the Hlutdaw. He asked for an armistice, declaring that the British Government had not understood that time was necessary to do all that they had requested from the Burmese King. Prendergast replied that no armistice could be granted, but that if the King surrendered himself, his army and Mandalay, and if the Europeans in Mandalay were found unharmed in person and property, the King's life would be spared and subjects in dispute would be negotiated under orders from the Viceroy. An answer was demanded by 4 a.m. on the 27th.⁷

The flotilla then advanced to a point some thirteen miles below Ava, capturing a fully-armed royal steamer and taking a number of prisoners. Next morning the steamers weighed anchor at daylight, but again they were delayed by thick fog. No answer had come from the Burmese envoys, but at 10 o'clock when the force had advanced to about 3,000 or 4,000 yards below Ava, they again appeared, having given orders that

the Burmese were not to open fire, and bearing an unconditional accep-
tance of the terms offered. Prendergast insisted that the troops holding
Ava and Sagaing should lay down their arms, but there was a considerable delay in agreeing to this, as the commander was senior in rank to
the chief envoy. At this point Prendergast showed great restraint and
diplomacy. His staff, impatient at what they considered to be obvious
delaying tactics on the part of the Burmese, urged an immediate assault
on the forts, but the General, mindful of Dufferin's advice, held his
hand—a fact which the Viceroy afterwards remembered to his credit.

Sagaing presented greater obstacles than those encountered at Minhla.
Not least of them was the difficult nature of the river channel, with a reef
running out from Ava and sandbanks on the other side below the
Sagaing redoubt. The Burmese had very skilfully blocked the channel
just above Ava by sinking a steamer, three flats and a number of small
boats filled with sand and stones in the middle of the fairway, and it
would have been 'a dangerous if not impossible operation' for the fleet to
move up river until the forts on either bank had been secured. While the
negotiations went on, however, a naval survey party, using the steam
launches, discovered a safe channel and marked it out with buoys. The
ships were placed in the best position by signal, and in fighting order,
and the troops were put ashore. These manoeuvres complete, Prendergast again pressed for the immediate surrender of arms, and this time
with success, the royal mandate having been telegraphed from Mandalay eleven miles away.[8]

White, ordered to disarm Sagaing, found that 'there was not only no
opposition, but the soldiers and people were quite cheerful over the
change of masters'. In his diary he noted that the commandant of the
fort, a 'fat old general', had wanted to finish his dinner before meeting
him.[9] In a letter to his sister Jane he gave a fuller account of the incident.
'I sent an order to my predecessor, the Burmese general, to come and
hand over to me. He was discovered in his hut eating his dinner, and
when told to come at once he said he would like to finish his dinner.
However, it was hinted to him that his dinner of tomorrow night might
be unnecessary if he got my dander up, so he leisurely lit a cheroot and
lounged out, and immediately sat down and appeared entirely uncon-
cerned. Long before I got to his fort I told him I would show him where
I had intended to assault it, and took him to the place. He said, "Yes,
you could have got in there." '[10] It was a fair sample of the Burmese
attitude to the conqueror.

Early next morning, while White was collecting the Burmese iron and brass cannon and some hundreds of Martini rifles, the rest of the fleet steamed past him to Mandalay. By mid-morning the ships were in the harbour, and some of the European residents, including Andreino, came down to welcome them. At Sagaing, Sladen had intimated that it would expedite matters if the King would come with the Kinwun Mingyi to submit himself on board the General's ship. There was, of course, no likelihood that Thibaw would do anything of the kind. A message was sent to the ministers that the troops would land and move up to the palace, but still no reply came from the Golden Feet. 'No communication having been received from the palace,' Prendergast tersely recorded, 'I landed the troops at 1 p.m.'[11]

He had drawn up plans for the assault of the city, but, in the reasonable expectation that they would not be needed, he had also made arrangements for its ceremonial occupation. All three brigades were to land and march by separate routes to the palace. General Prendergast, with an escort of mounted infantry, led the 1st Brigade. As he approached the south gate of the palace enclosure at about 3 p.m. the Kinwun Mingyi suddenly appeared, and earnestly requested that Sladen should accompany him to the palace to allay the fears of the King and his court. This Sladen agreed to do, and the Kinwun Mingyi conducted him to the Hall of Audience, where Thibaw, who appeared much affected and frightened, said he hoped that the English would spare his life. Meanwhile Prendergast had entered the south gate and occupied the enclosure. At each of the four gates the guards were disarmed and replaced by British sentries, and the troops were drawn up in line facing the entrances. At 5 p.m. Sladen and the Kinwun Mingyi returned to him with the King's submission. Thibaw had declared that he would leave the palace and go into a summer-house in the royal gardens, and it was arranged that the formal surrender to Prendergast should take place there on the following day.[12] Prendergast had decided to leave small detachments to guard the palace, and to withdraw the rest of his troops to the ships. The decision was a mistake, and not the only one to be made that night.

The western gate of the palace, which led to the Queen's apartments, had been occupied by White and the Hampshires, and once they were in position, he refused to allow anyone to enter or leave, even though 'crowds of smartly dressed young ladies came to the gate with great urns of lacquer work, some of them jewelled (the urns), with the dinners of the ladies of the palace, which were apparently all cooked outside'.[13] The ministers requested permission for the Queen's ladies to come and go as they wished. Prendergast hesitated, for he was suspicious that Thibaw might well attempt to escape dressed as a woman, but in the end he agreed to the request. It was, as it later turned out, a terrible blunder. During the night Supayalat's attendants all deserted her, while the women of the city poured in to the royal apartments and out again with as much loot as they could carry. 'Colonel Sladen . . . sent me word that the ladies might be allowed to come and go freely,' wrote White. 'I entered a protest that everything of small size and great value would be passed out by the ladies.' But Prendergast took their side, and as a result, White lamented, 'thousands of pounds worth of booty were, I am sure, lost to the army.'

There is some evidence that Prendergast was not entirely happy with the situation at the palace, but his greatest fear was that Thibaw might escape. The 67th Hampshire Regiment had been detailed to remain at the palace and guard its gates, and at the last moment Prendergast asked White to stay and take command. Conditions in the outer palace enclosure, where the rain had turned the ground into a marsh, were extremely uncomfortable, and White passed a miserable night. 'I had nothing with me, and the place we occupied was a morass. I held Theebaw tight, however, and only got a bad cold for my damp and cold night.' And in addition to these discomforts he could hear a good deal of firing in the city, which made him uneasy about the general military situation.[14]

The next day, White recorded, was the most remarkable of his life, which had not been devoid of incident. 'Early in the forenoon Colonel Sladen became uneasy about Theebaw, as he showed signs of fright, and he feared he might try to escape. I strongly advised to put him in charge of a guard at once, and a guard of the 67th Regt. was marched into the sacred confines of the Palace, and had the Lord of the White Elephant surrounded in a twinkling.' The King seemed not to be afraid of the white soldiers, but 'when the officer of the Guard's servant (a black man) came in with the officer's luncheon, Theebaw was much disturbed, and asked if he was the executioner'.[15]

At noon Prendergast arrived from his ship, and accompanied by Sladen and White, went to the summer-house. They found Thibaw sitting in the corner of an open verandah with his two Queens and the Queen Mother. 'His eyes roamed about uneasily, but he was dignified.

He did not attempt to rise, and the ladies of the Court crouched on their knees before and behind him. He was asked to come to the ship that was sent to take him away at once, but he said he would be ready tomorrow. However, he had been told he must be ready to start when called for, and he was given ten minutes. These ten minutes were prolonged to an hour and two hours. At last he was ordered to come, and after a vain attempt had been made to get him one of his own highly-gilded coaches, he was offered conveyance in a hospital doolie. This he scorned for himself and his Queens and boldly started on a walk, the longest of his life, I should think, from the way he waddled along.' White was much struck by the demeanour of the *mingyis*, who had really handed over his kingdom. They appeared in great awe of him, and crouched before him like the crowd. Even the 'evil-faced' Taingda Mingyi 'showed outward veneration at all events for his fallen lord.'[16]

At this moment Thibaw showed a dignity which could not fail to command the respect of the British officers who were so hurriedly bundling him into lifelong exile. The King bore uncomfortably little resemblance to the gin-soaked tyrant of popular imagination they had expected to encounter, and the scene was one not to be forgotten by those who were present. The Royal Gate, never used except by the King, had been thrown open, and the whole grandeur of the palace exposed to the view of the waiting crowd. At 3.30 p.m., after a long delay, the procession appeared at the top of the stairs. General Prendergast and his staff, in sombre khaki, led the way. The Queen Mother came next, then Thibaw, holding one Queen by each hand, began the descent. 'I was sorry for him,' White wrote, 'He showed a great deal of dignity, I thought, and the tenderness with which he treated his Queens was chivalrous at such a time.' The royal party was followed by 'an immense crowd of servants bearing large bundles, probably containing the wealth of the palace. The Burmese crowd pressed heavily upon the party, and would have looted them, I am sure, had they not been kept back by our troops. Some of the bundles contained a fortune. I saw one servant, the moment she got out of the Palace Gate, dash through the ranks of the sepoys with a bundle on her head and disappear in the crowd. She had probably stolen a good haul.'[17]

At the gate the royal party were helped into two small bullock carts and taken to the landing stage, through streets lined by troops, and put on board the steamer *Thoreah*. 'At first the numbers of Burmans were very small, and no demonstration was made. As darkness came on and the river was approached along the roadsides and at the street corners the crowds became very large. No attempt at a rescue was made and all were safely put on board the *Thoreah*.' The name of the ship meant 'sun' in Burmese. Two companies of the Liverpool Regiment, who, with the Naval Brigade, had lined the landing place, embarked as the King's escort. The Kinwun Mingyi also went on board. The *Thoreah* at once put into mid-stream, and early next morning she sailed for Rangoon.[18]

Meanwhile General Prendergast was writing to Lord Dufferin an account of operations since the fall of Pagan and how he had interviewed Thibaw and escorted the royal family to the quayside. 'I should recommend that they leave Burmah at once. The poor people are quite subdued, and it was a sad duty to hurry them off. They were very anxious to remain for four months, or for a few days; but no work can be done till they are out of the country, so I insisted upon immediate departure, and they will be on board the *Thoreah* under escort . . . in ten minutes without any trouble.' The last paragraph of the letter betrayed a faint tinge of uneasiness, as though the General scented trouble of which he could not exactly define the nature or identify the source. 'A few dacoits are about the town tonight, and the Continental gentlemen are very frightened, so I have five regiments and a battery on duty in the town. The dethroncment of the King has occupied till dark, so I have learnt nothing of the state of affairs. For the present the four Woon Mingies or ministers are retained in office. Mandalay is a hotbed of intrigue. I am not sure that Colonel Sladen is very clever, but he understands the Burmans, and knows how to treat them, and he will do well I think.'[19]

During the next few days the initiative was to pass to Sladen, as the political officer. His intention, from the beginning, was to carry on the administration of government through the Hlutdaw, at least until the future status of Upper Burma was determined, but the Kinwun Mingyi's decision to accompany Thibaw was a disappointing setback. The Kinwun Mingyi had remained the nominal head of the King's government throughout the reign, but there were really two parties struggling for control of the council, the other being led by the Taingda Mingyi. The Kinwun Mingyi was regarded by the British as enlightened and progressive, and possessed of a wide and long experience of the outside world, whereas Taingda, the creature of Supayalat, was notoriously zenophobe. Nevertheless Sladen was obliged to recognize him and to work through him, and was agreeably surprised to find him extremely co-operative.

Sladen framed a proclamation which the General now issued, calling upon all officials of the Burmese Government to recognize and accept the authority of the Hlutdaw with Sladen as its President. The Hlutdaw met on 3 December and made a number of important decisions. They strongly recommended that a small movable column should be sent to scour the country around Mandalay, and that all the princes of the royal blood should be deported from Upper Burma without delay. They agreed to lend some *kyaungs* or monasteries as rest-houses for the British troops, saying that the plan was good and would help to protect Mandalay, and to withdraw Burmese troops from the Shan States and let those states administer their own affairs as tributaries. They also agreed to order all Burmese troops south of Mandalay to give up their arms at Minhla, Pagan, Myingyan and Nyingyan.

Prendergast was able to write to the Viceroy in very reassuring terms next day. 'Sladen reports that "all is most satisfactory, Church and State are hand in hand, and working faithfully for mutual interests. My opinion is that the tranquillity of the country is already secured, and that no serious opposition is possible anywhere beyond a little jungle fighting with dacoits and marauders." I think the Colonel takes a bright view of the state of affairs,' Prendergast added drily 'but, at any rate, measures have been taken to draw the teeth of the opposition. . . .'

He could hardly be blamed for sharing Sladen's satisfaction to some extent. He had done all that had been asked of him, and carried out a difficult military operation with the minimum of force. It is the fate of such an expedition that if it succeeds it is dismissed as 'little more than a military promenade' and if it fails it is condemned as a costly shambles. It was with considerable justification that Prendergast was able to sum up the campaign. 'Attention to your Lordship's direction to strike quickly and vigorously has resulted in the present state of affairs, and the very small loss that has been suffered by Her Majesty's and by Thee-baw's forces. If a day had been lost, the Channel at Sinboungweh would have been blocked by Camotto who would have sunk the King's steamer and two barges in the Channel under the shore; this would have caused delay, and there would have been more time to block the river and strengthen the defences above. If Molinari, a Captain of Italian Engineers, had designed works for the defence of Ava, it would have been taken only after severe loss. There were 100 guns bearing upon the river; he would of course have looked to the flanks and rear. It seems that Theebaw's project was to endeavour to stop or delay the force at Myingyan; if he failed, then he would have caused a stout defence of Ava, and ultimately have ordered a stubborn resistance at Mandalay. It would have been undignified for the King to remain to witness such scenes, so he would have retired to Mount Shobo, and thence, if necessary, to Bhamo and the north-east. Money for his expenses had already been sent to Bhamo. I hope that you will not consider the preparations for the expedition too costly. By using heavy artillery at long ranges I proved to the enemy that fighting was useless and they retired more frightened than hurt.' When he had signed the letter General Prendergast added another line: 'P.S.—I deported the *Times* correspondent for transgressing the Press regulations.'[20] There was no way in which he could have known it, but that short sentence contained not only the destruction of his own reputation, but the undoing of the success of the Mandalay campaign, and much else besides.

8

'A FISH TO FIGHT A DOG'

Sladen's decision to work with the Taingda Mingyi was not universally welcomed. In Rangoon the reaction was one of incredulity and anger. 'It will surprise and disquiet our readers,' the *Rangoon Times* reported, 'to learn that the Tynedah Mengyee is now the chief native ruler in Mandalay. The vile, cruel wretch who murdered all the king's relations ... is the trusted favourite of the British, and now struts about Mandalay with infinitely more insolence then ever he displayed when King Theebaw reigned. This reflects the deepest disgrace on those responsible for it.' The *Rangoon Gazette* declared that it surpassed all belief that Taingda should not only be allowed to remain in the country, but be associated with its government. It ill-became the British Government to encourage and seek aid from such ruffians.[1]

Bernard shared these feelings, and when he arrived in Mandalay on 20 December he saw at once that Sladen's attempts to rule through Taingda and the Hlutdaw were unlikely to work for long. There were many other problems awaiting his attention—more than one dacoit leader was rallying support in the Mandalay area by claiming to be the Alompra pretender to the throne and flying the peacock banner; there was the difficult question of the future status of the semi-independent Shan States; and he was endeavouring to calculate the revenue of Upper Burma in Thibaw's time—but Bernard sought first of all for evidence implicating Taingda in the massacres of 1879 and 1884.[2] It was not to be found, for the Hlutdaw had taken all decisions collectively. Sladen, who had come to Mandalay prepared to execute Taingda if necessary had now begun to believe that 'the grim old minister was somewhat the victim of prejudice'. Nothing if not a political realist, Taingda had unceremoniously abandoned Thibaw the moment the British arrived, and it was he who wakened Sladen on the morning of 29 November to warn him that there was great confusion in the palace, and that the King was preparing for flight.* Certainly the British had every reason to be grateful to him.

Nevertheless, Bernard had decided within a week that Taingda must go, and on 27 December Mandalay was electrified by the news of his sudden arrest in the Hlutdaw. The circumstances were intensely dramatic. At 5 p.m. that afternoon, while the Hlutdaw was in session, Taingda was informed that the Chief Commissioner wished to speak to him without delay. Bernard had previously informed Sladen of his intention, and the latter begged to be excused the duty of arresting the minister, 'of whose conduct as a colleague he had no reason to complain'. Bernard said that he perfectly understood, and he agreed to send Sladen's objections to the Viceroy, but he insisted that Taingda must be removed from the ministry and the country forthwith. Brought to Bernard's office, the minister was informed of this decision. Having no warning of it, he assumed that he was to be executed, and he begged Sladen to spare his life. By 5.30 he was on his way to the docks with an escort of the Hampshires. Bernard, in spite of his reputation of being soft-hearted and pro-Burmese, had not dared to allow him even to return home and bid farewell to his wife lest he might create mischief. An armed guard was placed on his house, but three boxes of money and belongings were sent after him to the steamer. On the way to the river the escort found its way obstructed by a bullock-cart just outside the city walls, much to the annoyance of the officer in command, and Taingda fearfully asked if he had been brought thither to face a firing-squad. The bullock-cart was bringing into the city Grattan Geary, the editor of the *Bombay Gazette*, newly-arrived from India. It was the kind of scoop that journalists dream about.[3]

Taingda was taken to Rangoon and subsequently deported to Calcutta, despite Sladen's request that his help should be publicly acknowledged. At Calcutta Dufferin sent for him, and reported that he was 'an intelligent old man'; when he found 'he had not been sent for to have his head off' he became quite cheerful. Dufferin told him that he would be treated as a guest, and sent back as soon as Burma was tranquillized.[4]

---

* Sladen appears in fiction as the hero of F. Tennyson Jesse's novel *The Lacquer Lady*, which deals with the events of Thibaw's fall.

The Government of India tried to retrieve the situation by sending back the Kinwun Mingyi, but the other members of the Hlutdaw now felt insecure, and the institution had in fact lost its authority over the provincial officials. It remained in existence until Dufferin abolished it in February 1886, but it was no longer possible for Bernard to work through it. This breakdown precipitated, if it did not cause, the rapid increase of disorder and dacoitry.

After the King's departure, Prendergast had asked White to secure the palace and its valuables. This task White did thoroughly, and for ten days, assisted by Colonel Sanford and Captain Woodward, R.N., he searched the buildings and packed into crates all the movable property. The work was done by parties of bluejackets, who made some remarkable discoveries. In one dark corner they found a sum of 10,400 rupees, in another a chest full of infants' feeding bottles and several boxes full of empty photograph albums. 'The quantities of boxes of French silk were fabulous,' White told his wife, 'more like the turnout from some great shop in Paris than a supply for private use.' He wished that she had been there to help him 'sift the wheat from the chaff' as they had no experts. A great quantity of 'gold vessels, crown jewels, ivory and ladies' wearing apparel' was discovered. 'I was disappointed in the amount of jewels that we found,' he reported sadly, 'I thought we should have found quantities of rubies, as part of the revenue is paid from the ruby mines. One or two beautiful pieces of French jewelry were turned out of odd corners. One tiara must have cost much more than £1,000. We also found a case of very lovely little watches. One was a beetle; when you touched the spring, its highly jewelled wings were spread and opened out the face of a little watch of most perfect finish.'

There were a good many empty jewel-cases lying in the royal apartments, evidence of the extensive looting that had gone on during the night of the occupation. But pearls which White picked up crumbled to dust between his finger and thumb, and he considered that the royal family had been greatly cheated by the French. More valuable were the sacred solid figures of Buddha weighing about a stone each; some smaller images had lost their shape by being profusely overlaid with gold leaf, each leaf put on by a devout Buddhist being a work of merit.[5]

A prize committee was appointed to evaluate the confiscated property and to organize its sale for the Government of India. White declined to be prize agent (though he had done most of the work) since the appointment was a lucrative one and 'rather beneath the dignity of a General officer'. The total value of the prize was eventually estimated at Rs 826,424, and was something of a disappointment.[6]

Mackenzie Wallace had telegraphed to Prendergast that the Viceroy thought a few standards or similar trophies might be sent to Queen Victoria. To Bernard he intimated that His Excellency would also be glad to have some souvenirs of the expedition 'say a couple of Burmese cannon and a jingal or two' and 'something curious in the shape of a bell.' An inventory of jewels from the palace at Mandalay to be sent to England, dated 20 March 1886, reads;

For H.M. the Queen—Theebaw's best crown.*
*Eight stones have fallen out of the crown and
are sent in a sealed envelope in the same case
with the crown itself.)
   Necklace, with diamond peacock and gold comb.
   3 emeralds from Theebaw's second crown.
For H.R.H. The Prince of Wales
   2 carved ivory tusks
For H.R.H. The Princess of Wales
   a gold figure of the Buddha.[7]

The spoils of war at Mandalay also included a sacred white elephant. In Burma, as in Siam, the rare albino elephant was regarded with extreme veneration because of its association with the Gautama, or Buddha. 'Poor fellow! he was a fraud as regards his complexion,' White recorded. He was, however, much too holy to survive for long the dethronement of the semi-divine king, and after ten days 'he yielded up his great soul to Gautama, who had given it'. To bury him presented a major problem. The Buddhist priests wanted him to be left within the palace precincts, but White ordered that the elephant was to be taken away and buried outside the walls. Military carpenters set to work to construct a huge wooden sledge on which the elephant was dragged to his last resting place. 'There was another holy infant elephant—the Lord of the Silver Bowls.' White had come upon an elephant shed in his search rounds, and struck the huge vessels with his stick, deciding that they were tin. 'I afterwards heard the title I have applied to the little elephant, and on further investigation found that the vessels in which his food was cooked were solid silver, and all his drinking utensils of the same.' White also discovered the tusks of 'a former very celebrated white elephant' and had a photograph of himself taken with them. He sent one copy to the *Graphic* and another to Sir Victor Brooke.[8]

Prendergast had been anxious to establish communication with Bhamo, because as yet his authority extended only as far as the gunboats had gone up the river, a distance of about fifty miles. On 19 December, having got the Viceroy's authorization, he left Mandalay with six steamers and a force consisting of a half battalion of the Royal Welch Fusiliers, a half battalion of the 25th Madras Infantry, thirty-six mounted infantry and 300 sailors. Thereafter, as far as those left in Mandalay were concerned, he vanished into the blue, and no message was received from him for nearly a fortnight. He did not reach Bhamo until 28 December, having been much delayed by the difficulties of navigating the intricate channels and awesome defiles of the Upper Irrawaddy.

He found the country quiet and the people along the river banks well-disposed. Two miles below Bhamo, the *wundauk* of the district came to meet him, declaring that the town was calm and expressing pleasure at seeing him. The 'head man of the Chinese' whom he met on shore was also friendly; after reading the General's printed proclamation he said, 'The scene is the same, only the actors are changed.' Prendergast discovered, however, that the *wundauk* had had no instructions from the Hlutdaw since the fall of the Mandalay, although runners had brought the news of Thibaw's deposition to a merchant living near Bhamo on 2 December. 'This seems to show', he complained in his first message to the Viceroy, 'that the Hlutdaw, as at present constituted, is not doing its duty.' When Sladen received a copy of the letter, he scribbled below it 'What have the *mingyi* to say to this?'[9]

Prendergast had become increasingly critical of Sladen, and the handling of the political side, and what he had seen in Bhamo increased his suspicion of the Hlutdaw. 'It is evident that Prendergast is hostile,' Sladen told Bernard, 'but I can meet him, and will do so at the proper time . . . Prendergast could not get to Bhamo without a force—How did he expect the Hlotdaw to do so—after he has taken all their steamers and did not leave them a launch even—or a soldier, or a policeman. He even boned 20,000 Rs. of government revenue and took the money away to Bhamo—though he had 20,000 on board. The Hlotdaw made several attempts to get out their proclamations. They were interested in doing so.'[10]

On the more important question of the Chinese attitude to Bhamo, the results of Prendergast's expedition were reassuring. As Dufferin wrote to Churchill, 'Last night we received the gratifying intelligence of Prendergast's peaceful arrival at Bhamo, without having had to encounter either Black Flags or any opposition on the part of Chinese troops. Though I did not think it likely that the latter would have had time to put in an appearance, I was afraid that the occupation of Bhamo might prove a less satisfactory business than that of Mandalay.'[11] But all was still quiet when Prendergast left the town on 6 January, and there was only a small garrison of Chinese in evidence at the frontier. He left General Norman in charge, instructing him to clear the jungle for 1,000 yards around the town, to strengthen the palisade, to make frequent reconnaissances and to report on the activities of the Chinese. The Chinese had in fact approached the border at Bhamo to see what was being done, and the civil officer there was instructed to inform them that the British were only interested in keeping the peace in Bhamo, and were anxious to promote trade with China without encroaching upon Chinese territory.[12]

While Prendergast was in Bhamo the command in Mandalay devolved upon White, who grumbled that the General had taken nearly all the staff officers with him. General Foord had succeeded Prendergast for twenty-four hours, and had suddenly appeared at the palace, the first time that White had seen him, but 'as he was drawing 200 Rs less pay . . . than in India he asked to be sent back.' Prendergast, who was very anxious to have White in command, had complied with this 'most extraordinary request'. His intuition was sound. White assumed his responsibility with great energy and an utterly realistic appreciation of the situation. The opportunity was one which he eagerly seized, for he was much concerned about his career and future promotion, but his letters home show that he was in a particularly critical mood. 'I cannot help showing impatience with much that is around me, and I will be no favourite with the Madras Army. I shall be curious to see the official dispatches and whether General Prendergast will make out that the troops behaved gallantly and are the invincibles that soldiers are generally described as, after the fighting is over. . . . The Madras officers, especially the old ones, are an indolent unmilitary lot . . . the sepoys are sleepy and want waking up dreadfully.'[13]

But apart from the Ulster habit of candour, White was also deeply concerned and uneasy about the military situation, which seemed to his soldier's eye all wrong. 'Our position too here is ill-considered and much too extended. Sir Harry will find considerable modifications on his return.' He suspected in fact that Prendergast preferred to leave the worry of Mandalay to him, and as he preferred command to being a subordinate, the arrangement suited them both. 'This country will remain in a ferment until its future is settled. I fear that Lord D.'s visit means that nothing will be done till then. The people are now afraid to side with us beyond the walls of Mandalay. They say—as the Jagis said in the Kurram Valley, as the Afghans said in Kabul, as the Kandaharis said in Southern Afghanistan, as the Arabs of the Bayuda said on the Upper Nile, and as the Hadendowas said at Suakim—"If you will assure us that you will stay with us we will throw in our lot with you, but our throats will be cut if we do so and you go away." '

The speed and success of the Mandalay campaign created a totally misleading impression of conquest. The districts around Mandalay were covered with jungle and there were few roads. The British force, without any form of land transport, was virtually beseiged in the capital, while the thousands of disbanded Burmese soldiers turned dacoits and began at once to attack the British pickets and patrols. On the first day he assumed command, White had to send out columns in all directions, the beginning of many campaigns in which the British losses far outstripped those of the advance on Mandalay. 'Mr. Bernard and I work very well together,' he wrote, 'We have had risings in every direction to meet, and I think we have shown energy and precision in hitting the right points . . . Bernard gets the information, tells me of the combinations against us, and the threatened points, and then with a Burmese map on my table I try to plan a campaign. So far they have been a success. The country is the most difficult I ever saw or thought of to plan operations in—everywhere water and jungle, both of which defy calculations as to time of march. The natives know nothing of distance and the country is unsurveyed. We have little or no land transport. I knew when we started this would anchor us . . . I made no secret of it to others. I told the Quartermaster-General of the Madras Army that he had equipped a force as a fish to fight a dog. It is coming true . . . .'

Nor had White any illusions about the political situation. On the eve of Prendergast's return to Mandalay he wrote, 'It is a mistake to suppose that these people were anxiously awaiting annexation. The more I see and hear, the more convinced I am that they are very loyal, in their easygoing way, to the house of Alompra. The standard of Royalty, no matter where raised, attracts many adherents. The Ministers who delivered Theebaw into our hands are now threatening to resign if they are not given another prince. There is something more than mere political feeling in this . . . The mercantile class in Rangoon have cried out for annexation as the surest road to advanced profits in their trade. I am against annexation, for two strong reasons.

'1st. We have sacrificed much of late to establish confidence amongst our neighbours and feudatories that we no longer wish to remove our neighbour's landmark. The annexation of Burma would reawaken their slumbering suspicions.

'2nd. In annexing Burma we march with China at Bhamo. It has been said that China advances claims to Bhamo, which is now garrisoned by British soldiers—the usual handful. China may have been squared for the present, but after conquering some 30 or 40 thousand Frenchmen she will be very confident and have hordes of men set free to act elsewhere . . . It will be most disastrous for us to fight China. She is our best ally in the East against the aggression of Russia.'

But White confessed that he did not see how government could be carried on in a protected state. The *mingyis* had already shown that they were not to be trusted. 'They sit in Council, and ape the tricks of other ministries. They pass resolutions, and threaten to resign if not granted "home rule". But the district over which they preside is the most disturbed in the country. Our annexation must be followed by a rain of district officers all over the country, civilians whose courts must be hedged in by British bayonets for a long time to come.'

It was an astonishingly prescient view of the problem, and on the same evening White sent a long telegram to the Government of India pointing out that much military action was still required, that the troops were now overworked, and that the season for operations was short. He expected to be snubbed, but he felt that he had said what needed to be said.[14]

9

ANNEXATION

'I cannot but think that money, anxiety, and life will be saved if Upper Burma be annexed to Her Majesty's dominions,' wrote General Prendergast to the Viceroy just before the frontier was crossed, 'for you would then be sure of the policy of Upper Burma.'[1] Prendergast, who took his responsibilities seriously, renewed this advice more than once after Mandalay had been occupied. But as Dufferin explained, 'it would not be a very opportune course to take in the midst of a general election, which may possibily result in the return to power of a Government whose first step would be to annul any such proclamation as that which you desire to issue. Quite independent of any reason of this kind, however, there are several circumstances with which of course I cannot expect you to be acquainted, which militate against such a proceeding at present.' After indicating what they were, Dufferin continued, 'You must not, however, suppose from the foregoing that I am personally opposed to annexation. As at present advised, I think it may prove the lesser of two evils; but the decision must not be arrived at without due deliberation; nor, as I am the responsible person in the matter, must my hand be forced.'[2]

Just before the expeditionary force left Thayetmyo Churchill wrote to Dufferin that 'the Government as a body are strongly in favour of annexation pure and simple and I expect you will be forced into it by the difficulty of finding a prince who would have any chance of maintaining himself or of giving any guarantees of value for good government. In this office I find that Bernard's opinions carry little weight. He is considered essentially a weak, timid, undecided person. I should not wonder if he was in communication with Lord Ripon'. Sir James Scott, a leading authority on Burma, had advised Churchill against annexation, and in favour of a protected principality. The difficulty was that no suitable prince was available, for the acceptable Nyaungyan prince had died at Calcutta early in 1885, and his younger brother the Myingun prince, Nyaung Ok, was under French influence.

'But, even if you were successful in finding a decent prince, or if you decided to tolerate a bad one,' Churchill asked, 'can you have any security against foreign European intrigue? It is French intrigue which has forced us to go to Burmah; but for that element we might have treated Theebaw with severe neglect . . . Now the Indian Government have a unique opportunity, which may never recur, for dealing very summarily with Burmah. The French are sickened of colonial extension, and will certainly not try any tricks if Lord Salisbury's government remains in . . . There can be no question of foreign intrigue in territories absolutely under the British Crown. If on the other hand this opportunity of protecting India effectually on the east is allowed to pass, then events may follow a course analogous to what has happened in the north-west. European and Asiatic politics cannot well be separated, and, with all due submission, I would suggest that against the difficulties and expenses of annexation you must balance the danger of European aggression and determine whether annexation will prevent aggression . . .'[3]

It was difficult for Dufferin to withstand this kind of forceful advice. Already in October he had told Churchill that he now considered annexation preferable to placing another prince on the Burmese throne. Churchill was pleased, because this seemed to bring Dufferin and the Indian Council into line with the views held by Salisbury and himself. The Queen, moreover, had agreed with Salisbury that the annexation of Thibaw's kingdom was 'quite inevitable and necessary'. At the last moment Dufferin's resolution wavered, a reflection partly of his own underlying doubts about the consequences of annexation, but even more of the advice of senior members of the Indian Civil Service.

There was no lack of such advice, and the tenor of most of it was against annexation. On 12 October C. H. T. Crosthwaite, who had been Commissioner for British Burma, sent the Viceroy's private secretary a memorandum on the subject. 'The question how far the French are to be allowed to establish their influence in Upper Burmah is a pressing one. It is not yet but it will soon be too late to deal with it. It is a serious matter. Upper Burmah is merely separated from the British Province by an imaginery line, the people and the country are one and the same. We cannot lose our influence over the Mandalay Government without sensibly weakening our power and authority in our own Province.' Pointing out that crime and dacoitry had increased during the previous four years, Crosthwaite argued that there had been a loss of confidence in the British authorities. In no province of the British Empire were the evidences of English power fewer or less apparent to the people, and if Upper Burma were to fall under French influence the mischief caused, not least to trade, would be considerable. He then outlined the demands which ought to be made to Thibaw, in terms which Dufferin adopted, almost word for word, in the ultimatum. If the King rejected the conditions 'we should be justified in treating him as an open enemy; and I should be prepared to depose him and instal one of the rival claimants in his room.'

Crosthwaite strongly advised against outright annexation. 'In the first place it will compel us to increase the garrison of Burmah greatly. It would probably be necessary to double it. The expense of keeping troops in Burmah is very heavy. In the second place it will give us a frontier of a very wide range bordering on countries held by wild tribes of Shans and others. It is possible that these tribes might be more friendly to us than they have been to the Burmese. On the other hand it is possible that they may continue to be troublesome and that we should be involved in difficult and costly operations against them. In the third place, I doubt if the revenue of Upper Burmah would be sufficient to pay for administering the country according to our methods; my information on this point is very deficient . . . Annexation would certainly not be popular with the officials. We would certainly have a rough time of it at first.'[4]

Sir Charles Aitchison, the Lieutenant-Governor of the Punjab, wrote on 22 October: 'There are two things, I hope, Government won't do. I hope they won't annex Upper Burma, and I equally hope they will not establish a Resident at Mandalay, unless they support him by a British brigade . . . Briefly, the reasons for non-annexation are—(1) you will be brought into contact with China, and your Burma politics will thereafter be dragged into the European and American sphere; (2) you will touch on the north a hilly and jungly country, inhabited by wild tribes which you cannot govern, and who will be very difficult to tame; (3) the cost of occupation will be greater than the revenues the country will yield, and all the surplus you now get from Lower Burma will be absorbed.'[5]

In reply, the Viceroy's secretary said that he perceived clearly the force of two of Aitchison's arguments against annexation, the expensiveness of governing the country according to English ideas, and the difficulty of

8. The Flotilla anchored at Pagan, 22 November 1885. The scuttled steamers in the foreground belonged to Thibaw

9. Colonel Sladen receives the surrender of Burmese arms at Ava, 27 November 1885. Thibaw's envoy, the *wun* with his golden umbrella, stands beside him

10. The arrival of the Flotilla at Mandalay, 28 November 1885

11. General Prendergast (seated centre) with some of his staff at his Headquarters in the Hall of Audience in the palace at Mandalay. Brigadier-General Foord and Colonel Bengough are second and third from the left in the top row. Surgeon-General Donnelly sits on General Prendergast's left, with Colonel Sanford seated on the step between them

defending the frontier, 'but I do not clearly understand your repugnance to having China as a neighbour. There are, no doubt, certain objections to getting within easy striking distance of a great Power, but, on the other hand, there are compensating advantages which ought not to be left out of sight.'[6]

On 2 November Aitchison wrote . . . 'I conclude that the annexation of Upper Burma is as good as determined on. Well, of course, there are arguments for that course, and I hope the decision will turn out for the best. But I have more than misgivings . . . Don't imagine that Theebaw is such a tyrant that the people groan under him and will welcome us as deliverers, and troops will not be needed. Nothing of the kind. When Theebaw murdered all his blood relatives, our own people in Lower Burma thought it quite a natural thing . . . For, believe me, the annexation of Upper Burma is not a thing to be undertaken by Lord Randolph Churchill in the easy-going, jaunty way, in which he seems to have announced it.'[7]

To Bernard on 3 November Dufferin wrote: 'The really important question which it is desirable to settle is whether Upper Burmah should be permanently annexed to Her Majesty's dominions, or converted into a feudatory State. I perceive that you incline to the latter course, as does also Sir Charles Aitchison, a public servant for whose judgment and opinions I have the greatest respect, and in this view Lord Ripon, I see, also coincides. I confess, however, that my own instincts point rather the other way. In the first place, the quality required in a buffer state is that of elasticity and the power of resistance. These characteristics may to a certain limited extent be said to attach to Afghanistan; but even so, the arrangement, as our daily experience is proving, is anything but satisfactory. Burmah is of a soft and molluscous consistence, and is consequently far less adapted to subserve the required purpose.'

With regard to being brought into contact with China, which was the chief reason for Ripon's objection to annexation, Dufferin was inclined to hope that it might prove an advantage. 'It is possible it may pave the way for the establishment of a trading route, which seems to me to be the best counterpoise to any advantages of the sort which France may acquire by the approximation of her territories to Eastern Yunnan.'[8]

After the fall of Mandalay, M. E. Grant Duff, the Governor of Madras, gave his views on annexation in a confidential memorandum to the Viceroy. 'I take it for granted,' he began, 'that all those who have thought seriously, and to any purpose, about the Empire, are convinced

H   113

that the assumption of new responsibilities is *per se* an evil.' He would personally have preferred the *status quo* of a few years earlier to the situation which now existed, but since that was past praying for, the prospect of annexation had now to be considered. It would no doubt be welcomed by those who cherished 'golden dreams about a *great* trade to come down from China to the seaboard of our provinces'. In his opinion no great trade would come down by the Irrawaddy, or any other route, to the Bay of Bengal. The main stream would follow the Yangtse and other rivers flowing towards the east, until a way was found through the mountains of Assam. But *some* trade would find its way from Yunnan if Upper Burma was well-governed. As for direct benefits from Upper Burma, 'all the rich alluvial plains are already ours, and the country beyond our border, though a fine one, does not appear to be anything super-eminent.' A large body of troops would be needed to hold the new territory, and the British would be expected to endow it with 'European government in exchange for an Asiatic revenue'.

On the other hand, to retire 'having shown our irresistible power' was out of the question: that would merely mean having to repeat the expedition at some more inconvenient time. And if Upper Burma fell into anarchy, the British provinces would inevitably be imperilled. As for putting a nominee on the throne, no one he had spoken to had been able to give him much comfort on this point, as there was little reason to think that any of the princes of the reigning house were at all better than the 'wretched man just taken into safe-keeping', and *he* had had the benefit of a European education.

Also to be considered was the attitude of France, which had deliberately taken advantage of the Anglo-Russian crisis over Afghanistan to meddle in Burma. 'The Burmese have learned to intrigue in Europe, and are not likely to unlearn that lesson as long as a semblance of independence is preserved.' There was further the question of China, and what attitude she would take. Even if, as it was rumoured, she was not unfriendly to the idea of the extension of British power along the Irrawaddy, would she continue to be so when European traders began to insist on more trade with Yunnan? Might not the wild frontier tribes stir up trouble for both governments? Would the Kachins give trouble, or would their trading instincts prevail, and cause them to take as their motto *Olim Marte nunc arte* (happily translated by a Scots judge as 'formerly robbers, now thieves'). Such sobering reflections seemed to point to outright annexation, though annexation was 'rightly unpopular'.[9]

Dufferin had been loth to embark upon the campaign in the first place. He knew only too well what the consequences of such an expedition might be. To Reay, the Governor of Bombay, he confided that he was vexed at having been 'driven into the Burmah business', his hope was that by sending an overwhelming force he might reach a definite settlement without bloodshed, the thought of which filled him with horror, 'but when once the ball is set rolling, one has alas! very little control over the issues, as far as some of the principal interests of humanity are concerned.'[10] His intention had been to go to Burma himself as soon as Mandalay was secured, but a sharp attack of fever in the first week of December made it certain that his visit would be postponed until after the Delhi manoeuvres. There was some advantage in this accident, as Mackenzie Wallace told Bernard, for by the end of January Bernard would have had time to assess the situation and China's attitude would undoubtedly have become clearer.[11]

The Viceroy's first reaction to the news of the fall of Mandalay was therefore one of relief. While still recovering from the fever, he wrote to Prendergast to express his satisfaction. 'It does you the greatest possible credit; and I am happy to say that your services have been fully appreciated both at home and in India itself. The Queen is delighted, so is the Secretary of State, and so is the Government of India.'[12] Prendergast had shown himself prudent, skilful and humane: he had carried out his instructions to the letter and despite the worrying reports of confusion on the night of the entry into Mandalay, and of Prendergast's handling of the press, Dufferin was at this moment well pleased with him.

The question had now been removed to the political and diplomatic field, where Dufferin was more at home, and more confident of being able to control the outcome. He was very reluctant to incur the responsibility of outright annexation. Even if the Chinese claims could be satisfied, the financial burden for the Government of India would be considerable, and might prove ruinous to his Indian policies. As a Whig, Dufferin was opposed to annexation on principle; his natural political sympathies on Imperial matters were with Gladstone: but as an aristocrat and a landowner, he had on some other issues more in common with Salisbury and the Conservatives. One of these issues was Ireland, and there was irony in the fact that at the very moment when Gladstone's intention to work for Irish Home Rule was made public, Dufferin should be faced with the decision whether or not to annex another country to the British Empire. Britain had reached both the high water-mark of her imperial expansion and the point at which the United Kingdom itself seemed about to break up.

Dufferin was well aware that Churchill, with the backing of the chambers of commerce, was strongly in favour of annexation, and that he had hoped for the fall of Mandalay in time for the election—failing that, he now wished to present the next government with a *fait accompli*. Dufferin obtained his permission to leave the question open at least until he could himself go to Rangoon and Mandalay, and consult with the men on the spot. The hiatus thus created gave rise to a number of awkward problems, the most pressing of which concerned Upper Burma's relations with foreign powers. Churchill had suggested that the country might be declared to be, by conquest, part of Her Majesty's dominions, without declaring it at the same time to be part of British India. The Legislative Department of the Government of India advised Dufferin that conquest without annexation and re-grant did exist. Foreign treaties could be abrogated by reducing Upper Burma to the position of a Native State and thus annihilating its sovereignty for international purposes. This doctrine was open to question, however, and they suggested annexation and re-grant as the safer course. For administrative purposes it would be more convenient that the country should not be part of British dominions until it was more settled.

The Government of India could not annex territory without the previous sanction of the Crown. This, and the question of whether there was any distinction between annexation to the British dominions and to British India in particular, were matters for the English Law Officers to decide, and Dufferin sought guidance on whether he would require any special powers to administer the country. Salisbury therefore asked the Law Officers of the Crown to give their legal opinion, which was telegraphed to Dufferin on Christmas Eve.

'First. Events in Upper Burma have given the Crown the right to extinquish independent existence of Burmese State.

Second. If this be done, all Burmese treaties with Foreign Powers will therefore cease to exist.

Third. The fact of their cessation may in that case be properly communicated to Foreign Powers.

Fourth. Unless formal notification be now given that Burma has become part of the Queen's Dominions, Treaty Powers may contend, in case sovereignty of Upper Burma is hereafter ceded to a native ruler, that the

Burmese Government has only been suspended and that Treaties are still in force.

Fifth. Territory thus acquired by conquest may be hereafter ceded without authority of Parliament, so long as power of Crown is not limited by its own acts or by legislation, and may meanwhile be administered during pleasure by officers under the immediate orders of the Crown.

Sixth. If the Viceroy is to discharge this duty, he must receive special authority and instructions.'[13]

The Government therefore authorized Dufferin to proclaim Upper Burma part of Her Majesty's dominions, and to administer the country during the pleasure of the Crown. The Government of India was to have financial control and responsibility.

Churchill had gone over to Ireland to spend Christmas at Howth with his friend Lord Justice FitzGibbon, but before leaving London he had settled with Lord Salisbury the draft of the proclamation about Burma to be issued simultaneously on 1 January in London, Calcutta, Rangoon and Mandalay.[14] It read: 'By Command of the Queen Empress, it is hereby notified that the territories formerly governed by King Theebaw will no longer be under his rule, but have become part of Her Majesty's Dominions, and will, during her Majesty's pleasure, be administered by such officers as the Viceroy and Governor-General of India may from time to time appoint.'[15] Sir Winston Churchill, in his biography of his father, writes 'Lord Randolph arranged that the proclamation should be made on January 1st 1886, as "a New Year's present to the Queen". On the last day of December he was staying with FitzGibbon for his Christmas Party; and as the clock struck midnight he lifted his glass and announced, with due solemnity, "Howth annexes Burma to the British Empire." The next morning the Viceregal proclamation was published. It is one of the shortest documents of the kind on historical record.'[16]

IO

THE TIMES CORRESPONDENT

By one of those turns of chance against which no human plan of action is proof, someone else besides General Prendergast had interviewed Thibaw on the morning of 29 November. A handful of newspaper correspondents and the artists for the *Graphic* and the *Illustrated London News* had travelled with the expedition, or joined it in time to report the fall of Mandalay. Among them was one E. K. Moylan, the Rangoon correspondent of *The Times*. As such he was cordially received by Prendergast, and given special privileges to enable him to report fully on the dethronement of Thibaw. He was on good terms with Sladen, and somehow managed to accompany him to an interview with the King on the morning of the 29th, thus obtaining something of a scoop. He dispatched his copy by the military field telegraph to Minhla and thence to Rangoon. It appeared in *The Times* on 5 December, and was read with considerable interest.

At the interview in the summer-house, the royal party consisted of Thibaw, Supayalat, her sister, the Queen Mother and Thibaw's sister. No one else was present except an interpreter. Sladen and Moylan remained standing during the interview, and, as Moylan informed his readers, Sladen was the first European allowed to come into the presence of any Burmese king without taking off his shoes and assuming a crouching attitude. Supayalat sat beside the King, and closely followed the conversation, in which she occasionally took part. Moylan found Thibaw 'a stout, young, good-looking man of about 30, with a weak face', but without 'the receding forehead which is the distinctive mark of the descendants of Aloungpra'. Since finding that he had no violence to fear, the King had recovered his nerve and displayed a good deal of quiet dignity.

Sladen introduced Moylan as the correspondent of *The Times*, where-upon Thibaw immediately said that he knew *The Times* and that his ministers took a copy to learn English public opinion. He added that he was anxious that the English people should hear his words, and he requested Moylan to write down what he said. This Moylan did, and at the end of the interview he read his notes over again to the King. 'I wish to be kept quiet,' Thibaw said, 'I have given over everything to the English. I want Sladen to govern the country now and in the future . . . I have been badly advised.' He then launched a bitter tirade against his ministers who had deceived and betrayed him. At this point Supayalat, turning to the interpreter, said, 'Tell him that the day before yesterday I had 300 maids of honour. Yesterday evening only sixteen remained with me. We have two children alive, and three are buried in the northern garden.' Thibaw resumed: 'Let Sladen govern the country for five years . . . When he has got affairs in good order then I will come back and be guided by him. I have known Sladen since I was a boy, and have most confidence in him . . .'

Thibaw then embarked on a defence of his actions throughout his reign. 'You English think that I killed all my relatives, but it is not so. I was under guard myself, and they were murdered. The reason that I was not murdered myself was that before the King died he told the Queen I was the quiet son. A horoscope was also drawn by the priests and my name came out first. For the first seven months after I became King I was not allowed to interfere. I was not even crowned. I continued to wear the phongyee priest's robes. I ordered that my relations should not be killed but imprisoned, so that there might not be a disturbance in the country. I was sleeping in my bed when the order to kill them was given by the ministers. After eight months the Yenout Mengyee, who killed the princes, tried to murder me. The English people knew much that I did, but not what was going on behind me. I never left the palace. I wish the English people to know that I am not a drunkard. I am a religious Buddhist. I have given up all the Crown jewels, and I am sure that the English, who are a great people, will not object to me, as a king, keeping my ring, or my wife from keeping her jewels.' He indicated a magnificent ruby ring he was wearing, and Supayalat's diamond neck-lace. Sladen at once assented, and the interview ended. But Thibaw asked Moylan to return when Prendergast came to him, that the English people might know what happened.

Moylan did so, and his dispatch continued with an account of the

King's departure that afternoon. It did not end there, however, and the second half was a sensational report of events in Mandalay since the arrival of the British troops. After telling how, as a result of an order that any woman might be allowed to enter through the Queen's gate, the palace had been looted by several hundred women of the town, and the Crown jewels only just saved by Sladen, Moylan went on: 'Last night a disgraceful scene of riot and bloodshed occurred in Mandalay, and more lives were lost than in any engagement during the expedition. The Italian Consulate and other European houses were attacked. The military arrangements to protect the town were very deficient. The headquarters were on board of the steamers, three miles from the town. Many Europeans are leaving, owing to the danger.

'Last night the streets were occupied by gangs of armed Burmans, who looted and murdered almost unchecked. The Princesses of the Royal Family were robbed of their jewels in the streets. The Buddhist monasteries were plundered.

'Unless immediate steps be taken to restore order and provide for the civil government of the country very serious consequences will result, and Burmah will become completely disorganised.

'While I have been writing two men have been murdered by dacoits in daylight, at a short distance from this house.'[1]

Moylan had not submitted his copy for military censorship, as the Field Press Regulations required, and when he learned of the contents Prendergast was understandably furious. All the incidents which Moylan mentioned had occurred. Guards had had to be placed on the Italian and French consulates; robbery and murder had taken place in the streets; the princesses had lost their jewellery; at the 'Incomparable Pagoda', in the north-east of the city, a magnificent diamond had been stolen from the forehead of the Gautama by Burmese soldiers who were placed there to guard it, and a second large diamond and other jewels stolen from a pagoda in the south-west suburbs.[2] But Moylan had undoubtedly exaggerated these episodes to create a picture of total military incompetence. He had also written a letter, with two other Europeans, complaining to the military authorities about the lack of adequate protection during the night, and this roused the ire of Colonel Bengough, the Chief of Staff, who sent for him and treated him in a very harsh and intemperate manner. As a consequence, Moylan was summarily deported from Mandalay on the orders of the G.O.C., and on 3 December, he returned to Rangoon on board the S.S. *Burma*, a fellow passenger with Admiral Sir Frederick Richards (the naval C. in C.) who had been on a brief visit to inspect his ships.[3]

The Times accompanied Moylan's long dispatch on 5 December with a noticeably sharp editorial. 'The Burmese expedition is virtually over, and we are now able to review the position to which General Prendergast's brilliant successes have brought us. One unfortunate episode has marred plans which have been in other respects flawless. In the interregnum between the fall of King Thebaw and the assumption of power by Colonel Sladen dire confusion seems to have prevailed. The palace was looted by several hundred women in consequence of an inexplicable order; and for a day and a night Mandalay was given over to riot and bloodshed . . . Clearly the sooner a firm government of some kind is established the better; even Thebaw's rule is better than anarchy and lawlessness.'[4] On 9 December *The Times* announced that they could not continue their telegrams from the seat of operations, as General Prendergast had directed their special correspondent to return to Rangoon. 'We await an explanation of this peremptory act of the General in command.'[5]

That week *Punch* published extracts from the imaginary diary of King Thibaw, including a very obvious skit on the Moylan interview. Thibaw is represented as saying to Prendergast that he was well-acquainted with *Punch* and wished the people of England to be told how deeply he regretted not having studied the wise words of Mr. Punch all his life. He was extremely interested to hear that Mr. Punch's artists 'take off people's heads, even the heads of the greatest ministers'. There was also a sideswipe at the 'Anti-National League and destruction of British interests Association' which had promised to use their best endeavours to have Thibaw restored to the throne of his ancestors.[6]

When *Punch* heard of Moylan's treatment it gleefully announced, under the title 'The Sword is mightier than the Pen', that it had replaced him with its own special correspondent, whose first dispatch it was privileged to print. It was vituperative enough to have come from the pen of Moylan himself.

'The bravery of the troops in storming the ancient stronghold of Theebaw was admirable. Every soldier proved himself a hero, but the greatest of them all, the most heroic of heroes, was unquestionably Prendergast, who is known as "Bull-ee", which, being translated from the native *patois* into English means "The Wild Lion of the Fierce Battle Wagers" . . . His administration of the country, after the sanguinary combat which delivered the place into his hands, equalled his martial prowess. In twenty minutes he had introduced into the "Land of the Shining Moon" Magna Charta, the Habeas Corpus Act, the sixpenny loaf at twopence-halfpenny, the cheap parcels post and the self-acting sewing machine. With all this he is as merciful as he is clever, good-natured as he is clear-headed, beautiful as he is well-read. . . . Major-General Prendergast is a mixture of all that is best in Napoleon, Shakespeare, Bolton M.P., Sir Robert Walter Camden, and the cleverest performers (inclusive of the damsel who plays with equal facility the big drum and the German flute) of the Ladies' Viennese Orchestra. The conduct of Prendergast is magnificent, and may be called, with perfect truth, "the war".

'P.S. Please, Sir, I hope you will like the above. If not adequately complimentary, kindly supply the required epithets, etc.'[7]

Moylan had determined to have his revenge on Prendergast, and he was not without the means of achieving it. He had the full support of his editor, G. E. Buckle, who was a friend and confidant of Lord Randolph Churchill. Buckle immediately pulled strings to have Moylan returned to Mandalay, even going so far as to send Churchill Moylan's full statement of the events of 29 November, with the implied threat that *The Times* might publish it. Churchill had already been showing signs of impatience with what he regarded as Prendergast's slow progress up the Irrawaddy, and he was disappointed that the fall of Mandalay had taken place just too late to win votes in the election. (After Minhla he had confided to Dufferin: 'A government never fails to derive a certain amount of credit for successful military operations.')[8] Moylan's disclosures now turned him completely against Prendergast.

'I was desperately vexed with General Prendergast for his tactless treatment of the *Times* correspondent,' he wrote to Dufferin, 'The *Times* has been most loyal in support of your Burmese policy and carries great weight with the politicians; it has also generally been very favourable to the Government for some time past. Besides I knew that nothing in the nature of our operations in Burmah rendered any press regulations necessary or desirable, and I suspected that General Prendergast's ukase was called forth by the information sent home by the *Times* correspondent that there had been at Mandalay a good deal of avoidable looting and disorder. With the arrival of Mr. Bernard civil government resumes its powers and of course perfect liberty for the press recommences.'[9]

On 17 December he wrote: 'I have been concerned at the news from Mandalay as to the massacre of Europeans up country. I thought all

Europeans with the exception of Andreino had arrived safely in Lower Burma before the advance of our forces. I own, that until further informed, General Prendergast's proceedings appear to have deteriorated in intelligence and vigour. He must have known of the Europeans in danger when he first arrived, but seems to have either delayed making, or to have made no effort. I fear if this turns out to be so matters may go badly for him. The disturbance, crime and looting in Mandalay after the arrival of the British forces was most discreditable, and the treatment of the *Times* correspondent mischievous or silly. I make these remarks of course subject to what may appear from the General's dispatches, but the press is generally well-informed, and I greatly doubt the possibility of refuting much of its statements in this case. I was obliged to press for the reinstatement of the *Times* correspondent without delay.'[10]

On the previous day Buckle had written to thank him for the trouble he had taken in regard to Moylan. 'We have no desire to make mischief in Burma; and so *The Times* will let the matter drop provided that Prendergast does not insist on justifying himself, in which case of course we shall state our side. As soon as we obtain the necessary authorization we shall merely announce the fact in the same short way that we announced our correspondent's dismissal; and instructions shall be sent to our correspondent to guard him against allowing any irritation to bias him. He has always got on capitally with Bernard.'[11]

As soon as he received Lord Randolph's telegram, Dufferin instructed his private secretary, D. Mackenzie Wallace, to communicate to Bernard's secretary the authorization for Moylan's return. There was a twist to the situation, for Wallace had himself been one of *The Times'* most brilliant special correspondents, and some years later he was to return to the paper as head of its Foreign Department.[12]

A curious correspondence, not without elements of comedy, ensued between Moylan and E. S. Symes, the Commissioner's secretary, who informed him on 17 December that he was free to go back to the capital and fulfil his duties 'without hindrance or annoyance'.[13] Moylan replied: 'As you mention that the Government of India wish me to fulfil my duties without hindrance or annoyance, I desire to call your attention to the following matter: I understand that the military authorities at Thayetmyo still claim to exercise a right of censorship over all telegrams from Upper Burmah, and that they even carry this to such a length as to claim the same right over all telegrams sent from Thayetmyo which refer to Upper Burmah. I think the Government may perhaps not be aware of this fact, and I think it may be well to draw your attention to it.'[14] Symes confirmed that field telegraph offices in Upper Burma were still under censorship rules, and that the rules applied also to press messages from correspondents. He was not able to say how long the censorship would last. The Viceroy's instructions had been telegraphed to Bernard at Mandalay, but as the line was interrupted, and the message not likely to get through for some days, Symes also communicated with Colonel Auchinlech, in command of military telegraphs at Thayetmyo, asking him to arrange for Moylan to be allowed to go up country without let or hindrance.[15]

Moylan was still insisting that his position be made absolutely clear. 'I don't want to be troublesome, but the position I will assume is this:— I am not going as special correspondent with General Prendergast's sanction, or attached to any expeditionary force. No rules referring to military censorships are applicable to me. I go with the authority of the Government of India. I have a right to telegraph anything I wish, subject of course to the general right of the Civil Government to stop any telegrams containing any matter injurious to the public interests.' Symes had already sent him a copy of *Rules for working field service camp telegraph offices*, 1885. 'Please see Rule 2 in accompanying book. *All* private messages at field service telegraph offices have to be countersigned by the senior officer of the station or outpost, where the office is, and I do not think it can be intended that a special exception from this standing rule should be made in your favour. At the same time, I think you may feel certain that you will not receive hindrance or annoyance at the telegraph stations on the way up. Very likely orders will already have come down from Mandalay about you.' Moylan's reply was short. 'I am extremely obliged for your letter. I return book. I am sure the matter will be all right. I shall avoid making unnecessary difficulties.'[16]

On Sunday, 20 December, Moylan left Rangoon for Prome, where he caught the steamer *Ashley Eden*, arriving in Mandalay just a few days before Christmas. *The Times* quietly announced that 'owing to the courteous intervention of the Secretary of State for India and the Viceroy, our special correspondent in Burmah has been authorized to return to Mandalay . . .'[17] Moylan took up residence at the house of Moola Ismail, a Moslem merchant who under Thibaw had farmed the Burmese customs, and lost no time in showing that he was unaffected by the spirit of the season. Most correspondents in his position, while enjoying the discomfiture of the G.O.C., would probably have let the whole business be forgotten. But Moylan was no ordinary correspondent; he returned to Mandalay, says White, 'full of triumph and vindictiveness,'[18] and at once embarked on a bitter vendetta first against Prendergast and the soldiers, and later against Bernard and the civilians.

Months passed before the vindictive and spiteful character of his campaign was recognized in England, during which time he was able to pose as the fearless opponent of censorship, the champion of justice and the exposer of scandals. He threw the very considerable influence of *The Times* into the scales against what was held to be the ineptitude and callousness of the military authorities, and he did so with a shrewdness and cunning which kept him always just outside the range of his victim's counter-attacks. It subsequently emerged that his own hands were far from clean, but by that time the damage had been done, and it was futile to turn his own tactics against him. All this is not to say that he did not discover much about the military and civil administration in Mandalay which needed to be publicized, nor that the causes he espoused did not need a champion. He was an experienced and effective correspondent.

The source of Moylan's strength was succinctly indicated by *The Times* early in the new year. 'Though the confession is not altogether pleasant, it must be admitted that affairs of this kind are largely judged by the event. If annexation is well carried out and at small cost in money and life, a great deal of carping criticism is avoided, while the most necessary operation may be made to stink in the nostrils of the public by mismanagement.'[19] Moylan was finding a good deal to criticize. A dispatch dated 30 December from Mandalay, for example, began: 'The present position of affairs in Upper Burmah is critical. The blunders committed in allowing the Burmese soldiers at Ava and Mandalay to leave *en masse* with their swords, in delaying the dispatch of troops to the out districts after the capture of Mandalay, and in the mistaken policy of continuing the Tynedah in office are now felt. Serious disorder prevails in every locality not occupied by our troops.' Then, after a detailed account of operations against the Alompra pretender princes, he commented ominously on the absence of any news from the Bhamo force since leaving Mandalay. 'General Prendergast's action in proceeding to Bhamo while insurgents are ravaging the country is much criticized'. Subtle praise of the energy shown by White and Bernard was also by implication a criticism of Prendergast and Sladen.[20]

This was damaging enough, but worse was to follow. In the middle of

January Moylan had a conversation over dinner with Melton Prior, the special artist of the *Illustrated London News*, who was then engaged in depicting the glories of the palace at Mandalay for English readers, and with a Mr. Rose, the correspondent of the *Rangoon Gazette*, as a result of which he realized that the military had been delivered into his hands. A sensational dispatch from Moylan printed by *The Times* on 21 January reported that the Rev. Mr. Colbeck, the representative in Mandalay of the Society for the Propagation of the Gospel, had protested to Bernard about the attempt of the Provost Marshal to extract testimony from a Burman while he was covered by the presented rifles of a firing party. Such proceedings, Mr. Colbeck declared, could not fail to bring shame and discredit upon our name, nation and religion.

'The ghastly scenes which constantly recur in executions carried out by the Provost Marshal', Moylan went on, warming to his theme, 'constitute grave public scandals. The Provost Marshal, who is an ardent amateur photographer, is desirous of securing views of the persons executed at the precise moment when they are struck by the bullets. To secure this result, after the orders "Ready" "Present" have been given to the firing party, the Provost Marshal fixes his camera on the prisoners, who at times are kept waiting for some minutes in that position. The officer commanding the firing party is then directed by the Provost Marshal to give the order to fire at the precise moment when he exposes his plate. So far no satisfactory negative has been obtained, and the experiments are likely to be continued. These proceedings take place before a crowd of mixed nationalities, and cannot fail to have a demoralising effect on both soldiers and spectators.'[21]

This disclosure burst like a bombshell in the English press. The incident described was disquieting enough, but Moylan's careful choice of words, to suggest that such scenes occurred frequently, set in motion a wave of horror and indignation, as he intended they should. It was felt immediately in Parliament, where Salisbury's Conservative Government was reaching the last days of office against a political situation made very confused by uncertainty over Gladstone's intentions about Irish Home Rule. It was hourly expected that Gladstone would force a vote and the Government be defeated.[22] Moylan's dispatch appeared on the very day when Parliament reassembled after the Christmas recess. On the 22nd Dr. Cameron, the radical member for Glasgow, rose in the Commons to ask the Secretary of State for India whether he had seen *The Times* report, and called on him to order the ending of the practice described and the prosecution of the Provost Marshal. Mr. Justin McCarthy, the Irish Nationalist member for Newry, wanted to know if the statements were true, and Sir George Campbell, the member for Kirkcaldy, whether questions of life and death in Upper Burma were decided by Bernard, or by the military authorities ruling by martial law.

Lord Randolph Churchill's answers to these questions were guarded and vague. He was not certain whether the civil authority had yet superseded the military authority, but he had assumed that when Mr. Bernard went up to Mandalay, while General Prendergast was away in Bhamo, that civil government had recommenced, at least in Mandalay itself. He was not surprised that the members for Glasgow and Newry had put questions on 'the very grave and startling information' given to the public by *The Times* correspondent. He could not bring himself to believe that the report was true, and that any officer wearing the Queen's uniform would have allowed himself to perpetrate actions which 'would have disgraced the officers of King Theebaw'. He had telegraphed the Viceroy to find out the foundation of the allegations, and he had even broken protocol and telegraphed Bernard directly, on his own authority. If the allegations were true, immediate action would be taken against the officer concerned.[23]

To Dufferin he complained that the action of the Provost Marshal was the subject of the most unfavourable comment. 'Daily I became more convinced of the perfect unfitness of General Prendergast for his position in Upper Burma.'[24] The Viceroy replied, 'I cannot tell you how much annoyed I have been by the accounts of these executions in Burma. The one thing I had impressed upon both Prendergast and Bernard was that our operations were to be conducted with exceptional humanity, and Prendergast promised carefully to observe my wishes in this respect. Bernard has the reputation of being over-tenderhearted, so that I had no misgivings on this head; nor had I any knowledge of the way in which the military authorities were shooting their prisoners until a day or two ago.' He admitted, however, that accounts of how 'our troops cut up considerable numbers of the defeated enemy' had made him uneasy. He had warned Bernard that the execution of prisoners was an idea which would be very repugnant to English, to European and to Indian public opinion.

Dufferin now sent peremptory orders to Prendergast, Sladen and Bernard, forbidding military executions of any description. 'I fear that these untoward circumstances,' he wrote, 'will strengthen the hands of those who may be disposed to criticize our conquest of the country.'[25] Moylan's reports were indeed the very ammunition which Radical critics required for an attack on the Government's Burma policy; and Churchill had heard rumours that such an attack was planned as early as 14 January.[26] On 25th, Sir George Campbell asked whether the control of affairs in Upper Burma was under the Chief Commissioner, and whether the military authorities were amenable to his orders in their treatment of the Burmese. Osborne Morgan, a lawyer representing Denbigh East, asked whether the prisoners stated to have been shot on the Provost Marshal's orders had had any form of trial; and 'if so, how and for what offences, and under what law, if any, were they tried?'

Lord Randolph made brilliant use of the rather scanty information at his disposal. Skilfully evading Morgan's 'highly technical and legal' question (which was in fact the heart of the matter) he quoted Bernard's telegraphs to Dufferin to show that while Prendergast and Bernard were to establish civil jurisdiction as soon as the disturbed districts were pacified, civil and police officers had as yet been placed in command of only five districts—Mandalay, Minhla, Ningyan, Pagan and Mingyan. 'The rest of the country is nominally dominated by the Burmese Supreme Council . . .' (Here Lord Randolph paused. 'I cannot pronounce the native name for that body.') 'Rebels taken in arms on the field are liable to be shot; no-one is to be shot or punished by civil officers otherwise than after trial . . .'

'I am sorry to say,' he continued, 'that the information in my possession is far from satisfactory. The Viceroy telegraphs me that it is clear that the Provost Marshal had proceeded in a most unjustifiable manner, at any rate in one case. That alludes to the case where evidence was sought to be extorted by placing a prisoner apparently under the fire of soldiers.' The Viceroy had instructed General Prendergast that if a *prima facie* case was made out against the Provost Marshal on either of the counts mentioned, he and the other officers implicated were to be suspended from duty, and if proved guilty, to be punished with the utmost severity. A dispatch from Bernard said that it was true that the Provost Marshal did place a man suspected of treasonable correspondence in fear of instant death in order to induce him to give information which might incriminate two members of the Hlutdaw, and that when he heard of it he had pointed out that evidence extorted was valueless, and that it was contrary to all law to extort evidence by moral torture. (At this point Churchill was interrupted by cries of 'Oh, oh!'

12. The departure
of Thibaw and
Supayalat
from
Mandalay

13. Colonel Hooper's photograph of dacoits captured near Mandalay

14. The arrival of the Viceroy and Lady Dufferin at Mandalay, 12 February 1886. A salute is being fired from guns on the top of the Bund among the trees

from the Irish Home Rulers. 'I am giving the House the best information I can,' he said.)[27]

When the House divided, the Government had a majority of 28, Lord Randolph's spirited defence having caused the whole Opposition front bench to abstain from voting. On the next day the Conservatives announced their intention of introducing a new Coercion Bill for Ireland, and Gladstone finally decided to turn them out. In the evening the Government was defeated on a motion by Jesse Collings deploring the omission from the Queen's speech of any reference to measures for the benefit of rural labourers. The division took place at 1 a.m. on 27 January, and the Irish Nationalists, voting with Gladstone, defeated the Government by 79 votes, though 18 Liberals voted with the Conservatives. For the next five months, Home Rule for Ireland was to leave little indignation to spare for the annexation of Upper Burma, or the alleged atrocities of the Provost Marshal.

Meanwhile in Mandalay Bernard had continued his own investigations. Before sending his dispatch, Moylan had written to Sladen giving him the facts in detail. Melton Prior had been an eye-witness of the incident in which evidence was extorted from the Burman under threat of death. The man, whose name was U Kwet, had been forced to watch the execution of five dacoits near the south gate of the palace by a firing party of sepoys. He was then placed before the firing party and in consequence made hearsay statements implicating two members of the Hlutdaw. Under the Indian penal code, Moylan pointed out, such an action was punishable by transportation for life or ten years imprisonment. The executions had caused a feeling of horror in the community. 'The wretched men who were about to die, were used as models by amateur photographers, anxious—possibly for purposes of gain—to obtain a representation of their dying agonies.' Such proceedings were so opposed to decency that he hoped Sladen, as chief civil officer, would take immediate steps to end them, now that they had been brought to his notice. In the best journalistic tradition, Moylan declared that it was his duty to place the details of the photographic executions before the English people as fully as possible, and he demanded 'a full and impartial inquiry'.[28]

The Rev. Mr. Colbeck had also protested to Bernard, who replied 'that there could be no doubt wholly unjustifiable means were resorted to, to extort evidence'. Bernard had discovered that the facts were substantially true. The Provost Marshal, Colonel W. W. Hooper of the

I 129

Madras Army, had taken photographs of executions, although he had not delayed the order to fire in order to arrange his camera. The officer responsible for extorting information from U Kwet was not Hooper, but Lieutenant Burrows, the Assistant Provost Marshal, who candidly admitted the facts. The confession extracted implicated members of the Hlutdaw in a conspiracy to burn Mandalay.[29]

Bernard asked Sladen what number of prisoners had been executed under his orders between 28 November 1885 and 1 February 1886, and whether a record of the trials and executions had been kept. Sladen replied that there had been, in all, twenty-two executions at Mandalay. The men had been tried 'in a more or less summary manner', five by the superintendent of police, thirteen by the Deputy Commissioner and four by Sladen himself. These four were 'the pretender prince and three of his officers who were caught in open rebellion with arms and standards'. The others were tried and convicted for dacoitry and robbery with violence, being armed. 'I may mention,' wrote Sladen, 'that during the months of December and January we passed through a very critical and trying period in Upper Burma. In the rare instances in which dacoits were arrested, the severest measures were imperatively called for as a terror to evildoers and for the public safety.'[30]

He did not exaggerate. Since mid-December sullen acquiescence had given way to audacious guerilla activity, and the military, thinking the political officers too lenient, had hoped to stop the mischief by a few exemplary executions. Though the dacoits could now claim to be fighting for their country (and have been so represented by posterity) they were hardly patriots in the usual sense, for they tortured, crucified and burned their fellow-countrymen without compunction. On one of his first anti-dacoit patrols, Hooper had come upon a blazing *kyaung* and an elderly *pyongyi* murdered and with both hands cut off at the wrist. Such incidents were not isolated, and it is in the light of them that Hooper's actions must be seen. That is not how they *were* seen, of course, by the public at home, and in any case executions in cold blood were a different matter.

It is not surprising to learn that Colonel Hooper was anything but depraved in character. His bravery was a legend, and he was notorious among his men for his opposition to gambling and drunkenness. Repellent as his photographing obsession was, it had to be admitted that he had pursued it without regard to his own safety. Once in India he had coolly photographed a sepoy who had run amok and was shooting officers on sight; and at Minhla he had gone into action encumbered with camera and tripod. The irony was, as Grattan Geary unfashionably pointed out, that the cause of humanity might be advanced if there were *more* Colonel Hoopers 'to focus, fix and make widely known' the real horrors of war.[31]

11

THE LOOKING-GLASS PALACE

Dufferin left Calcutta for Burma on 3 February, accompanied by Lady Dufferin, Mackenzie Wallace, Lord William Beresford, his private secretary Mr. McFerran and his physician Dr. Findlay. He also took with him his eldest son Archie, Lord Clandeboye, and Major Cooper as his *aides-de-camp*. At Diamond Harbour they were met by the Commander-in-Chief Sir Frederick Roberts, and his Staff, and H. M. Durand, the Government of India Foreign Secretary. The viceregal party then embarked on the Indian Marine S.S. *Clive*, along with an immense number of servants, 'horses, cows, calves, chickens, sheep and quails',[1] and in the afternoon sailed for Rangoon. The calm and uneventful voyage gave the Viceroy a much-needed opportunity for rest and reflection. He enjoyed getting his sea legs again, but it was otherwise with the Army. 'Sir Frederick Roberts disappears a good deal either to sleep or to write,' Lady Dufferin recorded. 'Colonel Chapman is not very well, and Major Chamberlain is always miserable at sea, so that the army is in a much less flourishing condition than the civil department.'[2]

On 7 February the *Clive* anchored off the mouth of the Rangoon River. Bernard came aboard with the Government of India Home Secretary, Alexander Mackenzie, who was already at Rangoon, and further consultations were held while the party prepared for the official reception. It was on a magnificent scale. The warships in the harbour, *Bacchante, Woodlark, Turquoise* and *Sphinx*, were dressed overall and their yards manned, while great clouds of smoke and booming cannon announced the Viceroy's approach. The current was strong, and as the *Clive* manoeuvred slowly to the landing place the Vicereine had ample time to survey the scene. The banks were a mass of people, and beyond them more crowds were visible in the distance; on the wharf, which was laid with red cloth, lines of infantry were drawn up, and bishops, and ladies, and town councillors all waiting, and beyond them again Lady Dufferin saw something which completely astonished her. The Burmese, under the guidance of local officials, had painstakingly constructed in painted wood and canvas the front of Killyleagh Castle and the Town Rock. She was looking at the gateway of her own home. Then, when 'the prolonged agony of arrival' was over, the Viceroy landed and was received by officials, the chief merchants, the representatives of the various nationalities and a guard of honour of the Rangoon Volunteers. Behind the gateway of Killyleagh was a huge pagoda-like building where hundreds of people were waiting to see the presentation of the formal addresses. Dufferin, in his replies, carefully avoided any reference to the future of Upper Burma. A procession was formed, and the party, escorted by mounted volunteers, moved on to Government House through innumerable double arches and showers of rose-petals.

Bernard and his wife were the best of hosts, but the Residence could not be made comfortable. 'It is fine weather, but it is not warm,' complained Lady Dufferin, 'and we suffer from all the preparations that have been made to keep the house cool.' That evening there was a dinner for sixty people, and though she could scarcely believe that there were sixty doors in the room, there seemed to be one at everyone's back, and still the punkahs were kept going. She was much concerned about the Viceroy, who had caught a cold, and she asked for the punkahs to be stopped, but Dufferin shook his head at her across the table, and they went on again; '. . . hot sal volatile and a mustard poultice were the results; but we did our duty.'[3]

The next day was Sunday, part of which was spent in the ritual visit to the Shwe Dagon pagoda, and early on Monday they went by train to Prome and embarked on the river steamer *Mindoon* for the journey to Mandalay. The steamer was splendidly appointed (Lady Dufferin even had a boudoir smartly furnished with 'plush tables, stuffed armchairs, gold-headed scent-bottles') and its only fault lay in the arrangements 'for keeping up a perpetual draught'. Dufferin's cold became worse, and he had to take to his bed, which irked him since he had so much work to do. On Tuesday night the *Mindoon* anchored opposite the fort at Minhla and Lady Dufferin went ashore to see it. It reminded her of a graveyard in the twilight, and she wondered how Colonel Baker could sleep there with his tent looking 'as though it were pitched among tombs'. Few Buddhas remained in the pagodas, 'for the very first night the Mahometan troops got in, they defaced every image.'

As the steamer made its way carefully through the narrow twisting channels between sunken Burmese boats and sandbanks, Lady Dufferin was entranced by the outlook. 'The banks, covered with pagodas, are lovely . . . Out of every bit of jungle rises a spire, and it is impossible to convey the effect of it all. You can't bear to take your eyes off the scenery for a minute, lest you should lose some specially characteristic building. Burmah looks like a country of cemeteries, if you imagine each tombstone to be about the size of the Albert Memorial.'

It was not until noon on Friday the 12th, that they reached Mandalay, for the river was low at that season and navigation very difficult. Prendergast and Sladen came aboard on Thursday. Lady Dufferin sat beside the General at dinner, and found him a 'very straightforward-looking soldier . . . very kind, but determined'. At the landing stage they had to endure all over again the ordeal of an official reception before reaching the palace along a route lined for three miles by troops and bluejackets.[4] 'The Viceroy's State entry went off to perfection,' White reported, 'It was left entirely to me, and I did all I could to make it a success . . . It went off without a hitch, and Lord Dufferin sent for me and thanked me most warmly. I replied that if His Excellency thought the arrangements good, I was amply repaid for any trouble I had had on them. He repeated in his slow, rather forced manner, "Good! they were more than good, they were ideal—they were dramatic." '

White was delighted to see some of his Simla friends again. 'Lord Roberts is looking so young, and so are all his staff except Chapman, who is looking very wretched . . . Neville Chamberlain, Pole-Carew, Bill Beresford, Mr. Mackenzie, Morty Durand are all looking well.' That night he dined with the Viceroy and Lady Dufferin, and after dinner had a long talk with Dufferin in his study. 'I think we got on well and our views coincided. He is evidently bent on making this a great success, and does not want to be restricted by expense. I was very keen on this point also. He is, I think, very able, very earnest, and takes more of a Palmerstonian view of England's position than Lord Ripon. I was quite prepared on the point of protecting the people and thus scoring immensely over our late attempts elsewhere. I also dwelt much upon having the country full of troops to give efficient protection. I don't believe Sir Fred or Mr. Bernard contemplate anything like the reinforcements I spoke of. So probably they will be dropped.'[5]

It was not surprising that Dufferin listened to White's views with close attention. He had already formed a high opinion of his ability, and despite all the official courtesies, his first impressions of Mandalay had confirmed some of his worst misgivings. Durand remembered that at night as the steamer lay in the river the Viceroy had been surprised and far from satisfied to hear desultory firing from the environs of the city. Some of the circumstances of his arrival, too, had been disquieting. Although the European inhabitants and Burmese citizens had presented addresses under the benign guidance of Sladen, the Hlutdaw presented no address and extended no welcome. Dufferin had insisted that the Burmese officials should sit on chairs at the reception, and when he received the Ministers next day, they attempted to escape the ceremony by demanding that chairs be brought, and that they should wear their shoes. When Dufferin agreed, a hundred people arrived instead of the twenty who usually composed the Hlutdaw. Moylan was, as usual, at hand to underline the significance of this demonstration. 'The action of the Hlutdaw on the occasion of the Viceroy's arrival, was, in the opinion of those best qualified to judge, meant to be openly defiant . . . Petty officers, the subordinates of subordinates, who would not be allowed to remain standing in the presence of a Burmese woon attended as members of the Hlutdaw and attempted to monopolise all the front places, and to force the English officers and officials of high rank to remain behind them . . .'[6] Dufferin afterwards had separate talks with two of the senior ministers. Nevertheless he decided that the Hlutdaw should be abolished at once, and thus ended Sladen's attempt to carry on the government by this means. There was no doubt that he held Sladen responsible for some of the things which had gone wrong.

Yet another shock for Dufferin was to discover that nothing further had been done in the case of the Provost Marshal. Although he had instructed Prendergast that if the facts proved to be true, Hooper was to be punished with the utmost severity, he now found that he had been merely reprimanded. Foreseeing the consequences of this at home, Dufferin authorized the setting up of a court of enquiry, to be presided over by a senior police officer from Lower Burma. A letter from White to his wife, written on 1 February, shows that Moylan had been trying to find out what punishment had been meted out to Hooper. 'I have had a lot of unpleasantness about executions here. I only hope you have not seen my name mixed up with this report. I really have been the one man opposed to the system and made a stand against the whole-sale military executions the minute I took command here. However, I will not consent to tell newspaper correspondents what punishment has been inflicted on the Provost Marshal who is a colonel in this army. The fact is Sir Harry Prendergast has let him down too easy, I think.' Explaining that the colonel in question was an inveterate photographer, who had had the bad taste to photograph prisoners who were being shot, he added that the want of decorum was very distressing and created a bad impression at home. 'The *Times* correspondent is very bitter against these soldiers as he was turned away in what I consider a very foolish way by Sir Harry Prendergast at the instigation of the Assistant Adjutant General.'[7]

The important military decisions were taken on Sunday 14 February. Some idea of the pressure under which White was working at this time is given in a letter he wrote home that day. 'At 5.30 I was out of bed and wrote a minute about an expedition rendered necessary by a telegram received last night; at 6.30 I was in the saddle with Sir Frederick Roberts going round everywhere; at 20 minutes to 10 we came back, and I had to tub, shave and breakfast; at 10.30 I had to receive Lady Dufferin and to show Her Ex. where to sit in Church, or rather where to sit in the Grand Entrance of the Palace where the service is read. I had two gold chairs all ready, but the Viceroy did not turn up. About 11.30 Church was over, and I had all my work to do and arrange for a levee tomorrow. I had then an hour's talk with Sir Frederick Roberts about the future occupation of Burma. Had immediately afterwards to arrange the details of an expedition to start tomorrow morning to fight a Pretender.' While he was doing this, he received a telegram from the political department reporting a plot to burn down the palace and start a general rising. As the Viceroy was to come to the palace next day White had to turn out the hundreds of Burmese workmen who were there. At 6.30 he had to be at the river-bank to dine with the Viceroy. 'This means a ride of 4½ miles there, and of course the same distance back, and dining in all the splendour of the Viceregal uniforms in my Service-stained breeches (corduroy) and boots, not altogether unacquainted with the sands of Upper Nubia.'

Nevertheless, it was a good day for White; he wanted above all an independent command, yet he felt that if asked for his advice he must recommend that Mandalay be made the army headquarters. Roberts decided, however, that the headquarters should be at Rangoon, and that

White should retain the command at Mandalay while active operations in Upper Burma continued. White was jubilant, despite the responsibility and crushing work which he foresaw it involved. 'If I do well, I ought to be a Major-General before my 55th birthday.'[8] If Rangoon was made headquarters, Prendergast would have to go there, and White knew that Roberts wanted to give him as free a hand as was compatible with Prendergast's overall command in Burma, although the changes had to be made very tactfully.[9]

While the Viceroy was deep in consultation with his advisers, his wife was finding out a good deal about Mandalay and the last days of Thibaw's reign. She noticed on her arrival that outside the city the houses were mere matting sheds, and that the people looked very poor and naked. 'But the walls are beautiful and of a rich colour, being built of brownish-red bricks. They are in perfect repair and form a great square, each side a mile and a half long . . . There is something very grand and simple about the whole, and a moat right round it, wide as a river and full of water, adds to the effect. We drove through the finest gateway, and soon came to a high palisade which encloses the Palace; there gilded minarets and shining pinnacles and golden carved roofs began to appear, and when we descended from the carriage we found ourselves at the entrance of Theebaw's Hall of Audience. Then we walked through the Palace. A marvellous place it is. What is not gold is a sort of glass mosaic which is very bright and effective. There are glass latticework sides to some of the rooms, and golden pillars, and glasswork pillars, and great mirrors; and outside golden roofs beautifully carved, and more gold and glass palings, acres of gilt roofing, and shining pinnacles, and forests of teak pillars all gold!'[10]

It had been intended that the Dufferins should stay in the palace, but the ship was considered more healthy, and it was arranged that they should visit the palace again on the following Monday. When they did so, they were invited to inspect the 'prize'. 'Very poor prize it is! Theebaw's ladies were much too sharp for our soldiers, and managed to walk off with everything. There is positively only one jewel, and that is French—it is a necklace of small diamonds and rubies, and an ornament for the hair in the shape of a peacock, to match; one very big, but bad emerald, and three large good ones; that is absolutely all. There are a number of Geneva watches, and some small French ornaments, but nothing even worth buying as souvenirs, for these odds and ends are European things.'[11]

In the afternoon the Viceroy had a levee, standing before Thibaw's throne, surrounded by staff and with the *Illustrated London News* on one side and the *Graphic* on the other busily sketching, 'themselves a good subject for caricature in their evening coats and big sun hats'. Again there appeared to be some kind of demonstration by the Burmese, who did not at first appear. The Viceroy 'put on his helmet' and the levee seemed to be over; then it turned out that all the Burmese who had a right to come were there, 'but had got into some out-of-the-way corner.' The Viceroy resumed his place and they all passed by.[12]

A visit to the hospitals followed, and then to Mandalay Hill and its signalling station. Half-way up the hill there was a huge gold figure of Buddha, forty feet high, which Mindon Min had caused to be put up, with its finger pointing to the exact spot where the palace was to be built. On Tuesday, Lady Dufferin had a highly successful party for the wives and daughters of the Burmese officials. She was afraid at first that they would not come, but at 4 o'clock sixty of them appeared, exquisitely attired with flowers in their hair. The Viceroy and she welcomed them one by one, and gave them 'a cup of tea and a biscuit'. It was hard to know how to break the ice, but she eventually struck upon the idea of conducting them over the palace, an idea which they received with enthusiasm. They said they had been in the palace before, but 'not like this'.[13]

On Wednesday evening, Dufferin entertained at dinner Prendergast and his officers, and proposed their health in a speech warmly praising the General for having led a British Army into the enemy's capital with virtually no loss, a feat far more creditable than a costly victory, however glorious. He explained that in deciding to end the disastrous rule of a prince who was a curse to his own subjects and an impossible neighbour, he had chosen the lesser of two evils, and he announced that to give effect to the proclamation of 1 January, by which Upper Burma was annexed for ever to the British Empire, the country would be at once placed under the direct administrative control of British officers. It was to be regretted that the dacoitry which had been rife under Thibaw's rule was still prevalent, but he rejoiced that there was not 'the slightest sign' of anything approaching partisan warfare against the British troops. When the pen of history should eventually trace the causes and results of the conquest of Burma, the service which Sir Harry Prendergast and his companions had rendered their Queen and country would be honourably recorded.[14]

After dinner Dufferin went over to White and had another talk with him about the military situation, and White told him frankly that there were not enough troops in the country to protect those who had a right to look for protection. 'He was quite angry . . . and said rather brusquely for him, "You are the first person in an official position who has told me that." ' White replied that he had seen more of the sickening failures in that respect than any other official present.[15] Years afterwards Dufferin used to relate that one day when he was walking with White in Mandalay he had asked him how far British power in Burma then extended. White pointed to a sentry pacing up and down the rampart and replied, 'Up to that man and no further.' Dufferin had been angry at the time, but he acknowledged later that White's frankness had been of great service to him.[16]

Before Dufferin left Mandalay the new government of Upper Burma had been organized. Bernard was to be the supreme civil officer for the whole of Burma. White was to remain in Mandalay in command of the Field Force, on which all British authority still rested. General Prendergast was, for the present, to have the command of all the troops in Burma from his headquarters in Rangoon. A force of military police was to be raised in India and put under the control of the civil officers administering the various districts of Upper Burma, in order to release as many of the troops as possible. This would take some time, and in the interval the troops had the task of establishing order throughout the country, a task which, with the rainy season advancing and no transport available, was becoming more formidable every day.[17]

When the state farewells were made, General Prendergast on behalf of the Army presented Lady Dufferin with a small image of Buddha, and the Viceroy with the original and translation of Lord Dalhousie's ultimatum of 1852, which had been found in the palace. 'The Burmese appear to be a most pleasing, nice people to deal with,' Lady Dufferin recorded, 'but some of their very virtues make them difficult to govern and to depend upon. Their police are no good, and they neither stand and fight nor quite give way. However, for better, for worse, Burmah is annexed. It seems a rich country, and Mandalay is a lovely place, and we, at any rate, have had a delightful visit there. The soldiers hitherto have had an exciting time too, but now that the glamour is worn off, they have a full and rather dreary prospect before them.'[18]

THE RUBY MINES

In *The Times* on 17 March 1886 Moylan reported that the crown jewels and 'valuable rubies' found in the palace at Mandalay were to be sent to London to be sold there, but that the best furniture of the palace was to go to Government House at Simla. In the House of Commons Mr. Richard (Merthyr Tydvil) asked whether this had been done, and by whose authority. He was told that it had been intended to remove the furniture to the Viceregal Lodge for reasons of economy, but that later it had been decided to sell it on the spot.[1]

But by this time Dufferin, following up hints received at Mandalay, had found out some very interesting details about Moylan's past. Moylan, an Irish Roman Catholic, the son of a Lord Mayor of Dublin, had been educated in Bordeaux and at Trinity College, from which he graduated as a Bachelor of Laws in 1863. He then practised as a barrister. It was his career after 1880, however, when he was Attorney-General of the island of Grenada in the West Indies, that proved fascinating.[2]

Dufferin had obtained from the Colonial Office a full statement of charges made against Moylan in the West Indies. The gist of it was that in January 1883 Edward Kyran Moylan, the Attorney-General of Grenada, had been suspended on six charges, two of which were held by the Secretary of State to be clearly proved, 'viz, that in order to gratify a vindictive personal feeling, Mr. Moylan, being a high officer of the Government, and having been the confidential and trusted adviser of the Administrator, did conspire with a subordinate officer of the Government in an attempt to bring the Administrator into disgrace; that in furtherance of this purpose he imparted to the above-mentioned subordinate officer the substance of a conversation with the Administrator

which . . . was essentially confidential and of an official nature, together
with a statement which he had obtained from the Auditor by means of a
similar breach of confidence, and that in assisting the . . . officer to frame
an accusation against the Administrator, based on his own and the
Auditor's statements, he exaggerated and distorted the purport of those
statements.'

The Secretary of State further considered that Moylan's conduct had
been aggravated by the 'coarse and violent invectives' which occurred
repeatedly in his answers to the charges, and by the unfounded asper-
sions which he made upon two gentlemen holding high judicial appoint-
ments in the Windward Islands. Moreover this was not the first occasion
on which 'Mr. Moylan had misconducted himself since his introduction
to the Colonial Service'. Lord Derby had decided, however, 'not without
great hesitation', to give him a chance of retrieving his character as a
public officer in another colony, and he was offered the Attorney-
Generalship of British Honduras. Moylan first accepted and then con-
temptuously rejected the post, and his suspension was therefore
confirmed.

He remained in Grenada, practising as a barrister, until complaints
were made of his conduct in four cases. In two of these the Supreme
Court found that his character was seriously compromised, 'so compromised that we are of the opinion he is unworthy of the character
either of a barrister, or a gentleman.' In another, where it was alleged
that a number of peasant proprietors had been improperly deprived of
their land because of wrongful affidavits made by Moylan, the Secretary
of State decided that the affidavits warranted an indictment for perjury.
The Attorney-General (Moylan's successor) reported, however, that he
could not collect enough evidence to justify his taking criminal proceedings. By that time Moylan had left Grenada, having been disbarred in
the Colony for grave misconduct as a barrister and solicitor.[3]

The information was all the more valuable in view of Moylan's interference in the question of the ruby mines. These mines, which were
believed to be a source of immense revenue to the Burmese Government,
were situated in the Mogok area, east of the Irrawaddy and almost
encircled by its tributary the Shweli. The town of Mogok was 6,000 feet
above sea-level and almost inaccessible because of the surrounding
jungle.[4] In 1883 the Burmese embassy in Paris had granted to a M.
Charles Hecgnard a concession to work mines of coal, lead, sulphur,
silver, rubies and precious stones, and after the fall of Mandalay

Hecgnard claimed compensation from the British, alleging that he had already spent £4,000 in preliminary investigations. In January 1886 a certain Captain Aubrey Patton, described by Churchill as 'an adventurous speculating person, known to fame for his great proficiency in pigeon shooting', approached the India Office with the information that he had obtained Hecgnard's concession in conjunction with Messrs. Streeter, the jewellers.[5]

Patton then went to Calcutta, armed with a letter from Lord Harris, the parliamentary Under Secretary of State. Dufferin concluded that the India Office did not regard Streeter's application with disfavour, and that the Home Government would be content to leave it to him to settle with Streeter for a lease to work the mines. There was, however, another competitor in the field, the Calcutta firm of Gillanders, Arbuthnot and Co., who had already done business with the Shans who worked the ruby mines. Dufferin was nothing if not prudent, and when the new Government took office in February he informed Kimberley of Streeter's desire to obtain the concession, and asked him to find out if the proposals were *bona fide* and Streeter's syndicate good for the amount. Kimberley gave a reassuring answer on both counts, but he added that as the syndicate was to be formed *after* the concession had been received, it would be advisable to exercise caution.[6]

On receiving this information Dufferin invited tenders, and on 14 April was able to report that Streeter had offered a lakh of rupees more than the local firm. Bernard had recommended Gillanders Arbuthnot, but the Executive Council were strongly opposed to accepting their offer, as they had had some dealings with the firm which they considered unsatisfactory. Dufferin asked Kimberley if Streeter's bid might then safely be accepted. Kimberley thought that there were advantages in dealing with a local firm, but left it to Dufferin to decide whether they were outweighed by the extra lakh offered by the syndicate. The Government of India entered into no contract with Streeter at this stage, postponing definite engagements until the locality of the mines had been investigated and the conditions under which they were worked had been ascertained.[7]

What followed may best be described in Dufferin's own words. '. . . Moylan, as usual, has played an effectual part. Messrs. Gillanders Arbuthnot and Co. employed him as their agent. He accordingly filled *The Times* and the local papers with every kind of lie and accusation about the rival company, and tried even to get Lord Randolph Churchill to denounce Streeter's syndicate as principally composed of Frenchmen, the real facts being, I believe, the other way . . . As soon as Moylan learned that his principals had been outbid, he at once began to work up the "native claims", and he had the impudence even to report to *The Times* that much dissatisfaction was being caused by the Government of India's having over-ruled Bernard in regard to them, the fact being that, on the one hand, Bernard himself . . . does not attach much importance to the native claims, and, on the other, that the Government of India have refused to rush into an arrangement until the exact facts in regard to them have been ascertained.'[8]

So effective were Moylan's reports that in May Kimberley wrote to the Viceroy 'I do not at all like the notion of a French element in the Ruby Syndicate in the present state of Burmese affairs,' and on 9 June he telegraphed urgently 'Newspaper telegrams say that you are about to grant concession to French Company against Bernard's recommendation. Please telegraph facts to enable me to answer if questioned'. Dufferin at once replied that the report was unfounded, and that Streeter had guaranteed that his syndicate would contain no foreign elements. He added that the reports to which Kimberley referred seemed 'to have emanated from Moylan, who is agent of the rival syndicate, and who, as you know, stops at nothing.'[9]

The expedition had not set out when the rainy season came, and Bernard decided that it would have to be postponed. Then in November Cross, the new Conservative Secretary of State, sent Dufferin the following telegram. 'Ruby Mines. I gather arrangements with Streeter not finally concluded. Value of mines and rights of Government should be carefully ascertained before pledging Government, keeping me informed of result of local inquiry and of proposed arrangements, which should have my previous approval. Desirability of retention in hands of the Government well worthy of consideration.'[10] This attitude on the part of the Secretary of State entirely altered the complexion of the matter: the proposal to break with Streeter and re-open the question of whether the Government should itself work the mines or lease them to a company was a considerable embarrassment to Dufferin. Although no contract had been signed, he felt that the Government of India was committed to Streeter, who ought to have preference if any lease was granted. Moreover he was convinced that it would not be advantageous for the Government to work the mines directly.[11]

By the time an expedition was sent to occupy Mogok in 1887, Bernard had been succeeded as Commissioner by Sir Charles Crosthwaite.

Crosthwaite, with the whole of Burma in rebellion, disliked having to divert a substantial force for such an object: it was, he said, like polishing the door-handle of a house that was on fire.[12] He was even more vexed by the upshot, for he imprudently ordered his secretary to draw up a draft lease on fresh conditions based on his investigations. Fortunately the legal advisers of the Government of India were able to assure the Viceroy that this was not a binding agreement with Streeter's agents, since 'some elements of the contract remained to be settled, there was something that was yet *in fieri*'.[13] Crosthwaite was astonished at the hornet's nest which his 'purely local' decisions had raised about his ears. He wrote that if he 'had destroyed Mandalay or drained the Irrawaddy' there could not have been more disturbance than was caused by the grant to one of the prospectors of a few yards of worthless land at Mogok on which to erect a hut, and of an ordinary licence to mine.[14]

The cause of the disturbance was not far to seek. The exertions of Moylan had brought the matter of the ruby mines to the attention of Parliament, where it engaged the energies of no less a person than the redoubtable radical Charles Bradlaugh. On 28 January 1887 he asked whether the mines had been taken possession of by British troops, whether they had been leased, or were about to be leased to a London jeweller for an annual rental of £30,000, and who were the former owners of the mines. Three days later he wanted to know if any agent of Streeter's had accompanied the expedition. In answering these questions the Government spokesmen were able to point out that no binding agreement had been reached with Streeter, but they had to admit that Mr. Streeter, junior, had accompanied the expedition. By a further series of questions in the summer Bradlaugh was able to extract the information that one Captain Jackson, Streeter's engineer, had been escorted to Mogok by troops, and had set up machinery there which he was now working, though no agreement had yet been signed. Moreover it was revealed that in December 1886 a Paris jeweller named Ungar, who was acting as agent for a Rothschild syndicate which had shown interest in the mines, had applied for permission to visit the mines and had been refused.[15] Vainly did Dufferin supply Cross with all the available information. Questions continued to be asked in the House, and the ruby mines became yet another strand in the entangling net of Dufferin's Burmese difficulties. He bequeathed the problem to his successor, and the affair dragged on until 1889 when concessions were finally given to five promoters.[16]

13

CHINA

There was one cloud on the diplomatic horizon which grew steadily more menacing as the Burmese drama unfolded. Burma was one of those Eastern states over which the Chinese Empire claimed vague tributary rights, indefinable in Western terms, but vitally important in the Celestial *weltanschauung*. For most of the century China had been giving way to the assertive colonialism of the European powers, but the contest with France over Tonkin was to prove a turning-point in her history. For the first time Chinese troops had fought with a European army and not been defeated, and from that time an increased self-confidence was perceptible to those Westerners who had dealings with China. Kipling's line, 'An' the dawn comes up like thunder outer China 'crost the Bay' owed some of its emotive force to apprehension, or as he expressed it elsewhere, 'Their little difficulty with the French a few years ago has taught the Chinese a great many things which, perhaps, it were better for us that they had left alone!' Since a good deal of the British intervention in Burma was inspired by the hope of establishing a flourishing trade with western China, Britain was very anxious to keep on friendly terms with China, and this called for some cautious and skilful diplomacy.[1]

In October 1885 Dufferin had telegraphed to Nicholas O'Conor, the British *chargé d'affaires* in Peking 'Do you think annexation of Burmah would arouse any feeling in China? I presume distinct possibility of remonstrance.' O'Conor replied that if Burma appealed to China as a tributary state, the Chinese would certainly object to annexation. As he explained in another dispatch, Burma was traditionally regarded as a tributary of China, and a large tribute-bearing embassy had made its way to Peking in 1875. Such missions were decennial, but he could not

K

discover any evidence that they were sent also on the accession of a new king. Nor was there any record of an embassy having been sent by Thibaw, though one was now due, and he thought it unlikely that China would protect a vassal which did not maintain its allegiance. He considered that it would be bad policy to appear to anticipate or dread China's interference, or to treat the Burmese question otherwise than as one to be settled with the Burmese themselves.

But already there were ominous signs that the Chinese imperial government intended to assert its claims. The Viceroy Li Hung-chang had mentioned to H.M. consul at Tientsin that the matter was not one to be settled without consulting the Chinese Government. Although the link with Burma was weak, duty to a tributary state, and still more a sense of her own dignity, might compel China to remonstrate in a manner which would be likely to cause a coldness in her present friendly relations with England.[2] And on 30 October the Marquis Tseng, the Chinese minister in London, told the Foreign Office that he had been instructed to ask Lord Salisbury what the immediate and ulterior objects of the British expedition were, and to offer Chinese mediation in virtue of the influence which their position as regards Burma conferred upon them. Sir Halliday Macartney, the secretary and interpreter at the Chinese legation in London, called on the Foreign Office next day, declaring that China had no wish to quarrel with Britain over Burma, and that the Emperor had instructed his officials in Yunnan to proceed to Burma and counsel Thibaw to rescind his actions against the Bombay-Burma Trading Corporation. Macartney, a Scottish army surgeon who had entered the employment of the Chinese Imperial Government in the 1860s, was useful in negotiations with the British Government, but was understandably regarded with some suspicion by the Foreign Office. On the other hand the Marquis Tseng, his patron, an impulsive and hotheaded man, was not altogether trusted by his own government.[3]

In far-off Peking the Chinese authorities were able to call upon the advice of another Briton, Sir Robert Hart, the Inspector-General of the Chinese Customs. Hart, an Ulsterman, was born in Portadown, Co. Armagh, in 1835, the son of a Methodist distiller who gave up his business because of his co-religionists' attitude to alcohol, and educated at Wesley College in Dublin, and Queen's College in Belfast (then still a constituent college of the Queen's University of Ireland). When Hart was nineteen, the Foreign Office assigned to the college one nomination for the consular service in China. A competitive examination was to have been held, but when the authorities learned that Hart was interested, they gave him the nomination without further ado, so highly did they regard his abilities.[4]

Hart entered the service as an interpreter in 1854, and was for some time employed as such at Hongkong, Ningpo and Canton. In 1859 he resigned in order to join the new Chinese customs organization as Deputy-Commissioner; four years later he was appointed Inspector-General, and in that capacity he served the Chinese Imperial Government for the rest of his working life. The Chinese regarded him simply as the administrative head of the authority which collected the customs duties agreed by treaty with foreign powers. He had officially no political influence, and indeed his predecessor had been dismissed for too obviously endeavouring to acquire such power; but by his industry and sincerity Hart had become a trusted adviser of the ministers in Peking, and before 1885 he had several times played an important part in negotiations with other countries.[5]

The Burma question was one of obvious embarrassment for him. Hart upheld the Chinese interests as loyally as any Chinese national, and in no way compromised the trust placed in him. On the other hand he felt strongly that, by virtue of his unique position, he could advise the Foreign Office and act as an intermediary. He deliberated with O'Conor, and kept London closely informed of the Chinese point of view.

On 1 November the Chinese Foreign Minister, Prince Ching, told Hart of the British preparations for an expedition into Upper Burma. Burma was a tributary state, he pointed out, and sovereignty would compel China to interfere; but England was a friendly power and China desired an amicable settlement, believing that it was better to prevent a complication than to wait for one to arise and then to have to adjust it. He also told Hart that the Tsungli Yamen (the Chinese Foreign Office) was reluctant to pursue inquiries through the Marquis Tseng in London, or through O'Conor in Peking, since they feared the bellicose Tseng might create unnecessary difficulties and dangers, and that an approach to O'Conor might result in official coldness. Hart said that he was reluctant to touch on the matter while the legation was in Peking, but he thought it best to do so. He sent the substance of this conversation to London, adding: 'At this stage, best treat the matter thus, privately and not officially, through me: friendly understanding can be arrived at and made official afterwards—I show this to Legation.'[6]

Next day Hart sent another telegram, saying that China must interfere on Burma's behalf, and suggesting two possible solutions (1) that China should be allowed to settle the problem by compelling the Burmese to pay reparation, or (2) that England should take what action she liked, provided that she left the tributary status of Burma unchanged and permitted the decennial tribute to be sent to Peking. Hart thought that he might be able to get agreement on the second plan, which he preferred.[7] Salisbury, anxious not to give any appearance of recognizing China's claim until an answer to the ultimatum had been received, drafted a reply to be sent to Marquis Tseng and to Hart. It was to the effect that the British Government had only now learned that China claimed tribute from Burma, and some right of sovereignity over that State. King Thibaw had given great offence to Her Majesty the Queen, and the military measures undertaken could not be arrested until the King had been punished and the honour of Britain vindicated. 'When that has been accomplished, Her Majesty's Government will be prepared to discuss with the Chinese Government the future arrangements in relation to Burma, and in the meanwhile they will do nothing to prejudice the legitimate rights of China.' China's offer to interpose, though appreciated, had come too late to be of practical use, but H.M. Government did not apprehend that these actions in Burma would give rise to any difficulty between Great Britain and China, and they had every desire to maintain the relations of friendship happily subsisting between the two countries.[8]

Churchill telegraphed Dufferin that the attitude of China was 'very serious and ought not to be lightly treated'. If Burma were annexed at the expense of a quarrel with China, the commercial interests would profit very little and the ultimate results might be disastrous. He then suggested that Dufferin might consider dispatching a special mission to Peking to negotiate with China on questions arising out of Chinese rights in Burma. On 10 November he wrote that he hoped that Dufferin would approve of the idea. 'A clever envoy might be able to do much with the Chinese just now.'[9]

Meanwhile the Foreign Office thought it best to make vague but soothing noises to the Chinese at a time when the expedition was poised to cross the frontier. At the Lord Mayor's banquet on 9 November Salisbury 'indulged in an effusive compliment to China, and to the Marquis Tseng who was present'. He assured him that they would act in complete recognition of China's rights. The gesture was well-timed, for Tseng and Macartney showed signs of taking up a more intransigent position than the Tsungli Yamen in Peking.[10]

When the British forces did cross the frontier, the Tsungli Yamen told Hart, 'The expedition cannot now be recalled and English demand goes beyond what we could properly advise compliance with: if we interfere officially we shall only create complication therefore we authorize you to devise some settlement privately, which we can afterwards make official, and which will give England what English want, give China what Chinese want, and close the door forever against any third party, in that quarter.' Hart lost no time in acting upon this invitation. On 15 November he suggested to London a convention of two Articles with a preamble declaring that the tributary relation of Burma to China rendered an understanding desirable between the British and Chinese governments. By the first article Great Britain was to agree that Burma should continue to send decennial tribute to China, and China was to agree to respect whatever treaty Great Britain might make with Burma. By the second, China was to select a point on the Burmese-Chinese border to be opened to British trade, Britain agreeing that imports and exports there should pay the tariff duties in force at the treaty ports.

With characteristic eagerness Hart recommended that the convention should be ratified forthwith. He believed that if Britain were in favour of the convention he could secure the Yamen's agreement. 'I advise you accept exactly what I suggest, for suggestion is cast in form best calculated to win assent here, being more palatable in the lump than piecemeal. If you signify readiness to accept I shall proceed and suggest next step. Till then, please keep quiet, but strike here now while iron is hot, and no opposition afloat.'[11]

Lord Randolph Churchill had no intention of allowing Hart to destroy his chance of annexing Burma outright. A week earlier he had written to Dufferin 'I do not, I own, possess that unlimited confidence in Sir Robert Hart which some people do. I think he is very jealous of his own position, and will throw many obstacles in the way of outside interference and particularly of Indian interference. He wants to keep things in their old groove and to be the general and principal medium of all negotiation'.[12] It was natural also that the Foreign Office should assume that Hart was trying to get the best terms for China, and they preferred to listen to O'Conor, who secretly advised that Hart's convention proposals should be considered solely from a view of British and Indian interests and not as a necessary concession to the political feeling of the Chinese Government.

Hart was unaware that Salisbury's Cabinet had already resolved upon annexation—when he did learn that this was so, he reiterated his arguments. On 20 November Salisbury had informed him that a convention was premature. The future of Burma could not be decided at once, and the possibility of annexation had to be safeguarded. When that future was decided it would be easy to arrange things satisfactorily with the Chinese, but if annexation was decided upon England could never be a tributary power. Lastly, there was no record of tribute paid by Burma: the last treaty between China and Burma, dated 13 December 1769, merely stipulated an 'exchange of affectionate letters in gold every ten years'. But Hart insisted that if the tribute was discontinued China would interfere, and could not be ignored. 'Worthless tribute is just what proud China would wage hopeless war for rather than forego without a blow.' And even if she did not fight, all hope of frontier trade would have to be abandoned. Hart went so far as to suggest a form of 'limited annexation' under which China might authorize Great Britain to govern her tributary state of Burma.[13]

Salisbury, though very unwilling to go against the views of Hart, on whose knowledge of China he relied, was not tempted to make a bargain with the Chinese before a final settlement in Upper Burma was agreed. The Foreign Office therefore played for time, while steps were taken to investigate the precise nature of Burma's relationship to China. Salisbury told Tseng that he could not grant him an interview until after the Christmas holidays, and repeated his Mansion House assurances. At the India Office Sir Owen Burne studied the exchange of missions in 1874 from the records of the British Resident at Mandalay and of the British representative at Peking, and came to the conclusion that King Mindon had in no way acknowledged that he was the vassal of the Chinese Emperor, whom he addressed as his royal friend. But the Governor of Yunnan might have transmitted to Peking a forged, or at least a 'Chinese', version of the letter which Mindon dispatched. It was on this document, published in the Peking Gazette of 15 May 1875, that O'Conor had based his information. Burne's conclusions were supported by such formidable authorities as Sir Ashley Eden and Sir Henry Yule; 'it seems a great pity,' Eden wrote, 'that the F.O. were in such a hurry to accept the inaccurate statements of the Chinese and the Anglo-Chinese —Hart and Macartney.'[14]

On 29 December Salisbury instructed O'Conor to inform the Chinese Government that on 1 January 1886, Upper Burma would be annexed to the Queen's dominions. Attention now shifted from the question of tribute to the question of the frontier. Meanwhile the Chinese had shown no enthusiasm for the proposed mission from Calcutta to Peking; Churchill attributed this to the intrigues of Hart, annoyed because his convention had not been accepted. Dufferin had made preparations for the mission, and had selected Sir Lepel Griffin to lead it, but the Foreign Office made it clear throughout that relations with China were their responsibility and not that of the India Office, and the first opportunity was taken to kill the whole project.[15]

In February, advised by Bernard, Dufferin suggested to the India Office a solution which he thought would allow the Chinese to save face. Bernard had explained to him that the *Thathanabaing*, the hierarch whom the English generally referred to as 'the Buddhist Archbishop,' had formerly been recognized throughout Burma as the Head of the Buddhist Church. He was appointed by the King, and nominated all the subordinate dignitaries. The failure of the British to comprehend the true nature and organization of Buddhism in Burma, and still more the way in which that organization had been dislocated by the deposition of Thibaw, created confusion throughout the whole of Burma and added fuel to the flames of rebellion. Dufferin now proposed that the Chinese Emperor be invited to appoint the *Thathanabaing*, and that he would then undertake to continue the decennial exchange of letters and presents. Churchill was not enthusiastic about the idea, but left it entirely to Dufferin and his Council. The Burmese who were consulted rejected the scheme outright, and so did all the experts on Burmese affairs; only China seemed favourably disposed to it. But China was not a predominantly Buddhist country, and Chinese Buddhism was distinct from that practised in Burma. In any event, a Chinese-appointed *Thathanabaing* would inevitably become a focus for intrigue. The scheme was soon dropped, and it now seems hardly credible that the Indian authorities should have been so ill-informed on the subject of Burmese religion.[16]

At the same time the Marquis Tseng intimated to Lord Rosebery, Foreign Secretary in the new Liberal Government, that Bhamo might be ceded to China as a *quid pro quo* for waiving the claim to tribute. This idea, O'Conor informed Rosebery, was concocted by the Marquis with the approval of the Viceroy Li Hung-chang—no such proposal had been made by the Tsungli Yamen. Li Hung-chang had mentioned it several times to O'Conor, at first as a mark of goodwill and friendship which Britain ought to show China, but 'latterly as a claim which China was fully justified in making'. O'Conor made it clear in Peking that there was no question of giving up Bhamo, and Tseng was ordered back to Peking to provide personal explanations of his various proposals relating to the cession of territory.[17]

In March 1886 the Chinese made a final attempt to persuade the British to put a Burmese prince on the throne. Through Macartney the Chinese Imperial Government let it be known that they would be prepared to waive their claim to a continuance of the tribute missions if a Burmese prince was allowed to rule in Mandalay. But now an unexpected way out of the deadlock suddenly presented itself.

While these negotiations had been going on, a British commerical and scientific mission had been patiently waiting in Peking for visas to proceed into Tibet. In 1861 a road had been built through Sikkim to the Tibetan frontier at the Jelop Pass. The lamaist hierarchy in Tibet regarded this action with some justified suspicion, for the British in India had turned their thoughts to establishing commerce with this remote Himalayan kingdom, which was also a tributary of China, but under much more direct Chinese suzerainty. Colman Macaulay, the Financial Secretary to the Government of Bengal, obtained the backing of the Foreign Office in 1885 to travel to Peking and request Chinese passports for a mixed political and scientific expedition to proceed to Lhasa. With Hart's assistance (Macaulay was yet another Ulsterman, and like Hart educated at Queen's College, Belfast) he obtained the required Chinese permission. He then returned to India and prepared the mission, overlooking no detail which might contribute to its success.

The Tsungli Yamen, however, showed increasing disquiet about the project, for the Tibetan lamas were hostile, dreading Indian competition with their lucrative tea monopolies, and unwilling that foreign barbarians should penetrate their sacred mountain-guarded kingdom. The lamas brought pressure on the Yamen which Hart could not altogether counter, and indicated that if the mission proceeded that it would be resisted in the mountain passes. Such resistance would have proved very embarrassing to the Chinese Government, which began to look for a way of escape. The negotiations on Burma seemed to offer such a channel, and after a long interview with O'Conor in May, the Chinese ministers made it known that they would consider an immediate agreement about Burma in return for a concession over Tibet.

Dufferin had no hesitation in agreeing to withdraw the Macaulay mission at once, and although the Chinese continued some diplomatic hard bargaining over the form of the Burmese tribute, the issue had in fact been decided. By the Chefoo Convention, signed on 24 July 1886, Britain agreed that inasmuch as it had been the custom of Burma to send ten-yearly missions 'with articles of local produce' the highest authority in Burma should send the customary tribute. But this article was a dead letter, and no tribute was ever sent. Only at the very last moment, when he was about to set out from Darjeeling, was Macaulay officially informed of the countermanding of his mission. It was the central ambition of his life, and he died soon afterwards, a bitterly disappointed man.'[18]

14

FARTHER INDIA

'On the whole my visit to Mandalay has been pretty satisfactory,' Dufferin told Kimberley, 'though there are a great many matters which, of course, caused me worry and anxiety.' Foremost among them was Prendergast's leniency towards Colonel Hooper. The Viceroy had found Prendergast, whom he had not met previously, 'a plain, honest, straight-forward soldier, certainly not brilliant, but both liked and trusted by his officers and men.' He was dismayed, however, by his failure to act in the case of the Provost Marshal. As soon as Dufferin had heard the details of the allegations against Hooper he had instructed Prendergast to deal with him, if the case was proved, with the utmost severity, and it never occurred to him that this had not been done. When he arrived at Mandalay, and found that the culprit had merely been reprimanded, he consulted with the Commander in Chief as to what was to be done. 'Roberts seemed scarcely to know what to recommend. When Hooper was photographing, he was not on duty, and, however monstrous the act, it was doubtful whether it could be considered a military offence, and even in regard to the other matter, he seemed to think it was difficult to re-open the case.' Finally Roberts had suggested that in addition to the censure passed upon him, Hooper should be dismissed to India and his promotion stopped. The only alternative, he maintained, was to break him.

'Having no-one else to advise me,' Dufferin continued, 'and my mind at that moment being preoccupied with many other anxious questions, perhaps I did not think the matter out as thoroughly as I ought to have done. At all events I came to the conclusion that to deprive the unfortunate man of his commission for what was an error of judgement, however gross, in regard to a matter outside his professional duties, would be too severe a punishment. One of the most distressing parts of the business is that Colonel Hooper had done exceptionally good service, and had obtained a great hold over the Burmese, and had been expressly thanked by Bernard. He is an extremely religious man, and, at the same time, very popular with his brother officers.'

Dufferin presumed that it was for these reasons, combined with his own good nature, and the fact that the threatening of the witness with death had arisen 'from some misunderstanding by Hooper's young subordinate of his chief's instructions', that Prendergast had been so soft in the matter. 'Be that as it may, the result is disastrous. It has thrown an indelible stain on the Army: it will have done a great deal to make the war unpopular; and it will render public opinion in England very suspicious of all our doings. Unfortunately too, the *Times* correspondent, who is an ill-conditioned cad, was awkwardly handled by Prendergast's Chief of Staff, and as a consequence of the quarrel, he has done everything he could to write Prendergast down, apparently with considerable success, for Lord Randolph had turned completely against him as everyone else seems to have done. This appears to be rather hard, for Prendergast has undoubtedly executed a difficult task with great success. He has conquered a province bigger than the United Kingdom with the loss of a little over twenty men. Moreover it must be remembered that at a very critical period his desire to obey my instructions to avoid bloodshed enabled him to resist a temptation to which many military men would have succumbed . . . But he stood firm, and, as a result, entered Mandalay unopposed and captured the King. All this will really never be known, but I ask you to put it to the credit side of the General's account.'[1]

Prendergast was the first victim of Moylan's revenge, and the one who suffered most. His military reputation, which had been at its zenith on the fall of Mandalay, was destroyed overnight and his career was virtually ended. When selected to lead the Burma expeditionary force, Prendergast had been in command of the Secunderabad Division of the Madras Army. On 28 November he was promoted Lieutenant-General, and under the rules he would have ceased to belong to the Staff of the Indian Army from 31 March 1886. He could therefore only be retained in the Burma command by some special arrangement. The Government of India desired to make such an arrangement, and after the military decisions made in Mandalay, Dufferin telegraphed Kimberley on

17 February to suggest that all the troops in Burma should be brought under the Government of India and Prendergast retained in command. But on 19 February Kimberley replied that it would be necessary to have fuller grounds for severing the command in Lower Burma from the Madras Army, and that he did not think that the established rule should be departed from in Prendergast's case. The General was therefore informed that White would relieve him on 31 March. Dufferin agreed with Kimberley in allowing Prendergast to go, though he was sorry to lose a man who had learned a good deal about the country and had some excellent qualities. 'Everything he does will stink in the nostrils of the *Times* correspondent, and few reputations can withstand the erosion produced by the constant droppings of a special correspondent's acid telegrams.' It was a prophetic remark.[2]

In the palace at Mandalay White was wakened in the middle of the night by Bernard, who personally brought the telegram with the news, telling him that it was important. As White received several 'important' telegrams from Bernard every day, he was not very excited, but when he read it, he was 'not a little surprised' to learn 'that Sir Harry Prendergast's extension of service had been refused by the Secretary of State and that the commands in Burma were to be reconstituted; that I was to command in Upper Burma and to have two brigadier-generals under me; and that it was still to be considered a force in the field reporting direct to the C. in C. in India.' He was, however, to remain a brigadier-general in rank, a fact that was to cause him much annoyance and frustration. He was very sorry for Prendergast's sake. 'He had quite built on having his command prolonged till November and had taken a house in Rangoon. He is such a nice man, everybody likes him.'[3]

Later White told his wife that Prendergast had taken his disappointment admirably, but that it was 'something very bad for him', as he was not old enough to have earned his off-reckoning and had saved little. He believed that he was going to reside in India 'as it somehow gives him more pay'.[4] Prendergast was only fifty-one when the Burmese War brought his active military career to a close. He subsequently served briefly as Resident in several of the Indian States, and 'rendered valuable service in the Public Works and Railways Department'. Promoted full General in 1887, he retired at the age of fifty-seven and went to live in England. Dufferin considered that his treatment had been shabby, and he privately requested the Secretary of State and the Duke of Cambridge to do what they could for him.[5] In 1888 the India Office answered complaints by Prendergast (1) that he had been 'dismissed' from the command of the Burma Force, (2) that articles to his disadvantage 'in the London newspapers' had been believed at the India Office because the journals of operations in Burma after 31 January 1886 had not been sent punctually from India, and (3) that the military dispatch of 16 July 1886 had altogether ignored his share of operations in Burma after the fall of Mandalay. A memorandum rejecting these charges reveals that Prendergast had, in spite of repeated requests, withheld a supplementary report recommending officers for awards and promotions in connection with the campaign until 30 March 1886, the day before he relinquished his command.[6]

The next to go was Sladen. 'It is better, I think, that he should go home,' Dufferin told the Secretary of State. 'He has done excellent service and displayed considerable courage, and undoubtedly we are indebted to him for the capture of the King, and, to a certain degree, for there having been no fighting before Mandalay. I will, therefore, venture to suggest that he should be made a Knight. A K.C.S.I. would be too much I think. He is a foolish, vain man, and, I imagine, he was not quite loyal to Bernard. No-one was a stronger annexationist, but his notion was to set up the Hlutdaw and govern through it, with himself as Resident. The plan was an impossible one, and, I believe, it was self-interest which induced him to urge it.'[7] Sladen resigned as political officer in April, and received his knighthood in November. He was somewhat impatient to know what reward the Government of India proposed to give him, and more than a little disappointed to have to accept a K.C.B. instead of the expected K.C.S.I.

In June he wrote a letter to *The Times* defending his policies, and explaining how the Hlutdaw had been induced 'after a good deal of persuasion, to join temporarily in forming a Provisional Government to assist in the pacification of the country'. He asserted that the serious dacoitry only began in mid-December after the arrest of the Taingda Mingyi. The ministers had then resigned in a body and the Hlutdaw ceased to have administrative control.[8] His letter was supported by some Burma experts, but it also drew the fire of formidable critics; in July S. Holt Hallet, an engineer who with A. R. Colquhoun was associated with the plan for a railway through the Shan States, wrote that Prendergast had sent the Kinwun Mingyi away on Sladen's advice; and in the autumn, when an acrimonious debate on Burma took place in the columns of *The Times*, Hallet contributed a devastating indictment of Sladen's actions.

He alleged that in the first calculations made for the administration of Upper Burma, cheapness was to be the order of the day, and that Sladen had hoped to govern the country with twenty-five or twenty-seven European officers. 'Is it any wonder that such a castle of cards tumbled to the ground . . . and that your Rangoon correspondent on 13 July had to state "The attempt at cheap government has failed"?' Hallet declared that Bernard with Colquhoun, Adamson and Raikes had had to retrieve Sladen's mistakes. 'Under Sladen's rule blunder after blunder had occurred. First there was the desertion of Mandalay for the night, after securing the person of the King, thus leaving a large city, whence the police had fled, a prey to soldiery who had just been disbanded without pay, and in too many cases without being disarmed.' Sladen's second mistake had been the appointment of the Taingda Mingyi. The country was already in a fearful state before Christmas, thus refuting Sladen's claim that serious dacoitry did not occur until after the Taingda's arrest. Thirdly, Sladen had allowed the *soi-disant* princes to come and go freely, and one of them had resided in Mandalay for a month.

Hallet quoted a letter from a gentleman long resident in Mandalay who said: 'There is no doubt that Colonel Sladen was successful in taking Theebaw and Mandalay without bloodshed; but there his successes ceased . . . Colonel Sladen blindly trusted the Hlutdaw and was grossly deceived by them . . . It was with the greatest pleasure that we hailed his departure. I am convinced Bernard arrived in Mandalay just in time to save us from some serious disaster.'[9]

If Dufferin's visit to Mandalay had settled the question of annexation, it also proved to be a turning point in the contest with the dacoits. On his way down-river Dufferin had a good deal of time to consider the overall situation. He had summarily abolished the Hlutdaw, and told the Burmese that henceforth their sovereign was the Queen. Inevitably these announcements must provoke a renewal and intensification of the sporadic guerilla activities of the Pretender Princes and dacoit *bos*. 'I am well aware,' he had written from Mandalay, 'that though ultimately the acquisition of Burmah will prove advantageous to us, for some time to come it will breed nothing but trouble and annoyance. No-one can view with much complacency the extension of our Imperial responsibilities. Our first difficulty of course has been, and will for a long time continue to be with the dacoits.' Therefore when he reached Rangoon he told Bernard that additional reinforcements would be necessary, and he arranged for the 17th Bengal Infantry, the 26th Punjab Native Infantry, and an Assam regiment to be sent to Burma. The Punjab regiment was to be stationed at Bhamo.[10]

Meanwhile at home the long-impending debate on Burma took place in the House of Commons. Gladstone's Government was obliged to accept annexation as a *fait accompli*, and the only question before the House was to decide who was to pay for it; consequently the motion was 'That Her Majesty having directed a military expedition of her forces charged upon Indian revenues to be dispatched against the King of Ava, this House consents that the revenues of India shall be applied to defray the expenses of the military operations which may be carried on beyond the external frontiers of Her Majesty's Indian Possessions'.

Sir Ughtred Kay-Shuttleworth, opening the debate, assured the House that the cost of the expedition would not exceed £300,000. He drew attention to the fact that in British Burma the revenue had trebled between 1862 and 1885. Dr. Hunter, the member for Aberdeen North, argued that the time had been ill-chosen for increasing the burdens of the Indian Empire, since the Government of India had just been driven to impose an income tax. The first Burmese War had cost £15,000,000 and Upper Burma was likely to prove an insolvent province. Who had clamoured for annexation? He denied that there was a widespread feeling in favour of it in Britain, and it had certainly not been demanded by the people of India. The annexation had been brought about by the chambers of commerce, and the war was being fought to open up new markets for British trade. That being so, where was the justice of imposing the expenses of the war upon the Indian exchequer? Mr. Richard (Merthyr Tydvil) declared that the Burmese did not want their country stolen, nor did the Indians want to pay for the action, which was like the seizure of Naboth's vineyard. Other speakers denied that France posed any threat to British interests in Burma, and asserted that causes of dispute with the Court of Ava had been over trivial matters of ceremonial such as shoe-wearing. Mr. McIver argued prophetically that there was no general desire on the part of the Burmese to come under British rule, and that the violation of national sentiment centred on the Buddhist religion and the monarchy would set both Upper and Lower Burma against the British.

Gladstone insisted that the merits of the campaign were not under discussion. By the 'urgent and unforeseen necessity' clause of an act of 1858 the Government of India was not required to obtain the prior consent of Parliament for actions such as the Burma expedition. Even if it should be proved that the war was wanton and needless, it would not necessarily follow that a reversal of the annexation should occur, since such action now might do more harm than good. He accepted Lord Dufferin's appraisal of the situation. The war had been waged in good faith to protect the security, happiness and prosperity of India, and as such it was chargeable to Indian revenues. The motion was carried by 297 votes to 82.[11]

Dufferin was naturally pleased by the outcome of the debate, and expressed his thanks to Gladstone.[12] Moreover, circumstances over which he had no control now provided him with a much needed respite from public criticism in England. Gladstone's announcement that he intended to bring forward his Irish Home Rule bill as soon as possible began a period of political excitement unequalled in Britain since the seventeenth century. In the torrents of hatred and abuse released by this action, the problems of Burma were, for the moment, swept into oblivion. In February, when Dufferin was returning from Mandalay, Lord Randolph Churchill was in Belfast telling the Protestants of Ulster to organize and prepare, so that the catastrophe of Home Rule might not come upon them like a thief in the night.[13] Three months later, Sir James Stephen was writing to Dufferin that the only question as to civil war was precisely how, when and where it was to come about, and who was to have the law on his side; the worst horror he could envisage was a rising in Ulster against an Irish parliament put down by English troops.[14] The news of the political crisis over Ireland came to Dufferin 'like the sound of raging billows in a far-off sea', but he could not be indifferent to his own interests there. 'As for myself,' he confided to a friend, 'I am so tremendously busy from morning till night that I have not time even to think of what is in store for us in Ireland, though when I do consider the matter, it looks very much as though the few thousands I have invested in Canada is all that I am likely to call mine in a few years.'[15]

Nevertheless it was something to have the attention of Parliament directed away from the newest colony to the oldest. Lady Gregory wrote to him 'If there is any act of absolutism or illegality that your government wishes to commit, now is your time, for India is forgotten for the moment.'[16] But on 8 June the Home Rule Bill was defeated, and the Liberal Party irreparably divided. Gladstone went to the country and his policy was decisively rejected. By July, Salisbury was once more in office, and Dufferin had again to face the prospect of working with a Conservative Secretary of State.

Meanwhile the immensity of the problems facing White might have broken down a less ingenious or industrious soldier. One of his worst anxieties was that the palace and a large part of Mandalay might be destroyed by fire. A bad fire occurred in the city just after the Dufferins' departure. All the troops were called out and White had difficulty in preventing dacoits from looting from the refugees. Guards were placed on the groups of women and children, who spent the night in the streets, sitting besides their possessions. 'The palace itself in which we are all housed, and without which I cannot imagine what we should do, is all built of wood and there are now nearly 2,000 Burmese carpenters at work inside it. They all smoke and throw their cheroots about in the most promiscuous fashion. I expect to be burnt out before the season is over.'[17]

Outside Mandalay the military situation was deteriorating. The original ten military stations had to be increased to twenty-five, and the strength of the movable columns progressively increased. Formidable groups of insurgents operated close to Mandalay itself, led by three independent *bos* all acting on behalf of the Myingun Prince, a son of Mindon Min. White's general plan of campaign was to progress along the two great rivers, the Irrawaddy and the Chindwin, and by establishing military posts, close enough to support one another, to obtain control of the whole area. But Upper Burma was a vast area of mountain, plain and jungle, intersected by broad and often impassable rivers, and devoid of roads.

In March he wrote to his wife that the country was not falling in as he had hoped. The troops had been worked very hard, and he was afraid that if cholera broke out among them it would tell heavily.[18] In April he reported that the country was still very disturbed and that he was fighting in all directions. The Burmese, though they defied the British, and burned and looted the villages, invariably ran away when faced by the troops. Communication with his posts was very difficult, because of the absence of roads and telegraphs, and he was putting six to eight months supplies into all the inland posts before the rains came. It had been predicted that resistance would increase at the Burmese New Year (1 April), and this had proved to be true. He was 'taken quite aback by the energy developed by the organisation against us in the country everywhere'. All the outposts had been attacked and there was a continual cry for reinforcements.

At the end of the month another disastrous fire burned down a large area of Mandalay, though the palace again escaped. The temperature varied between 100° and 104°F., and only an iron constitution, hardened by years of campaigning in trying climates, enabled White to keep going, but it took 'something out of one, up half the night at fires, and at work again at 5 a.m.' A quarter of the 67th Hampshire Regiment was in hospital; scores of soldiers were being sent down-river in steamers and flats; the officers were 'rapidly breaking down'.[19] White was constantly out superintending his posts and directing the mobile columns, but the burden of paper work kept him from getting enough exercise in the steamy morass of Mandalay, and strained his eyes, causing him to use glasses at night. This troubled him, and made him fatigued and irritable. His quarters were in Thibaw's royal apartment. 'Worse luck, it has a flat roof, that flat roof is covered with Portland Cement, that Portland Cement is full of cracks; about three nights ago rain came down in torrents. My rooms . . . were flooded. I walked about trying to put my papers in a dry place, but failing, I resigned the papers to become *papier mâché*, put my India rubber tub over my mosquito curtain frame at the upper end, rolled myself, perspiring properly, in the blanket you bought for me, and went to sleep; awoke very wet and slightly chilled, took quinine, and viewed the desolation around. My most cherished books of reference, wet rags. My maps, corrected by the latest surveys in red paint, etc., were masses of red and blue blotches, and the mosquitoes more nippy than ever.'[20]

The fraying of his temper began to show in his letters home. He was worried about money, about the disobedient attitude of his small son Jack, then only seven but already proving 'difficult' at school. He was depressed by the death and sickness of his officers, and concerned for Bernard, who was looking very haggard and ill, and had suffered several bouts of dysentery. Above all he was obsessed by the fear that he would be retired at fifty-five without being made a Major-General. He believed that the senior brigadiers like Norman who had been put under his command were jealous, and that his name was anathema to the Duke of Cambridge. His worst fears were confirmed when in August he heard confidentially from Roberts that General Sir Herbert Macpherson was

'for political reasons' to be sent to Burma to take the direction of operations. 'This will probably be in every newspaper in England', he told his
wife, 'and will annoy and worry you and my friends at home, as it will of
course be added that I have failed.'[21]

15

THE BURSTING OF THE BUND

There was some speculation that the change of Government might have an effect on the Burmese situation. Kimberley wondered whether Moylan would be instructed to find only pleasant things to say, and wryly commented that after a decent interval all the blame could be put on the late Liberal Secretary of State.[1] But Moylan's energy showed no sign of diminishing as the summer passed. He attacked the civil government, the administration of justice, the conduct of military affairs, and the proposal to send Indian police to Burma.

'I see that Lord Randolph Churchill will be Chancellor of the Exchequer,' White wrote home at the end of July, 'I hope so as it will keep him from the India Office where we don't want him, especially we in Burma. He backs the newspaper people so shamefully. We have had a heavy loss this week in Captain Adamson, the Deputy Commissioner of Mandalay. He went down the river on Sunday morning quite broken down in health and I believe much on account of the attack on him by Mr. Moylan, the *Times* correspondent.'[2] Adamson, a hardworking and conscientious officer, was Moylan's current victim. Moylan alleged that he was an Artillery officer entirely ignorant of the law who passed summary verdicts on Burmese offenders and often held trials, of which no records were kept, in his own house. In fact Captain Adamson had been in 'civil' employment in Burma since 1871, for seven years as Assistant Magistrate in Rangoon, and since as Assistant and then Deputy Commissioner. He *had* held trials in his own house, when accommodation in the court was restricted, but the house was open to the public, and full records were kept in every case. Adamson had, however, decided some cases against Moylan's clients, and there was as yet no right of appeal from the authorities in Upper Burma. This was a justified grievance to which Moylan persistently drew attention in 1886. Bernard argued that the same situation had obtained in Lower Burma for a considerable time after the conquest, and he did not approve of its being changed. He was sure also that Moylan's agitation for the right of appeal was to create more work for himself as a barrister. Moylan based some of his charges against Adamson on the testimony of one Miller, whom Adamson had chastised 'for beating a French Jew'.[3]

Sir Richard Cross, the new Secretary of State, warned Dufferin that Dr. Cameron, the Glasgow radical, was going to raise questions about the matter in the House of Commons, and asked for precise details. This was the kind of thing which Dufferin found most irritating. Moylan's reports went direct to *The Times* and did not appear in the Indian press, so that it was sometimes seven or eight weeks before he was made aware of the 'ever-growing indictment'. Moreover Cameron would have full, if not accurate, particulars of any incident by letter, and to hope to counter this, the Viceroy had to be able to identify the incident in the first place. His only intimation of the Adamson affair had in fact been a letter which Moylan wrote to Mackenzie Wallace, in which he explicitly said that Cameron was the M.P. who would bring the matter up in the House. He obtained a fuller explanation from Bernard, and sent it to Cross.[4] With this information at his disposal, the Under-Secretary, Sir John Gorst, was able to deal effectively with Cameron's questions when they were raised in the Commons.[5]

Dufferin told Kimberley that he did not believe that the tone of Moylan's telegrams had been inspired from home, or for any political purpose. Moylan's animus was peculiarly personal; in the first place he was a man of brutal and vindictive temper, and in the next his main object was to terrorize those in authority into furthering his professional interests as a barrister.[6] At the same time Dufferin had decided that Moylan must be silenced by almost any means available, and he now took the unusual step of writing privately to the proprietor of *The Times*, John Walter, drawing attention to Moylan's past record and the complaints made against him, and requesting that he should be replaced by another correspondent.

Walter did not reply for a fortnight, pleading as an excuse the absence of Macdonald, the head of *The Times* foreign department. On his return, Macdonald had explained that Moylan's connection with the newspaper as an occasional correspondent went back as far as the Ashanti War of

1871, in which he had done very good service. He had been chosen by the famous editor Delane, who had later recommended him to Lord Carnarvon for a legal appointment in the West Indies. He had not been sent out to Burma by *The Times*, but, having gone out there on his own account, he offered his services as a special correspondent, and these were accepted.

Having explained the circumstances of Moylan's appointment, Walter made it quite clear that *The Times* intended to stand by him. They had had every reason to expect that he would prove an active and trust-worthy correspondent, and with regard to the salient points brought to their notice, his accuracy could not be impeached. Undoubtedly his criticism of General Prendergast's operations after the fall of Mandalay had given mortal offence, and even if his history and character had been unimpeachable he could never have regained, had he ever possessed, the goodwill of the military authorities. At that time, however, Moylan had been warned to be cautious and to avoid giving offence. Walter rarely interfered in editorial matters, but he was bound to say that when the news of the photographing business arrived he was so shocked that he had a telegram sent to Moylan asking for confirmation. It proved to be only too correct.

The story of the ruby mines belonged to another category. If it could be proved that Moylan, being the agent of a company, had concocted the paragraph in the Rangoon paper, with a view of telegraphing it to *The Times* for the promotion of the objects of the company, that would be an act wholly incompatible with his duty as a correspondent, and would forfeit their confidence. But, this aside, Walter did not think that a case had been made out against either Moylan's veracity or integrity. On the whole the tenor of his correspondence had been 'extremely fair and temperate', and they would not be justified in at once replacing him by another correspondent.

Then, with a sly thrust at Dufferin, Walter continued: 'It is not easy to find a gentleman qualified for such a position. Such a correspondent e.g. as Mr. Mackenzie Wallace is not to be found every day; and if we were fortunate enough to meet with such a person, we might find our-selves alas! suddenly deprived of his services by more tempting offers than we could make him.' Dufferin was assured that Moylan's telegrams would be closely scrutinized, and nothing that seemed likely to have been inspired by personal animus would escape the editor's supervision.[7] *The Times* was just as sensitive as other newspapers to the slightest suspicion of pressure from high places, and Dufferin's letter was regarded as an attempt to interfere with the freedom of the press. It probably made the situation worse, for *The Times* became more determined to defend Moylan than it would otherwise have been. Meanwhile Moylan was, according to White, 'rapidly making a fortune' in Mandalay. 'He takes on the cases of the natives and they know that the *Times* has great influence and consider him greater than the Chief Commissioner.' Because Moylan had returned to Mandalay in triumph after being sent away by General Prendergast, he was regarded by the Burmese as a *mingyi* of greater power than any of the officials, and was thus able to command his own price.[8] He now began to threaten Bernard that if he did not decide certain claims against the Government promptly and to his satisfaction he would attack his reputation in *The Times*. This was a mistake, for Bernard angrily rejected the suggestion and at once began to make his own inquiries into Moylan's background and professional conduct. Before long he discovered from some outside source what Dufferin had already known for six months.

On 28 August Bernard informed the Viceroy that he had received copies of official gazettes and files of newspapers from the Colony of Grenada which showed that Moylan had 'falsely and maliciously slandered' officials there from the Governor and Chief Justice down to the local magistrate. 'He was dismissed, after a full trial before the Colonial Council, and with the sanction of the then Secretary of State, from his office as Attorney-General. He then got hold of a newspaper, slandered people all round, and tried to incite sedition, with the result that his editor was sent to prison for six months, and the newspaper press was sold up, though Mr. Moylan escaped. He then practised as a barrister and solicitor with the result that he was brought before the courts for professional misconduct in two or more cases. The Supreme Court held that his conduct as a lawyer had been fraudulent and unbecoming the character of a barrister or a gentleman, and ordered that he be struck off the list of barristers and solicitors of the Colony.[9]

Bernard was in no doubt as to his duty in the matter: it was to bring these facts to the attention of the Government Advocate at Rangoon and seek his legal advice. This he requested permission from the Viceroy to do. While he thought that to enter the lists against the representative of so powerful an organ as *The Times* might not 'conduce hereafter to Bernard's peace or advantage', Dufferin agreed that the Commissioner was justified in trying 'to rid the Burmese Bar of such a scoundrel'. He would of course be accused of persecuting the press, but he would undoubtedly have taken the same action if the offender had not been a newspaper correspondent. After consulting Ilbert and Bayley, legal members of the Executive Council, Dufferin decided to let Bernard go ahead, on the understanding that he told them the Advocate's opinion before taking further action. In the meantime, as it was possible that Moylan might learn of Bernard's intentions, he sent a warning to Cross of what was on the cards.[10]

Once again, however, luck was on Moylan's side. This time it was nature which played into his hands. When Mindon Min built his new city of Mandalay, he protected it from flooding by building an embankment nine miles long from a point just north of the city to Amarapura. This embankment, or bund, was built by royal troops, and hundreds of elephants had been used to pack the earth hard; it was 40 feet high, 105 feet wide at the base and 60 feet wide at the top. During the reigns of Mindon and Thibaw stringent precautions had been taken to keep it in good repair. In the spring of 1886, at the time of the fires in Mandalay, threats had been made by dacoits that the embankment would be cut during the rainy season. These threats were renewed at the beginning of August, and the military authorities took the precaution of protecting the bund at night with small detachments of troops.

In the middle of August the Irrawaddy flooded its banks, and there was some concern about the condition of the earthwork. On the 16th, water bubbling up through the ground showed that the foundations had been undermined, and an uneasy feeling prevailed in the city all day. Shortly after 7 o'clock in the evening, part of the northern portion of the bund suddenly gave way and the floodwaters of the Irrawaddy poured in through a 30-yard breach which rapidly widened to 300 yards. A small number of people were drowned in the first onrush of the water, but the fact that there had been ample warning, and that the floods extended very slowly, enabled most Burmese to reach safety.

The water took an hour to reach the bazaar, three miles from the bund, and people in the low-lying areas had time to get out, and to bring some of their belongings with them. By 9.30 p.m. an area five miles long by two miles wide was inundated, and some 50,000 people had been left homeless. The *pyongyi kaungs* were crowded with refugees, and there was a great danger of a cholera epidemic. Moylan sent off what Dufferin called 'some of his usual malicious and exaggerated reports,' but *The*

Times held back his longer dispatches until 21 September, when it printed his criticisms in full.[11]

According to Moylan the Kinwun Mingyi and other Burmese ministers selected to help Bernard had some time previously represented to Thirkell White, the Secretary for Upper Burma, that it was urgently necessary to make the embankment secure. These representations were forwarded to Captain Adamson, who had done nothing about it. The present calamity was therefore directly attributed to the neglect of the authorities, and the persons chiefly to blame were Adamson, Carter (his acting Deputy Commissioner) and Thirkell White, a civilian who lacked experience. News of the catastrophe had not reached the military authorities in the palace until two hours after it had happened, and then their first concern was to secure the key buildings with detachments of troops. The distress of the Burmese had been greatly increased by the earlier action of the authorities in acquiring all the houses within the walled city and pulling them down to make room for cantonments. Moylan toured the inundated areas in a boat, noting the plight of the homeless, and the stench of death from the abandoned houses.[12]

All this was calculated to generate more controversy. 'Further statements in the *Times* today about the loss of life through inundation at Mandalay,' Cross wrote to Dufferin, 'consequently further questions in the House of Commons, which from your information we can answer satisfactorily. When Bernard is perfectly certain of his facts and can give figures, you will of course inform us, and we shall be able to lay this ghost, and by these effectual means thoroughly discredit the "correspondent." '[13] Questions *were* asked, on the basis of Moylan's information, and Sir John Gorst was able to reassure the House that only twelve lives had been lost, and that a pound of rice and half an anna were given daily to any destitute person who applied for it. The Government of India had held an inquiry, and it had been established that the bursting of the bund was not the result of any malicious act.[14]

Cross was understandably tired of all these questions on Burma in the House. He agreed that Moylan's conduct had been scandalous, but he cautioned that his iniquities might be more properly dealt with by the legal authorities in Rangoon and not by the Government of India.[15] Consequently Dufferin telegraphed Bernard, after due thought, that 'although under ordinary circumstances he would certainly be bound to provide for the purity of the Bar of Rangoon', the local administration had better not interfere in this instance, as such action would be at once denounced as persecution inspired by vindictive motives. If the judges chose to deal with the matter, that would be different.

The Rangoon Bench did take up the matter, and called upon Moylan for an explanation of his actions. This he furnished, along with a statement from the Benchers of his Inn in Dublin, which 'to some degree whitewashed him' by finding that the evidence of his misconduct in Grenada had not been sufficient to justify his being disbarred. 'Though I have no doubt that there was a great deal that was disgraceful in his conduct at Grenada', Dufferin reflected charitably, 'it may perhaps be that the general hatred which he seems to have the talent of inspiring in all societies he frequents may have prejudiced the action of the local authorities.'[16]

Dufferin was much more concerned about Moylan, however, than this comment suggests. His prediction that no reputation could withstand the acid droppings from a special correspondent's pen was coming uncomfortably true. Moylan was now all the more determined to destroy Bernard's prestige, and was even turning his baleful attention upon the Viceroy himself.

At the time of Dufferin's visit to Mandalay, Moylan had been praising Bernard and White as part of his campaign against Sladen and Prendergast. Once the latter had gone, he began to write Bernard down, and even then Dufferin had been obliged to defend Bernard to the Secretary of State. 'Of Bernard I have formed a very good opinion. He has his faults. He is too quick and jerky, and would do better if he deliberated more; but he is high-minded, disinterested, zealous, extremely intelligent, and most humane and friendly to the natives, on which latter account he has made himself unpopular with the Anglo-Indian community.'[17] Nevertheless Dufferin seems to have regarded Bernard, now Sir Charles Bernard, as partly discredited by the newspaper reports, at least in the eyes of the politicians, and there was some risk of his being made the scapegoat for the blunders which others had perpetrated. Just before he left the India Office in July, Kimberley had advised Dufferin to get Bernard away from Burma, and put a stronger man in his place. He suggested Crosthwaite, 'a quiet sensible man, rather worn out'.[18] Crosthwaite, who had been Commissioner for British Burma before Bernard, was fatigued and ill in 1886, and Dufferin, when he met him briefly, was not very impressed by him, though everyone spoke very highly of his ability. In fact he was to succeed Bernard in 1887, and he was to be the man largely responsible for the pacification of Burma.

But for the present Bernard remained at his post, surviving the increasing hostility of Moylan. When Cross renewed the suggestion in September that he should be replaced, Dufferin replied that he had no reason to be dissatisfied with him, and that he was certain that he had no-one under his hand who was likely to do better. 'Moylan has undoubtedly discredited him by a deliberate system of perverse cunning and malicious misrepresentation—his telegram about the bursting of the bund at Mandalay sufficiently indicates his methods—and of course it is always unsatisfactory working with a discredited instrument, for everything that goes wrong, even though it be beyond all human control, is at once supposed to be the fault of the convicted blunderer.' On the other hand, Dufferin could think of nothing more cruel and unjust than to remove Bernard for that reason. He proposed to keep Bernard at Mandalay until the winter or spring, and to release him then, so that he would not appear to have been got rid of to appease Moylan.[19]

Dufferin's idea was to recommend Bernard for the Punjab, but Lord Salisbury objected. Dufferin concluded that the reputation of no public servant could long survive 'with such a liar and hell-hound as Moylan upon his tracks'. In spite of themselves, people remembered what was written in *The Times*, even if it was not true, and in time it became part of the crystallized faith adopted by public opinion. Indian public servants could not defend themselves, and often did not know of the accusations made against them until months after they had been published. 'I cannot help sometimes smiling at the anomaly of a Viceroy of India in the midst of his many cares and anxieties being compelled to spend so much time as it has already cost me to refute and disprove the fabrications disseminated by a rowdy and discredited barrister, especially after his untruthfulness has already been so fully exemplified. But I suppose I must command my patience, as this is one of the characteristics incident to the new aspects of modern Parliamentary government.'[20]

In September, when the public disquiet about Burma was at its most intense, Cross asked Dufferin if he would supply him with a complete narrative of operations, civil and military, since the occupation of Mandalay. Kimberley had asked for such a report in July, but it had apparently not been furnished before he left office.[21] The memorandum which Dufferin now prepared was in effect a defence of his whole Burma policy, and it suggested an idea to him. A few weeks later he expanded it almost to the length of a pamphlet, had it privately printed, and sent it to some eighty of his most influential acquaintances at home and in India. The list included politicians, members of the aristocracy, soldiers, judges, old India hands and influential editors. Copies of the confidential memorandum were received by such eminent, if ill-assorted, late Victorians as the Duke of Cambridge, Gladstone, Lord Tennyson, W. T. Stead, and the Duchess of Manchester.[22]

'As I see that public opinion is becoming a little irritated in England at the prolongation of the struggle in Burmah,' Dufferin wrote, 'and especially as the Government of India has been accused of having stinted the Burmese authorities in the matter of troops, money and officials, I have thought it as well to draw up the following memorandum in reference to this and other analogous criticisms, which have been made in Parliament and elsewhere, on the progress of affairs in Burma generally.' The document showed very clearly the extent of Moylan's success in tarnishing the glamour of the Mandalay campaign, and the reputations of those involved in it. It began by outlining the reasons for the war, the swift and successful ascent of the Irrawaddy, and the comparative tranquillity of the period from the fall of Mandalay until his own visit to Burma in February. His impression then had been that the Burmese people had acquiesced in the conquest, but, on his way down the river, he had reconsidered the situation. The announcements made at Mandalay were in their very nature 'calculated to excite and provoke whatever dormant elements of turbulence and dissatisfaction' existed. Therefore, being a prudent man, Dufferin had arranged with the Commander-in-Chief to send another three regiments from India, one of which was earmarked for Bhamo, and to increase the numbers of military police to be recruited in the Punjab and North-West India. The process of reinforcement was continued until a body of 30,000 fighting men was at the disposal of the Burmese administration, 'that is to say, a larger force than the British Government sent to the Crimea, or to Egypt, and double that with which Lord Napier invaded Abyssinia.' No demand of any kind for troops, money, supplies or civil officers made by the proper authorities had been refused.

There followed a defence of White and the military policy, and of Bernard and the civil administration, in which Dufferin was at pains to defend also his own reasons for supporting them. White was an excellent officer, but it was true that he was unknown in England and had brigadiers under his command who were much senior to him. Therefore Macpherson was sent to Burma to have 'a soothing and re-assuring effect

at home.' Bernard was universally admitted to be high-minded, conscientious, intelligent, vigorous, and hard working. The only criticism
Dufferin had ever heard made against him was that he evinced more
sympathy for the Burmese than was altogether approved of by the mercantile community of Rangoon. His humanity was proverbial, he spoke
the language and his local knowledge was unrivalled. No Viceroy, even
if he had thought less of Bernard than Dufferin did, would have resorted
to the violent act of displacing, and thus disgracing, him.

Dufferin then went on to deal with the Hooper case, the legal code,
and the criticisms made of Adamson. All the counts in the indictment
against the local government had emanated from the same source, *The
Times* correspondent in Burma, a man who had used *The Times* 'as a
vehicle through which he endeavours to gratify his own personal resentment and advance his professional interests, and who is regardless of
truth in the pursuit of his sinister purposes.' When he first arrived he
had been treated with great kindness by General Prendergast, but had
almost immediately come into collision with the Chief of Staff. Prendergast had ordered him out the country and made him famous and a
martyr. Colonel Hooper's unjustifiable proceedings had given him a
most favourable opportunity: not content with relating the facts of the
case, which were bad enough, he had interpolated in his narrative, 'it
must be admitted in a very artistic manner', many exaggerations and
inventions. Happily, Moylan had now been found out, and the *Saturday
Review* and other papers, though unfortunately only too ready to accept
his general description of affairs in Burma, had shown up in a very
amusing way how he insinuated into the ear of the public his wilful
misrepresentations.

Finally, Dufferin attempted to refute the idea that the conquest of
Upper Burma had been carried out 'on the cheap'. The fact was that the
general public in England never seemed to have comprehended the real
character of the work in hand. 'They thought that the bloodless campaign of last November, and the capture of Theebaw and of his capital,
had finished off the business; and they were delighted with the idea of
having acquired a new Province in so inexpensive a manner. The
Government of India, on the contrary, never indulged in these sanguine
anticipations, and though, during the interval which took place between
the taking of Mandalay and my own visit to Burmah, the reports of our
officers gave some hopes that our experiences might, after all, prove less
troublesome than those of Lord Dalhousie, I never ceased, in spite of

the comparative calm which then prevailed, to have considerable misgivings on the subject . . .'

When all was said and done, it was more a question of time than of troops. The disturbances in Burma could not be ended by the mere weight of troops. The whole army of India could not do that; it would be like trying to destroy quicksilver by trampling on it. 'The present problem in Burmah is not unlike that with which we are contending in Ireland. In neither country would the great mass of the people, if left to themselves, be inimical to our rule, but in each, from different causes, a seething mass of disaffection and lawlessness is rife, fostered in a great measure in both by personal ambition and the love of plunder. But Ireland is not a big country, and only a small part of it is really disturbed. The English Government is a highly-organized machine with a large army and an effective police for its instruments, and the invaluable advantage of roads, railways, and telegraphs; and yet what difficulty there has been found in suppressing moonlighting, raids upon farms, murders, drillings, and party contests; and, after all, the tactics adopted by the dacoits are very much those which have been so successfully invented by the Moonlighters. They do not attack our posts (though now and then, under the auspices of one or two enterprising leaders, there have been exceptions to this rule), any more than the Moonlighters attack the barracks of the Irish Police. They carefully watch the movements of our people, and when a column sets out in one direction, they descend upon some unsuspecting village in another, or if they hear of a weaker party than usual marching out, they take advantage of the opportunity to waylay and annoy it by a volley or two from the jungle, just as the Irish assassin waylays and shoots an obnoxious landlord.'

The truth was that the function of troops was not to suppress disorders at the point of the bayonet, but to produce an effect upon the imagination and moral sense of the people, to make them feel that the inevitable had overtaken them. Unfortunately 'the inborn conceit, lightheartedness, and impulsiveness' of the Burmese rendered them impervious to salutary impressions of that kind; 'neither their religion nor their temperament permits them to suspect their inferiority.' The process of pacification would necessarily be slow. Dufferin was able, however, to end on a cheerful note. He had frankly been sceptical that Upper Burma would prove a rich or a paying province. He was now informed that its mineral wealth was considerable, and that there were indications of the establishment of satisfactory mercantile relations with the Chinese. Meanwhile substantial brick houses were rising rapidly in Mandalay, and the price of land outside the town had trebled in value.[23]

The pamphlet had something of the desired effect, though the replies of the recipients showed the consolatory cheerfulness of people who are thankful not to be burdened with the same problems. Gladstone's letter was vague and evasive to the point where it conveyed nothing except good wishes for the health of the Dufferin family.[24] Goschen wrote 'You certainly make out a very strong case. That *Times* correspondent has certainly played the devil.' Buckle was coming to see him that day, but he was afraid the matter was too delicate to take up with him.[25] Henry Reeve, of the *Edinburgh Review*, assured Dufferin that 'no serious distrust or irritation has been shown here in spite of the evident malignity of the *Times* correspondent, and the feeble attacks in the House of Commons.'[26] F. D. Finlay, another Scots editor, took the liberty of showing the memorandum to one of the attackers, the radical Dr. W. A. Hunter of Aberdeen. Hunter said that he retained his original view as to the expedition having been undertaken, but he accepted that Dufferin had completely vindicated his policy since, and overturned the imputations and misrepresentations of the *Times* correspondent and others. Finlay commented: 'to that extent, therefore, his gun is spiked.'[27]

16

THE RIVER OF LOST FOOTSTEPS

Bernard's discovery of Moylan's antecedents had given great satisfaction to White. Jubilantly he wrote to his wife: 'We now have absolute information about Mr. Moylan, the *Times* correspondent who has vilified Bernard and me so much . . . I believe the *Times* knows that he is a blackguard and yet they employ him.' He hoped that when Bernard reported his information a move would be made to turn Moylan out of the Rangoon Bar. 'To us who know the wonderful good work the soldiers, at all events, have done, it is most disgusting to know that a convicted slanderer and defaulter can turn the whole tide of public opinion against us, and that a man in high place and with such a reputation as Dufferin should pander to the popular cry and bend to it, sacrificing in public the man he knows well has done first-class work as he has me.'

White continued with a vituperative attack on Dufferin. 'I look upon him as one of the most miserable men in an official position I ever met. I neither have respect for nor trust in him. His falseness is only equalled by his weakness and he peddles behind the popular prejudice with his finger on the pulse of the press!' This was a most unjust criticism, as White was soon to see and acknowledge, but he had been stung by the appointment of Sir Herbert Macpherson as his superior, taking him away from the command of his friend and patron Sir Frederick Roberts, and by the continued refusal to grant him the rank commensurate with his responsibilities. He believed that 'the wily and crooked Dufferin' had, in correspondence with the Duke of Cambridge, turned down the lead suggested to him by Roberts, and had 'in the most marked way' omitted all reference to his service in the government order in which Macpherson's appointment had been announced.[1]

But, unknown to White, Dufferin was striving by subtler and more diplomatic means to achieve what White so anxiously desired. Macpherson's appointment was beyond doubt a gesture to calm the hysteria of public opinion at home. Macpherson was known in England, White was not; and Dufferin, who had the highest opinion of White's ability, did not want his name to be too closely associated with the lack of military success in Burma. He was in fact trying to obtain for White either the rank of major-general or a knighthood, but against opposition in high places. White's suspicions of the Duke of Cambridge were completely justified. The Duke was scandalized at the high position White, a junior colonel in 1885, now occupied, and was adamant that he should not be advanced over whole pages of colonels, 'including some *very* good men'. Dufferin found it very provoking that the Duke should be so stiff about White, who was an excellent officer, and had done admirably in a position entailing great labour, anxiety and responsibility. But in late September Cross wrote: 'I had a long conversation with the Duke of Cambridge about White, but he will do nothing as to military rank. I will see what I can do as to the K.C.B.'[2]

At the beginning of September White had left Mandalay 'to meet Sir Herbert at Prome and dry-nurse him'. He had served under Macpherson at Kandahar, and the two men got on well together when they met. A few days later White was cheered to receive a letter of three pages from the Viceroy, appreciative of his work. In the postscript Dufferin confided that he was doing his best to obtain for him either his rank of major-general or a K.C.B., and that he had been much vexed at the delay in the issue of the Burmese honours, and the way in which the lists he had submitted were cut down by the authorities at home.[3]

White soon learned, however, that there was no chance of his being made a major-general, and he remained rather critical of the new C. in C.'s activities. Macpherson was 'not a good man to do business with' though very pleasant as a person. When he went up to Bhamo to take stock of the situation there, White pointed out that 'we could not all picnic and that I had better command the forces'. The situation was soon to be resolved in a way that White would not have wished nor could have foreseen. In October General Macpherson died suddenly from fever. The news reached White as he was about to board a river-steamer at Kyouk-Myong. 'I was greatly shocked as I had soldiered so much with him and liked him so much. He could not shake off the fever and I fancy the complication of gout in the system made his chances much worse.'[4]

Macpherson's death left Dufferin with no alternative but to ask Sir Frederick Roberts to go to Rangoon and take command himself of all military operations in Burma. Roberts arrived with his Staff on 9 November, and was met by White. The sending of Roberts had a calming effect on opinion in England, but he was under no illusion about the nature of his task or the length of time it would take. He was careful to pay generous tribute to the 'two able officers at the head of affairs', White and Bernard, and to draw public attention to what they had achieved.[5]

In December White learned that he had been knighted. 'How do you like being Lady White?' he asked his wife, 'I think ladies like the title and I hope you do. The belief that you will be proud of it is my greatest, I may truly say my only, pleasure in being K.C.B.' He felt that he was being chaffed 'when they Sir George me', and that it would be made the excuse for not giving him any further reward. But if he could hold on until Christmas 1887 he thought he must be safe to avoid extinction as a colonel. He was now commanding an army corps of 21,500 men in six brigades.[6]

Bernard at last resigned in January 1887. 'I shall never get on so well with anybody else as I have with Bernard,' wrote White, 'I have the highest respect and affection for him and his ability is undoubted. He fell upon difficult times, and has one bad fault as an official: he is too conscientious to throw money about recklessly and therefore makes many enemies.' Three weeks later he was still lamenting 'the greatest loss I have had since I arrived in Upper Burma, the departure of my friend Sir Charles Bernard. Hounded by the press, and abused by the communities in Rangoon, whose interests he would not push on at the sacrifice of the Native part of the community, and too indifferent to his own personal interests to feed or flatter the newspaper correspondents, he had been freely abused. Lord Dufferin, who knows his value, was not, I imagine, sorry to get a letter from Sir Chas., when he was really very ill in Rangoon, saying he could not trust to being able to continue his arduous work throughout the hot weather. The offer of resignation was closed with, and now, although much better, he is on his way home. With him goes my one adviser in whom I have confidence, and whose superiority over myself I felt at every point.'[7]

In the same month there appeared in the *Edinburgh Review* an anonymous article on 'The Conquest of Burma' in which the author attempted to explain for readers at home the difficulties facing the administrators of the new province. 'We can well understand that it was not with a light heart that the Indian Government accepted the responsibility of under-taking the direct administration of this great country.' The problems of the government of the Indian Empire already taxed the capacities of Viceroys to the utmost, and the occupation of Burma necessarily involved at the outset the employment of a considerable portion of the Indian Army. The civil administration, hastily organized, did not attempt to occupy the whole of the country; its operations were restricted mainly to the districts bordering on the Irrawaddy and the line from Toungoo to Mandalay. The British public had not understood the original military strategy. The aim was not to pacify the country, for that could not be done during the rainy season, but to keep the troops healthy until the dry season when they could again take the offensive. In fact, the author believed, White's mistake had been to attempt too much too soon in response to the civil authorities.

He had had to deal with an enemy 'who never made a stand at any point; whose headquarters were not in any large centres of population, but in some remote and inaccessible jungle, from which they sallied forth when opportunity offered to harry and plunder the more cultivated districts. Under these circumstances all notion of moving in large columns according to the maxims of ordinary warfare had to give place to a special mode of action suited to the circumstances.'

The ease with which the annexation was accomplished had not pre-pared the British public for such resistance, and this disquiet 'was prob-ably aggravated by the tone of the correspondent of a great newspaper, who persistently from the first placed the worst construction on all the acts of the local administration, exaggerating its failures and minimizing its successes. That so much weight should be attached to the opinions and statements of an irresponsible newspaper correspondent is a curious feature of modern sentiment.' Most correspondents to newspapers of that standing had been distinguished by their honest desire for truth and their good judgement, but the rule was not invariable, and when people read the statements of a correspondent they did not stop to ask whether he was a man of unimpeachable character and antecedents; whether he might not have clients to serve by misrepresentations, or a grudge to pay off for injuries, real or fancied; 'they see the statements in a paper with a world wide circulation, which generally shows judgement in the choice of its correspondents, and they believe them.'[8]

The other side of the story was given later in the year by an article in *Blackwood's Magazine*, written by one of the officers engaged in the 'pacification'. Though it had been customary to designate the Burmese forces which took the field against them as dacoits, he asserted that this term was erroneous. Undoubtedly some of the Burmese leaders had been dacoits under Thibaw's rule, 'but in taking up arms against the British army of annexation they may reasonably be credited with at least partially patriotic motives.' The Burman was adept at jungle warfare; it mattered little to him who was master of the terrain, provided that he was able to inflict serious loss and sustain little himself. The British had won a pyrrhic victory, and the reader was warned not to put his trust in official figures, since it was a well-known and quite irresistible tendency in warfare to minimize our own and magnify our enemy's losses.

Nor was the Burmese bullet the worst foe with which the troops had to contend. The arch-foe had been, and would be again during the coming hot and rainy season, disease . . . 'the ravages of cholera, malaria, dysentery and heat-apoplexy'. The average death-rate from disease, from May till October 1886 had been 100–150 a month. The soldier's life in Burma was stifling heat, roads feet deep in water, flooded rice-fields and swollen rivers, and his favourite refrain was 'One more river to cross'.

The author of the *Blackwood's* article reflected wryly that though many distinguished travellers had spent the cold weather in India, few had come to Upper Burma, yet nothing was easier than a voyage up the Irrawaddy. 'Not that such a voyage would give the globe-trotter any insight into the nature of the military operations in Upper Burma. That could only be acquired by a trip into the interior.'[9] Two years later, one such globe-trotter (he so described himself) visited Rangoon and longed to make the trip into the interior. During 1886, 1887 and 1888 the progress of the pacification of Burma was reported by the papers for which Kipling worked, and indeed written up by Kipling himself, so that he was familiar with every detail of the military operations. While public opinion in Britain and in India was critical of the conduct of the affairs in Burma, Kipling's sympathy was with the men in the jungle, the subalterns of his own age who with a handful of Tommies and sepoys went after the dacoit *bos* and their gangs.

When he first saw the Irrawaddy in 1889, he wrote, 'I reflected that I was looking upon the River of the Lost Footsteps—the road that so many many men of my acquaintance had travelled, never to return, within the past three years. Such a one had gone up to open out Upper

Burma, and had himself been opened out by a Burmese *dah* in the cruel scrub beyond Minhla; such another one had gone to rule the land in the Queen's name, but could not rule a hill stream and was carried down under his horse. One had been shot by his servant; another by a dacoit while he sat at dinner; and a pitifully long list had found in jungle-fever their sole reward for "the difficulties and privations inseparably connected with military service," as the Bengal Army Regulations put it. I ran over half a score of names—policemen, subalterns, young civilians, employees of big trading firms, and adventurers. They had gone up the river and they had died. At my elbow stood one of the workers in New Burma, going to report himself at Rangoon, and he told tales of interminable chases after evasive dacoits, of marchings and counter-marchings that came to nothing, and of deaths in the wilderness as noble as they were sad.'[10]

EPILOGUE

It took five years in all to re-establish peace and order in Burma, and the employment of 32,000 troops and 8,500 military police. But that is another story, told sixty years ago by Sir Charles Crosthwaite in his book *The Pacification of Burma*. For long afterwards, British troops were engaged in campaigns against the peripheral peoples—the Shans, Kachins, Karens and Chins. The golden dream of a great lucrative trade with western China never materialized. The internal commerce of China operated, as it had done for centuries, within its own political and economic structure, and it could not be drawn off through Burma without the destruction of that system. The merchant's ambition of a commercial revolution combined with political stability proved to be illusory. A complicated system of railways, already begun in Lower Burma in 1870, was extended to the whole country and completed in 1915. The enormous outlay in capital was never recovered, but was defended on administrative and strategic grounds. The Irrawaddy Flotilla Company continued to operate what was a virtual monopoly of river traffic until it was nationalized in 1948. The development of Burma's considerable mineral resources did not really begin on a large scale until after 1914, although the only really large, profitable, industrial undertaking to follow the conquest, the Burmah Oil Company, began operations in 1886.

Upper Burma was a province of the British Empire for only sixty years, though in retrospect the association appears to have been much longer. The decision to make the whole of Burma part of the Indian dominion was, from every point of view, a mistake. The insouciant Burmese were quite unlike any of the Indian peoples; their civilization, religion, customs and laws were alien to those of India, yet Indian laws, Indian judges, Indian police and officials were imposed upon them. The deposition of Thibaw dislocated the delicate interdependence of the monarchy and Theravada Buddhism, and, from the highest motives, the British, by declining to interfere in religious matters, undermined and destroyed the Buddhist hierarchy.

The basic British assumptions that the Burmese were so oppressed by Thibaw that they would welcome the invaders as deliverers, and that they would prefer efficient and just government to capricious tyranny, proved to be false. The Burmese had groaned under Thibaw, but they revered the monarchy with its semi-divine status, and even found many good things to say about the last of the Konbaung dynasty. The demoralization of the *Sangha*, the Buddhist monastic order, was amply demonstrated by the number of *pongyis* who became active rebels between 1886 and 1890.

In 1888 Dufferin asked Salisbury to relieve him of his post as Viceroy, bequeathing the problem of Upper Burma to his successor Lord Lansdowne. In September of that year he was created a marquis; he wished to add to his title that of Quebec, but Queen Victoria did not approve, and she suggested that he take instead some Indian title such as Delhi. Dufferin replied that he thought that this might cause resentment in India, though a Burmese title might be more acceptable. The first ones he thought of sounded to him too much like names 'out of one of Offenbach's operas or the *Mikado*', but finally he chose Ava, the name of the ancient temple-studded capital below Mandalay. On 10 December 1888, he formally handed over his office to Lord Lansdowne, and left India four days later.[1]

In the autumn of 1890, after he had finished his first novel *The Light that Failed*, Kipling was ordered by his doctor to take a long sea-voyage. In London he had called upon Dufferin, who had just been appointed British ambassador to Italy, announcing himself modestly as 'Mr. Lockwood Kipling's son'. Dufferin, who was pleased to see the young reporter he remembered in Simla, now transformed into a famous author, invited him to pay a visit to his villa at Sorrento. Kipling went to Naples in October, and while there acted upon the invitation. In his autobiography, *Something of Myself*, he wrote that Dufferin received him with great kindness, and that one evening between lights he had talked—sliding into a reverie—of his work in India and the world at large. 'I had seen administrative machinery from beneath, all stripped

184

and overheated. This was the first time I had listened to one who had handled it from above. And unlike the generality of Viceroys Lord Dufferin *knew*. Of all his revelations and reminiscences, the one sentence that stays with me is: "And so, you see, there can be no room" (or was it allowance?) "for good intentions in one's work." '[2]

King Thibaw never saw his palace again. He lived out the rest of his life in exile at Ratnagiri on the Kolkan coast of India, with a generous government pension, and Supayalat always by his side. When he died, on 16 December 1916, she was allowed to return to Rangoon, where she lived in a small private house, 'a pathetic old lady, strangely different from the feline personality who had dominated Thibaw in the tragic days before the monarchy came to its sudden inglorious end.'[3]

Lord Dufferin's distinguished career did not end with the Indian viceroyalty. He was still to be British ambassador at Rome (1887–91) and at Paris (1891–6). Although to be ambassador in Paris was recognized as the ultimate prize of the diplomatic profession, the post was scarcely a comfortable one for Dufferin. The French had distrusted him ever since his mission to the Lebanon in 1861. They saw him, not unnaturally, as the man who had defeated their interest first in Egypt and subsequently in Burma, and suspected him of pursuing the same objective in Siam in 1893. In his last years heavy misfortunes fell upon him. He received the news that Archie, his eldest son, had died of wounds at Waggon Hill in South Africa. Dufferin had been inveigled into accepting the chairmanship of a dishonestly-conducted company, the London and Globe Finance Corporation, in which the leading figure was Whitaker Wright, and when at last he realized that it was about to collapse he honourably refused to resign from it. He was in no way to blame for the disaster, but he felt that it had involved him in irreparable disgrace, since so many of the investors had trusted to the security his name provided. The scandal gradually sapped his strength, and he died at Clandeboye on 12 February 1902.[4]

Lady Dufferin survived her husband for more than three decades. In 1935, when she was in her ninety-third year, she attended at the India Office the celebration of the fiftieth anniversary of the 'National Association for Supplying Female Medical Aid to the Women of India', which she had founded in August 1885 on the suggestion of Queen Victoria.[5] It was for the 'Countess of Dufferin's Fund' (as it was usually known) that Kipling wrote the 'Song of the Women'.

EPILOGUE

'How shall she know the worship that we do her?
The walls are high and she is very far.
How shall the women's message reach unto her
Above the tumult of the packed bazaar?
Free wind of March against the lattice blowing
Bear thou our thanks lest she depart unknowing.'

White did not finally escape from Burma until 1889, when he was given the command of a division at Quetta, but by then the Duke of Cambridge had withdrawn his opposition to his major-generalcy and had expressed warm appreciation of his services in Burma. He became famous in 1900 as the heroic defender of Ladysmith, although his strategy on that occasion was criticized by his friend Lord Roberts, and a government enquiry. His son Jack, tidings of whose childish wilfulness had worried him in Mandalay, fulfilled his early promise as a rebel against every orthodoxy cherished by his caste. Modelling his life, he said, on the teaching of Christ and Lenin, he tried to set the world to rights in his own way: he was that Captain John White who formed the Irish Citizen Army, which James Connolly was to lead into insurrection in Dublin in 1916.[6]

Moylan died at Rangoon in 1893; his son, Sir John Fitzgerald Moylan, became a distinguished civil servant, the author of works on Scotland Yard and the British Police, and Under-Secretary at the Home Office during the Second World War.[7]

Sladen retired in 1887, and went to live in England, where he died three years later. Bernard on leaving India was appointed Secretary in the Revenue and Statistics Department of the India Office. He died at Chamonix in 1901.[8]

The palace enclosure was afterwards renamed Fort Dufferin. Sixty years after General Prendergast's triumphal entry into the city, Kipling's exhortation was fulfilled. The British soldier came back to Mandalay, but this time he was stubbornly opposed. When British and Indian troops of the 33rd corps of General Slim's 14th Army reached the out-skirts of Mandalay on 9 March 1945, they found the Japanese dug in on Mandalay Hill and occupying Fort Dufferin. On Mandalay Hill they fought to the death, while the defences of the fort appeared impregnable, even to the weapons of the twentieth century. Repeated low-level attacks by Mitchell bombers with 2,000 lb bombs failed to breach the great red walls, and an infantry assault across the moat on 17 March was thrown back with heavy losses. At 12.40 on 20 March, as smoke and dust from a heavy air attack began to clear, six Burmans suddenly emerged from the fort, carrying a white flag and a Union Jack. They reported that the last of the Japanese troops had withdrawn under cover of the bombardment. Later that day, a fire started by the air attack took hold on what remained of the palace, and the magnificent carved teak buildings of vermilion and gold, which had seen the splendours and miseries of Thibaw's reign, disappeared for ever in the flames.[9]

CHRONOLOGY

1586   Ralph Fitch reaches Burma.

1617   East India Company sends agents to Syriam and Pegu.

1755   Alaungpaya (Alompra) defeats Mons of Lower Burma and builds Rangoon.

1785   Bodawpaya (his son) annexes Arakan.

1824
1826   FIRST ANGLO-BURMESE WAR.

1826   Treaty of Yandabo. Arakan, Assam and Tenasserim ceded to the East India Company.

1837   Tharrawaddy rebels against his brother Bagyidaw and seizes the throne.
Captain McLeod reaches China via the River Salween.

1840   British Resident withdrawn from Ava.

1846   Death of Tharrawaddy. Succeeded by Pagan Min.

1851   Two British merchant captains, falsely charged by the Burmese, submit claims to Calcutta.

1852   Commodore Lambert, dispatched to Rangoon by Lord Dalhousie, shells Burmese forts when fired on.
SECOND ANGLO-BURMESE WAR.

1853   Mindon Min succeeds by a palace revolution.
British fix the frontier at Myédé.
Thomas Spears becomes unofficial British representative Mindon's Court.

1855   Yule Mission to Ava.

189

1857   Mandalay built by Mindon.

1862   British sign commercial treaty with Mindon.
Dr. Clement Williams appointed Resident at Mandalay.

1863   Dr. Williams reaches Bhamo by the Irrawaddy.

1866   Rebellion against Mindon suppressed. Murder of the *Einshemin*.

1867   New treaty with Mindon signed.
Sladen Mission to Momein.

1872   Burmese Mission to Europe. Received by Queen Victoria.
Visits Scotland and Ireland.

1873   The French occupy Hanoi.
Collapse of Panthay Rebellion in China.

1875   Murder of A. R. Margary by the Chinese.
Forsyth Mission to settle status of the Red Karens.
British Resident ordered not to remove his shoes when received
in audience by Burmese King.
Mindon refuses to receive him.

1878   Death of Mindon, and accession of Thibaw.

1879   Members of royal family murdered.
British Residency staff withdrawn from Mandalay.

1884   Chinese irregulars attack and burn Bhamo.
Further massacres in Mandalay.
Thibaw negotiates a treaty with the French.

1885   22 Oct. British ultimatum to Thibaw.
THIRD ANGLO-BURMESE WAR.
11 Nov. British Expeditionary Force advances on Mandalay.
17 Nov. Capture of Minhla.
29 Nov. Fall of Mandalay. King Thibaw sent into exile.
4 Dec. *The Times* correspondent deported to Rangoon on the
orders of General Prendergast.
20 Dec. *The Times* correspondent returns to Mandalay.
27 Dec. Arrest and deportation of the Taingda Mingyi.

1886   1 Jan. Upper Burma declared 'part of Her Majesty's dominions'.
21 Jan. *The Times* prints story of military executions in Mandalay.
27 Jan. Salisbury government resigns and Gladstone resumes
office.
12 Feb. The Viceroy visits Mandalay.
17 Feb. Formal annexation of Upper Burma.
22 Feb. House of Commons debate on annexation of Upper
Burma.

26 Feb. Burma becomes a province of the Indian Empire.

31 Mar. General Prendergast succeeded in command of the Burma Field Force by Brigadier-General White.

1 Apr. Colonel Sladen resigns as Political Officer.

24 Jul. Chefoo Convention with China signed.

16 Aug. Inundation of Mandalay.

17 Sept. General Macpherson, appointed to command of forces in Burma, arrives at Mandalay. Dies in October.

1 Oct. Lord Dufferin's Memorandum on Burma privately distributed.

9 Nov. Lord Roberts, C. in C. of Indian Army, assumes personal command in Burma.

1887   1 Jan. Sir Charles Bernard resigns as Chief Commissioner of Burma.

LIST OF BURMESE NAMES

Alaungpaya, Alompra	Founder of the Alompra or Konbaung Dynasty (1752–1885)
Einshemin	Crown Prince (lit. 'lord of the Eastern House')
Hlethin Atwinwun	Son-in-law of the Taingda Mingyi, and Master of the Royal Barges
Kinwun Mingyi	Minister of Foreign Affairs during the reigns of Mindon and Thibaw
Konbaung	See *Alaungpaya*
Myanma	Burma
Nyaungyan Min	Son of Mindon, died 1885
Myingun Min (*Nyaung Ok*)	Son of Mindon, claimant to the throne in 1885 and 1886
Sinpyumashin	Mindon's chief Queen
Supayalat	Thibaw's Queen
Taingda Mingyi	Minister of the Interior in Thibaw's reign
Thathanabaing	The Buddhist Hierarch appointed by the King
Thibaw Min	Son of Mindon, King of Burma 1879–1885

GLOSSARY OF BURMESE WORDS

Atwinwun	palace adviser
Bo	colonel, leader of any armed band
Daw	royalty, royal
Gyi	big or great (often used as a suffix)
Hlutdaw	royal council, council hall
Hti	golden umbrella placed on pagodas
Kala	foreigner (used opprobriously for the British and the Indians)
Kutho	merit (in Buddhism)
Kuthodaw	Buddhist shrine built by King Mindon at Mandalay, 'royal work of merit'
Kyaung	monastery
Ma	title of younger women
Maung	title of younger men, 'Mister' (used of oneself)
Min	prince or lord (retained by kings after accession)
Mingyi	great prince, title of the most senior ministers
Myo	town
Myothugyi	headman of a town
Myowun	royal governor
Nat	spirit, devil
Pyongyi	monk (lit. 'great glory')
Sangha	the Buddhist monastic system
Shwe	gold, golden
Thugyi	headman
U	title for respected elders, 'uncle' (never used of oneself)
Wun	Government official, 'burden-bearer'
Wundauk	Hlutdaw assistant to a *wungyi*, 'prop for a burden-bearer'
Wungyi	royal minister of state, 'great burden-bearer'
Zayat	rest-house

NOTES AND SOURCES

ABBREVIATIONS

AR   The Annual Register
DIB   Dictionary of Indian Biography
DNB   Dictionary of National Biography
DP   Dufferin Papers
D,VL   Hariot, Lady Dufferin, *Our Viceregal Life in India*
Home Corres. Home Correspondence, Secret and Political
Mil. Proc.   Military Proceedings, Burmah, 1885–1886
Parl. Deb.   Hansard, *Parliamentary Debates*
SP   Sladen Papers
WP   White Papers

NOTES

PROLOGUE

1. Charles Carrington, *Rudyard Kipling*, pp. 154–158.
2. Francis Adams, 'Mr. Rudyard Kipling's verse', *Fortnightly Review*, LIV (1893), pp. 590–603; Robert R. Buchanan, 'The voice of the hooligan', *Contemporary Review*, LXXVI (1899), pp. 774–789; R. Le Gallienne, *Rudyard Kipling*, cited Carrington, p. 342.
3. George Orwell, 'Rudyard Kipling' in *The Decline of English Murder and other essays* (Penguin edition), p. 58.
4. For a discussion of the place of 'Mandalay' in literary sub-culture and popular imagination, see D. A. Farnie, *East and West of Suez*, pp. 386–387.
5. Edmonia Hill, 'The young Kipling', *Atlantic Monthly*, April 1936.
6. R. Kipling, *From Sea to Sea*, i, 230–235.

NOTES

1. THE VICEROY

1. Biographies of Lord Dufferin: C. E. D. Black, *The Marquess of Dufferin and Ava* (1903); A. C. Lyall, *Life of the Marquis of Dufferin and Ava* (2 vols. 1905); H. Nicolson, *Helen's Tower* (1937).
2. Black, p. 14; Nicolson, p. 62.
3. *The Book of Helen's Tower* (privately printed).
4. Lyall, ii, 306.
5. Nicolson, pp. 34-40.
6. ibid., p. 143.
7. ibid., p. 153.
8. Black, p. 336.
9. Correspondence from St. Petersburg, 1879–1882 (DP. 1071 H/J1/1–5); Duke of Somerset—Dufferin, 21, 26 Jan. 1879 (DP. 1071 H/L2); R. J. Kennedy, *Russia* 1879–1881 (typescript in the Queen's University Library, Belfast), p. 27.
10. The most recent examination of Dufferin's domestic policy, and his handling of the Indian National Congress, is the exhaustive *New India 1885* by Briton Martin, Jnr., whose early death in 1967 was a grievous loss to historical scholarship.
11. Lyall, *Edinburgh Review*, Jan. 1889.
12. Black, p. 227.
13. Carrington, p. 62.
14. D, VL, i, 131.
15. Sir Ian Hamilton, *Listening for the Drums*, p. 209; Carrington, p. 78.
16. D, VL, i, 192.

2. THE CONQUEST OF LOWER BURMA

1. *Hakluytus Posthumus, or Purchas his Pilgrimmes* (Maclehose reprint), X, 165.
2. ibid., X, 192–194; D. G. E. Hall, *Europe and Burma*, pp. 20–21.
3. *Purchas his Pilgrimmes*, X, 185–187.
4. *Hakluyt Society*, series II, LXVI, 47–48. An abstract of Methwold's letter is printed in Foster, *The English Factories in India*, i, 207–208.
5. D. Woodman, *The Making of Burma*, p. 33.
6. G. S. Graham, *Great Britain in the Indian Ocean*, p. 350.
7. Hall, *Europe and Burma*, p. 113.
8. O. Warner, *Captain Marryat, a Rediscovery*, p. 68. Marryat's recollections of the Burmese war are to be found in his *Diary on the Continent* (*Olla Podrida*, collected edition), pp. 94–102.
9. *Anonymous Sketch of the Madras European Regiment in Burma* (cited Woodman, p. 71).
10. J. J. Snodgrass, *Narrative of the Burmese War*, p. 8.
11. See Hon. J. W. Fortescue, *A History of the British Army*, XI, 272–273. The Burmese tree-top observation post equipped with guns is illustrated in Snodgrass.

12. Woodman, p. 76.
13. ibid., p. 80; Hall, *Europe and Burma*, p. 119; *South East Asia*, pp. 516–517.
14. He was the author of a three-volume *History of the Indian Archipelago*.
15. Hall, *Europe and Burma*, p. 123.
16. Sir H. Yule, *A Narrative of the Mission sent by the Governor-General of India to the Court of Ava in 1855*, p. 222.
17. Hall, *Europe and Burma*, p. 123.
18. Hall, *Dalhousie—Phayre Correspondence*, p. xvii.
19. *Papers relating to hostilities with Burma*, C.1490, p. 14.
20. Hall, *Europe and Burma*, p. 140.
21. Dalhousie—Sir George Couper, 23 Jan. 1852 (cited in Baird, *Private Letters of the Marquess of Dalhousie*, pp. 188–189.
22. Baird, p. 261.
23. Hall, *Europe and Burma*, p. 140.
24. Hall, *Dalhousie—Phayre Correspondence*, p. xxii.
25. Hall, *Europe and Burma*, pp. 142–143.
26. Hall, *Dalhousie—Phayre Correspondence*, p. xxxviii.
27. Dalhousie—Couper, Baird, pp. 251–252.
28. Cobden—Richards, 24 Aug.; 10 Aug. 1852 (cited Woodman, p. 145). For Cobden's attitude to the war see also J. Morley, *Life of Cobden*, II, 144 and Cobden's *Speeches* (ed. J. Bright and T. Rogers), II, 508.

3. THE GOLDEN DREAM

1. Yule, pp. 193–194.
2. Hall, *Dalhousie—Phayre Correspondence*, p. xxviii; *The Times*, 21 Dec. 1885.
3. The best account of Spears is in Hall, *Dalhousie—Phayre Correspondence*, pp. xli sqq. Professor Hall learned much about Spears from his last surviving son, William, who died in Rangoon in 1929.
4. ibid., No. 97, 27 Mar. 1854.
5. Yule, *passim*.
6. *Journal of the Asiatic Society of Bengal*, vol. 5, 1836; Woodman, pp. 103–112.
7. Fytche, *Burma Past and Present*.
8. *Copy of the Report upon the Income and Expenditure of British Burmah*, by R. Temple and Lt. Col. H. Bruce, 1860. H. of C. paper 405, 1865.
9. J. S. Furnivall, *Colonial Policy and Practice*, p. 78.
10. DIB, p. 453; Woodman, pp. 176–179.
11. Fytche, i, 212–214.
12. ibid., i, 100; Appendix E. Memorandum on the Panthays, 15 July 1867.
13. ibid., i, 102–110; SP.

14. Woodman, p. 187.
15. ibid., p. 189.
16. Fytche, i, 113–114.
17. Robert Bruce, 'King Mindon of Burma', in *History Today*, Nov. 1969, p. 771.
18. Woodman, p. 191.
19. *The Times*, 16 July; 13, 16 Sept. 1872.
20. Maung Maung, *Burma in the Family of Nations*, p. 51.
21. Browne, *Reminiscences of the Court of Mandalay*, pp. 61–68.
22. Woodman, p. 207.

4. THE LORD OF THE WHITE ELEPHANTS

1. Cady, *A History of Modern Burma*, pp. 111–112; Browne, pp. 145–149; Grattan Geary, *Burma After the Conquest*, pp. 126–128.
2. Hall, *Europe and Burma*, pp. 166–167.
3. Aitchison—Mackenzie Wallace, 22 Oct. 1885. DP.
4. *Annual Register*, 1879, p. 279.
5. W. Joest, *Kölnische Zeitung* (reprinted in *Belfast Newsletter* 16 Dec. 1885).
6. *Correspondence relating to Burmah since the accession of King Theebaw.* Oct. 1878. C.4614. 1886. p. 61.
7. ibid., p. 97.
8. Woodman, p. 221; S. Gopal, *The Viceroyalty of Lord Ripon*, pp. 48–56.
9. P. G. Camaratta—Sir A. Rivers-Thompson, 31 Aug. 1885. DP; D, VL. pp. 322–325.
10. A succinct summary of the causes of rivalry is given in the introduction to L. K. Young, *British Policy in China* 1895–1902, pp. 13–14.
11. This is the thesis of Miss Woodman in *The Making of Modern Burma*.
12. Hall, *Dalhousie—Phayre Correspondence*, p. lxi.
13. Hall, *South-East Asia*, pp. 544–545.
14. H. McAleavy, *Black Flags in Vietnam*; M. Billot, *L'Affaire du Tonkin*; D. R. Watson, 'The French in Indo-China,' *History Today*, Aug. 1970.
15. C. 4614, p. 122.
16. ibid., p. 123.
17. ibid., p. 122.
18. Lord Randolph Churchill—Dufferin, 14 Jan. 1886. DP; Letters relating to concessions to the French, Bernard—Sladen. SP. 290/11.
19. C. 4614, pp. 134–135.
20. ibid., p. 125.
21. Cady, p. 118; Hall, *Europe and Burma*, pp. 175–176.
22. C. 4614, pp. 169–170; Thirkell White—Sladen, 6 Jan. 1886. SP.
23. *Home Corres.* 1886, vol. 85; C. 4614, p. 177.

24. Conversation with M. Harmand relating to M. Ferry's Burma policy, 28 July 1886. DP.
25. *Home Corres.* 1885, vol. 80.
26. See Cady, p. 115n.
27. C. 4614, p. 221.
28. *Home Corres.* 1885, vol. 81; C. 4614, p. 228.
29. C. 4614, pp. 256–257.

5. THE OLD FLOTILLA

1. Dufferin—Grant Duff, 22 Oct. 1885. DP.
2. DNB, xvi, 301; *The Times* 19 Nov. 1886.
3. Sir O'Moore Creach and E. M. Humphries, *The V.C. and D.S.O.*, i, 65; *The Times* 26 July 1913.
4. Dufferin—Prendergast, 21 Oct. 1885. DP.
5. Dufferin—Prendergast, 3 Nov. 1885. DP.
6. *Mil. Proc.* No. 885.
7. ibid., No. 279.
8. Letters from Sir George White to his wife Amy. Eur. F. 108/101 D; M. Durand, *Life of Field-Marshal Sir George White* (includes long extracts from the letters).
9. *Mil. Proc.* Diary of operations, 29 Oct. 1885; M. E. Grant Duff, *Out of the Past*, ii, 178.
10. White, Diary, 31 Oct., 2 Nov. 1885; White—Mrs. White, 7 Nov. 1885. WP.
11. White, Diary, 4 Nov. 1885; White—Mrs. White, 7 Nov. 1885. WP.
12. *Mil. Proc.* 28 Oct. 1885; Lt. Col. O. R. Newmarch—Mackenzie Wallace, 24 Oct. 1885. DP.
13. *Mil. Proc.* Nos. 42–46.
14. Bernard—Mackenzie Wallace, 8 Nov. 1885. DP; Bernard—Sladen, 14 Nov. 1885. SP. The last four pages of Forchhammer's list are in the Sladen Papers.
15. Bernard—Mackenzie Wallace, 10 Nov. 1885. DP.

6. AT THE MINHLA REDOUBT

1. *Mil. Proc.* Diary of operations, 11 Nov. 1885.
2. ibid., 14 Nov. 1885.
3. ibid., 15 Nov 1885.
4. Prendergast—Dufferin, 23 Nov. 1885. DP.
5. *Mil. Proc.* 17 Nov 1885.
6. ibid., 17 Nov. 1885.
7. White, Diary, 17 Nov. 1885; White—Mrs. White, 18 Nov. 1885. WP.
8. *Mil. Proc.* 17 Nov. 1885.

9. White—Mrs. White, 18 Nov. 1885. WP.
10. Carrington, *Rudyard Kipling*, p. 111.
11. Kipling, *From Sea to Sea*, i, 228–229.
12. Report of Depy. Surgeon-General J. McN. Donnelly, principal medical officer to the Burma Field Force. *Mil. Proc.*
13. ibid; White, Diary, 18 Nov. 1885; Kipling, *Something of Myself*, p. 56.
14. Report of . . . medical officer, *Mil. Proc.*; White, Diary, 4, 6, 7 Dec. 1885. WP; Prendergast—Dufferin, 4 Dec. 1885. DP.
15. Operations of the Toungoo column. *Mil. Proc.*

7. THE ROYAL GEM CITY

1. *Mil. Proc.* 18 Nov. 1885; Prendergast—Dufferin 23 Nov. 1885. DP.
2. *Mil. Proc.* 18, 19 Nov. 1885.
3. Prendergast—Dufferin, 23 Nov. 1885. DP.
4. *Mil. Proc.* 24 Nov. 1885; White, Diary, 24, 25 Nov. 1885. WP.
5. White, Diary, 26 Nov. 1885. WP.
6. White—Mrs. White, 7 Dec. 1885. WP.
7. *Mil. Proc.* 26 Nov. 1885; Prendergast—Dufferin, 29 Nov. 1885. DP.
8. *Mil. Proc.* 27 Nov. 1885, and map of Sagaing and Ava; Prendergast —Dufferin, 29 Nov. 1885. DP.
9. White, Diary, 27 Nov. 1885. WP.
10. White—Jane White, Nov. 1885. WP.
11. *Mil. Proc.* 28 Nov. 1885; White—Mrs. White, Nov. 1885. WP.
12. *Mil. Proc.* 28 Nov. 1885, and plan of Mandalay; Divisional orders issued by Gen. Prendergast; Prendergast—Sec. of Military Dept. 2 Dec. 1885 (in *Mil. Proc.*).
13. White—Jane White, 5 Dec. 1885. WP.
14. ibid.
15. White—Mrs. White, 7 Dec. 1885. WP.
16. ibid.
17. ibid.
18. *Mil. Proc.* 29 Nov. 1885.
19. Prendergast—Dufferin, 29 Nov. 1885. DP.
20. Prendergast—Dufferin, 4 Dec. 1885. DP.

8. 'A FISH TO FIGHT A DOG'

1. Reprinted in *The Times* 12 Dec. 1886.
2. SP. 290/11; Dufferin—Churchill, 5 Jan. 1885. DP. Bernard calculated the revenue at 103 lakhs of rupees, including 3 lakhs from the 'earth-oil' (petroleum) monopoly. His estimate made in October had been $78\frac{1}{2}$ lakhs. But these totals were never realised in the prevailing conditions.

NOTES

3. Geary, pp. 202–226.
4. Dufferin—Churchill, 26 Jan. 1886; Dufferin, Diary, 25 Jan. 1886. DP.
5. White—Mrs. White, 7 Dec. 1885. WP.
6. ibid.; miscellaneous notes by the Viceroy. DP.
7. Miscellaneous notes by the Viceroy. DP.
8. White—Mrs. White, 8 Dec. 1885. WP; Helen Bruce, 'The White Elephant', in *History Today*, Jan. 1971.
9. *Mil. Proc.* Nos. 508–510, 513, 514, 516; Prendergast—Dufferin, 29 Dec. 1885, endorsed by Sladen. SP.
10. Sladen—Bernard, undated, in reply to a letter of 2 Jan. 1886. SP.
11. Dufferin-Churchill, 5 Jan. 1886. DP.
12. Miscellaneous notes by the Viceroy. DP.
13. White—Mrs. White, 20 Dec. 1885. WP.
14. White—Mrs. White, 3 Jan. 1886; White—John White (his brother), 10 Jan. 1886. WP.

9. ANNEXATION

1. Prendergast—Dufferin, 11 Nov. 1885. DP.
2. Dufferin—Prendergast, 29 Nov. 1885. DP.
3. Churchill—Dufferin, 10 Nov. 1885. DP.
4. Crosthwaite—Mackenzie Wallace, 12 Oct. 1885. DP.
5. Aitchison—Mackenzie Wallace, 22 Oct. 1885. DP.
6. Mackenzie Wallace—Aitchison, 25 Oct. 1885. DP.
7. Aitchison—Mackenzie Wallace, 2 Nov. 1885. DP.
8. Dufferin—Bernard, 3 Nov. 1885. DP.
9. Memorandum enclosed with Grant Duff—Dufferin, 6 Dec. 1885. DP.
10. Dufferin—Reay, 31 Oct. 1885. DP.
11. Mackenzie Wallace—Bernard, 12 Dec. 1885. DP.
12. Dufferin—Prendergast, 29 Dec. 1885. DP.
13. *Home Corres.*, 1886, vol. 85.
14. Churchill—Dufferin, 31 Dec. 1885. DP; *Home Corres.*, 1886, vol. 85.
15. *Home Corres.*, 1886, vol. 85.
16. W. S. Churchill, *Lord Randolph Churchill*, i. 525.

10. 'THE TIMES' CORRESPONDENT

1. *The Times*, 5 Dec. 1885.
2. *Mil. Proc.*, 29, 30 Nov. 1885.
3. ibid., 3 Dec. 1885; Prendergast—Dufferin, 4 Dec. 1885. DP; Geary, pp. 31–33.
4. *The Times*, 5 Dec. 1885.
5. ibid., 9 Dec. 1885.

6. *Punch*, 12 Dec. 1885.
7. ibid., 19 Dec. 1885.
8. Churchill—Dufferin, 20 Nov. 1885. DP.
9. Churchill—Dufferin, 11 Dec. 1885. DP.
10. Churchill—Dufferin, 17 Dec. 1885. DP.
11. Buckle—Churchill, 16 Dec. 1885. DP.
12. See *The History of The Times*, vol. iii.
13. Symes—Moylan, 17 Dec. 1885. DP.
14. Moylan—Symes, 18 Dec. 1885. DP.
15. Symes—Auchinlech, 18 Dec. 1885. DP.
16. Exchange of notes between Symes and Moylan on 18 Dec. 1885. DP.
17. *The Times*, 19 Dec. 1885.
18. White—Mrs. White, 1 Feb. 1886. WP.
19. *The Times*, 4 Jan. 1886.
20. ibid., 8 Jan. 1886.
21 ibid , 21 Jan. 1886.
22. R. R. James, *Lord Randolph Churchill*, pp. 230–231.
23. *Parl. Deb.*, 3rd series, 1886, cccii, col. 189.
24. Churchill—Dufferin, 22 Jan. 1886. DP.
25. Dufferin—Churchill, 26 Jan. 1886. DP.
26. Churchill—Dufferin, 14 Jan. 1886. DP. 'Ireland is our weakest point and most anxious care. On all other matters we can well afford to meet any amount of hostile criticism. I hear rumours of an attack upon the annexation of Burma from the Radicals . . .'
27. *Parl. Deb.*, 3rd series, 1886, cccii, cols. 314–317.
28. Moylan—Sladen, 18 Jan. 1886. SP; Geary, p. 238.
29. Sladen—Prendergast, undated; Burrows—Hooper, undated, and U Kwet's confession. SP.
30. Thirkell White—Sladen and Sladen—Thirkell White, undated, Feb. 1886. SP.
31. *Mil. Proc.*; Geary, pp. 243–244.

11. THE LOOKING-GLASS PALACE

1. Dufferin, Diary, 3 Feb. 1886. DP; D, VL. p. 292; Dufferin, *Speeches in India*, pp. 91–92.
2. D, VL. p. 293.
3. ibid., pp. 294–295.
4. ibid., pp. 303–306.
5. White—Mrs. White, 14 Feb. 1886. WP.
6. *The Times*, 15 Feb. 1886.
7. White—Mrs. White, 1 Feb. 1886. WP.
8. White—Mrs. White, 14 Feb. 1886. WP.
9. White—Mrs. White, 22 Feb. 1886. WP.
10. D, VL. pp. 307–309.

11. ibid., pp. 315–316.
12. ibid., p. 316.
13. ibid., pp. 319–320.
14. Dufferin, *Speeches in India*, pp. 97–101.
15. White—Mrs. White, 22 Feb. 1886. WP.
16. Durand, *White*, i, 324; another version of the story is given by Black, p. 257.
17. Miscellaneous notes by the Viceroy, DP
18. D, VL. pp. 326–327.

12. THE RUBY MINES

1. *The Times*, 17 Mar. 1886; *Parl. Deb.*, 3rd series, ccclv, cols. 750–751.
2. G. D. Burtchaell and T. U. Sadleir, *Alumni Dublinenses* . . . 1593–1860, p. 85 (supplement); *Catalogue of graduates . . . in the University of Dublin*, p. 416; Middle Temple Registers, ii, 535; *The Times*, 8 May 1893.
3. Confidential statement from the Colonial Office, 8 Mar. 1886. (Misc. notes by the Viceroy, DP.)
4. Crosthwaite, *The Pacification of Burma*, p. 45. A vivid description of penetrating the jungle to reach Mogok in 1886 is given by General Sir Ian Hamilton in *Listening for the Drums*, pp. 191–193.
5. Churchill—Dufferin, 14 Jan. 1886. DP.
6. Dufferin—Kimberley, 25 Feb. 1886. DP; Sec. of State—Viceroy (undated). *Home Corres.*, 1886, vol. 85.
7. Dufferin—Kimberley, 14 Apr. 1886; Misc. notes by the Viceroy; Dufferin—Cross, 17 Jun. 1887. DP; *Home Corres.*, 1886, vol. 85.
8. Dufferin—Cross, 25 Oct. 1886. DP.
9. Kimberley—Dufferin, 14 May; 9, 11 Jun.; Dufferin—Kimberley, 11 Jun. 1886. DP.
10. Cross—Dufferin, 18 Nov. 1886. DP.
11. Dufferin—Cross, 17 Jun. 1887. DP.
12. Crosthwaite, p. 44.
13. Dufferin—Cross, 17 Jun. 1887. DP.
14. Crosthwaite, p. 45.
15. *Parl. Deb.*, 3rd series, ccx, cols. 161, 260, 1087, 1557–1558, 1769; cccxv, cols. 1028–1029, 1073–1075, 1580–1581; cccxvi, cols. 409, 1027; cccxvii, cols. 68, 790, 949, 523; cccxviii, col. 1843.
16. Crosthwaite, p. 46.

13. CHINA

1. *From Sea to Sea*, i, 303; E. V. G. Kiernan, *British Diplomacy in China*, p. 185.
2. *Home Corres.*, 1885, vol. 81; correspondence respecting the affairs of

Burmah. Confidential (5218). Printed for the use of the Foreign Office. *Home Corres.*, 1886, vol. 85.

3. DNB; for an account of Marquis Tseng and Macartney in London see H. McAleavy, *Black Flags in Vietnam.*
4. S. F. Wright, *Hart and the Chinese Customs*, pp. 159–176.
5. ibid., pp. 176; 250–253; 258–553 *passim.*
6. *Home Corres.*, 1886, vol. 85.
7. ibid.
8. ibid.
9. ibid.; Churchill—Dufferin, 10 Nov. 1885. DP.
10. Churchill—Dufferin, 10 Nov. 1885. DP.
11. *Home Corres.*, 1886, vol. 85; Wright, pp. 555–557.
12. Churchill—Dufferin, 10 Nov. 1885. DP.
13. *Home Corres.*, 1886, vol. 85.
14. *Home Corres.*, 1885, vols. 81 and 82; 1886, vol. 85; Woodman, pp. 258–260.
15. Churchill—Dufferin, 11 Dec. 1885. DP.
16. Churchill—Dufferin, 14 Jan. 1886. DP.
17. O'Conor—Rosebery, 27 Feb., 6 Mar. 1886; *Home Corres.*, 1886, vol. 85.
18. *Home Corres.*, 1886, vol. 85; Churchill—Dufferin, 31 Dec. 1885; Dufferin—Cross, 24, 27 Aug. 1885. DP. For a detailed account of the Macaulay Mission see Alaistair Lamb, *Britain and Chinese central Asia: the road to Lhasa, 1767–1905*, pp. 143–173.

14. FARTHER INDIA

1. Dufferin—Kimberley from SS *Clyde* at sea, 26 Feb. 1886. DP.
2. ibid.; The case of General Sir H. Prendergast. DP.
3. White—Mrs. White, 19 Mar. 1886. WP.
4. White—Mrs. White, 5 Apr. 1886. WP.
5. *The Times*, 26 Jul. 1913.
6. The case of General Sir H. Prendergast. DP.
7. Dufferin—Kimberley, 26 Feb. 1886. DP.
8. *The Times*, 29 Jun. 1886.
9. *The Times*, 6 Oct. 1886.
10. Dufferin—Kimberley, 14 Feb. 1886; Memorandum by Dufferin on Burma. DP.
11. *Parl. Deb.*, 3rd series, cccii, cols. 939–988.
12. Dufferin—Kimberley, 21 Mar. 1886. DP.
13. W. S. Churchill, *Lord Randolph Churchill*, ii, 62–63.
14. Stephen—Dufferin, 9 May 1886. DP.
15. Lyall, ii, 113.
16. Lady Gregory—Dufferin, May 1886 (cited Lyall, ii, 113).
17. White—Mrs. White, 26 Feb. 1886. WP.
18. White—Mrs. White, 28 Mar. 1886. WP.

19. White—Mrs. White, 11, 25 Apr. 1886. WP.
20. White—Mrs. White, 15 May 1886. WP.
21. White—Mrs. White, 12, 26 Jun., 9 Jul., 7 Aug. 1886. WP.

15. THE BURSTING OF THE BUND

1. Kimberley—Dufferin, 18 Aug. 1886. DP.
2. White—Mrs. White, 24 Jul. 1886. WP.
3. Dufferin—Kimberley, 20 Sept. 1886. DP.
4. Dufferin—Cross, 10 Sept. 1886. DP.
5. *Parl. Deb.*, 3rd series, cccviii, cols. 1184–1185.
6. Dufferin—Kimberley, 13 Aug. 1886. DP.
7. Walter—Dufferin, 31 Aug. 1886. DP.
8. White—Mrs. White, 24 Jul. 1886. WP; Moylan was said to have one of the most lucrative practices at the Indian Bar (*The Times*, 8 May 1893).
9. Bernard—Dufferin, 28 Aug. 1886. DP.
10. Dufferin—Cross, 10 Sept. 1886. DP.
11. *The Times*, 21 Sept. 1886; Dufferin—Cross, 27 Aug. 1886. DP.
12. *The Times*, 21 Sept. 1886.
13. Cross—Dufferin, 22 Sept. 1886. DP.
14. *Parl. Deb.*, 3rd series, cccviii, col. 542.
15. Cross—Dufferin, 6 Oct. 1886. DP.
16. Dufferin—Cross, 11 Oct. 1886. DP.
17. Dufferin—Kimberley, 26 Feb. 1886. DP.
18. Kimberley—Dufferin, 30 Jul. 1886. DP.
19. Dufferin—Cross, 27 Sept. 1886. DP.
20. Dufferin—Cross, 25 Oct. 1886. DP.
21. Cross—Dufferin, 8 Sept. 1886; Dufferin—Cross, 18 Oct. 1886. DP.
22. List of persons to whom Lord Dufferin's memorandum on Burma was sent. DP. H.M. 13/11B.
23. Memorandum by Dufferin on Burma (secret and confidential). DP. H.M. 13/11B.
24. Gladstone—Dufferin, 20 Jan. 1887. DP.
25. Goschen—Dufferin, 26 Nov. 1886. DP.
26. Reeve—Dufferin, 19 Jan. 1887. DP.
27. Finlay—Dufferin, 18 Jan. 1887. DP.

16. THE RIVER OF LOST FOOTSTEPS

1. White—Mrs. White, 4 Sept. 1886. WP.
2. Dufferin—Kimberley, 13 Aug.; Dufferin—Cross, 27 Aug.; Cross—Dufferin, 22 Sept. 1886. DP.
3. White—Mrs. White, 4, 12, 26 Sept. 1886. WP; Dufferin—White, 16 Sept. 1886 (cited Durand, i, 350–351).

NOTES

4. White—Mrs. White, 4, 24 Oct. 1886. WP.
5. Durand, i, 354–355.
6. White—Mrs. White, 19 Dec. 1886. WP.
7. White—Lady White, 21 Feb. 1887. WP. Dufferin wrote to Cross on 25 Jan. 1887 that Bernard, though told by his doctors to leave before the next hot weather, 'showed an inclination to hang on, on the plea that his health had improved.' DP.
8. 'The Conquest of Burma', *Edinburgh Review*, Jan.–Apr. 1887.
9. A. C. Yate, 'Burma Reformed', *Blackwood's Magazine*, 1887, vol. 141, pp. 711–714.
10. Kipling, *From Sea to Sea*, i, 217.

EPILOGUE

1. Black, pp. 322–323; Nicolson, p. 208.
2. Kipling, *Something of Myself*, p. 94.
3. *The Times*, 20, 21 Dec. 1916; Hall, *Europe and Burma*, p. 181.
4. Nicolson, pp. 268–279.
5. ibid., pp. 209–211.
6. *The Times*, 8 May 1893.
7. *Who's Who*.
8. *Who's Who*; DIB; DNB.
9. *History of the Second World War*, United Kingdom Series, *The War Against Japan*, vol. IV, 'The reconquest of Burma', pp. 299–301; Field-Marshal Lord Slim, *Defeat into Victory*, pp. 468–470. Five days after the fall of Mandalay, an officer on the Headquarters Staff of the Mandalay sector was killed in a Japanese ambush. He was Basil Sheridan Blackwood, 4th Marquess of Dufferin and Ava.

SOURCES

A. Unpublished

In the India Office Records, Commonwealth Relations Office, London
Papers of Sir Edward Bosc Sladen. Eur.E.290.
Papers of Field-Marshal Sir George Stuart White, V.C., Eur.F.108.
India Office, Home Correspondence, Secret and Political. L/P and S/P.
Government of India, Military Department. Military Proceedings, Burmah, 1885–1886. 2768.
In the Public Record Office of Northern Ireland, Belfast
Papers of Frederick Temple Hamilton-Temple Blackwood, 1st Marquis of Dufferin and Ava. Indian Viceregal Papers. D.1071 H.M.

NOTES

B. Published

Hall, D. G. E., *The Dalhousie-Phayre Correspondence, 1852–1856*, 1932.
Hariot, Lady Dufferin, *Our Viceregal Life in India*, 2 vols., 1889.
Wallace, D. M. (ed.) Lord Dufferin, *Speeches Delivered in India, 1884–1888*.
Hansard, *Parliamentary Debates*.
The Times.

PARLIAMENTARY PAPERS

Copy of Major Sladen's Report on the Bhamo route. H. of C. paper, 165 (1871).
Correspondence relating to Burmah since the accession of King Theebaw, October 1878. C.4614 (1886).
Further correspondence relating to Burmah. C.4887 (1886).
Further correspondence relating to Burmah. C.4962 (1887).
Dispatch from H.M. Minister in China, transmitting Convention between H.M. and H.M. the Emperor of China relating to Burmah. Signed Peking, 24 July 1886. C.4861 (1886).

WORKS OF REFERENCE

Annual Register of World Events.
The Army List.
Buckland, C. E. (ed.) *Dictionary of Indian Biography.*
Burgess, J. *The Chronology of Modern India.* 1913.
Dictionary of National Biography.
Murray's *Handbook for India, Burma and Ceylon.*
Hunter, W. W. *Imperial Gazetteer of India.*
Index to events relating to India and the East in *The Times*, 1850–1889 (prepared for official use). In India Office Library.
Index to The Times.
The Statesman's Yearbook.

CONTEMPORARY ARTICLES

Blackwood's Edinburgh Magazine
——'England and France in Indo-China', 138, 1885.
——'Our New Eastern Province', 139, 1886.
——'Burmese Border Tribes and Trade Routes', 140, 1886.
Yate, A. C., 'Burma Reformed', 141, 1887.
McMahon, A. R., 'Cathay and the Golden Chersonese', 141, 1887.

Edinburgh Review
——'The Conquest of Burma', 165, 1887.
——'India under the Marquis of Dufferin', 169, 1889 (attributed to Sir A. Lyall).
Fortnightly Review
——'Our Task in Burma', 41, 1887.
Gentleman's Magazine
Farrar, J. A., 'The Burmese War', 252, 1886.
Westminster Review
——'France and Cochin-China', 123, 1885.
Journal of the Asiatic Society of Bengal
Pemberton, R. B., 'Abstract of a Journal of a Route travelled by Captain S. F. Hannay from Ava to the Amber Mines of Assam', 1837.
Macleod, T. E., 'Expedition to Kiang Hung on the Chinese border from Moulmein, 13 Dec. 1836', 1837.
Richardson, D., 'From Moulmein to Ava, 1836-7', 1837.
Phayre, A. P., 'History of the Shwe Dagon Pagoda', 1859.
Williams, C., 'Journal of a trip to Bhamo', 1865.

SECONDARY ARTICLES

History Today
Bruce, Helen, 'The White Elephant,', Jan. 1971.
Bruce, R., 'King Mindon of Burma', Nov. 1969.
Lunt, J., 'Simla: the British in India', Sept. 1968.
Martin, B., Jnr., 'The Viceroyalty of Lord Dufferin', Part I, Dec. 1960; Part II, Jan. 1961.
Mohl, R. A., 'Confrontation in Central Asia, 1885', Mar. 1969.
Watson, D. R., 'The French in Indo-China', Aug. 1970.

BOOKS

BAIRD, J. A. *Life and Letters of the Marquis of Dalhousie*. London, 1910.
BANNERJEE, A. C. *The Annexation of Burma*. Calcutta, 1944.
BILLOT, M. *L'affaire du Tonkin*. Paris, 1888.
BLACK, C. E. D. *The Life of the Marquess of Dufferin and Ava*. London, 1902.
BODELSEN, C. A. *Aspects of Kipling's Art*. Manchester, 1964.
BOND, B. (ed.) *Victorian Military Campaigns*. London, 1967.
BROWN, H. *Rudyard Kipling*. London, 1945.
BROWN, R. G. *Burma As I Saw It, 1889–1917*. London, n.d. (1926).
BROWNE, H. A. *Reminiscences of the Court of Mandalay*. Woking, 1907.
BUCKLE, G. E. (ed.) *The Letters of Queen Victoria*, vol. iii, 1879–1885. London, 1928.
CADY, J. F. *A History of Modern Burma*. Ithaca, New York, 1958.
CARRINGTON, C. E. *Rudyard Kipling, his Life and Work*. London, 1955.

NOTES

CHURCHILL, WINSTON S. *Lord Randolph Churchill,* 2 vols. London, 1906.

COLLIS, M. *Siamese White.* London, 1935; *The Land of the Great Image.* London, 1943.

CORNELL, L. L. *Kipling in India.* London, 1966.

CROSTHWAITE, C. E. *The Pacification of Burma.* London, 1912.

DAUTREMER, J. *Burma under British Rule.* Trans. by Sir George Scott. London, n.d. (1913).

DODWELL, H. H. (ed.) *The Cambridge History of India,* vol. vi. Cambridge, 1932.

DURAND, H. M. *The Life of Field-Marshal Sir George White, V.C.,* 2 vols. London, 1915.

EDWARDES, M. *The West in Asia, 1850–1914.* London, 1967.

FARNIE, D. A. *East and West of Suez: the Suez Canal in History.* Oxford, 1969.

FERGUSSON, B. *Return to Burma.* London, 1962.

FORTESCUE, THE HON. J. W. *A History of the British Army,* 13 vols. London, 1899–1930.

FYTCHE, A. *Burma Past and Present with Personal Reminiscences of the Country,* 2 vols. London, 1878.

GEARY, G. *Burma after the Conquest.* London, 1886.

GOPAL, S. *The Viceroyalty of Lord Ripon,* 1880–1884. London, 1953.

GORDON, C. A. *Our Trip to Burma.* London, n.d. (1875?).

GRAHAM, G. S. *Great Britain in the Indian Ocean, 1810–1850.* Oxford, 1967.

GRANT-DUFF, M. E. *Out of the Past,* 2 vols. London, 1903.

GREEN, R. L. *Kipling and the Children.* London, 1965.

HALL, D. G. E. *Burma.* London, 1950; *Early English Intercourse with Burma, 1587–1743.* London, 1928; *Europe and Burma.* London, 1945; *A History of South-East Asia.* London, 1968.

HALL, H. F. *The Soul of a People.* London, 1926.

HAMILTON, GENERAL SIR IAN *Listening for the Drums.* London, 1944.

HARVEY, G. E. *British Rule in Burma, 1824–1942.* London, 1946.

KIERNAN, E. V. G. *British Diplomacy in China, 1880–1885.* London, 1939.

KIPLING, R. *Barrack Room Ballads.* London, 1892; *From Sea to Sea,* 2 vols. London, 1892; *Something of Myself.* London, 1932; *Stalky and Co.* London, 1899.

LAURIE, W. F. B. *Our Burmese Wars and Relations with Burma.* London, 1885.

LEE-WARNER, W. *The Life of the Marquis of Dalhousie.* London, 1904.

LYALL, A. *The Life of the Marquis of Dufferin and Ava,* 2 vols. London, 1905.

MCALEAVY, H. *Black Flags in Vietnam.* London, 1968.

MCMAHON, A. R. *Far Cathay and Farther India.* London, 1893.

MALCOM, H. *Travels in the Burman Empire.* Edinburgh, 1840.

MARTIN, B. *New India, 1885,* Berkeley and Los Angeles, 1969.

MAUNG MAUNG. *Burma in the Family of Nations.* Amsterdam, 1956.

NOTES

MOORE, R. J. *Liberalism and Indian Politics, 1872–1923*. London, 1966.
NICOLSON, H. *Helen's Tower*. London, 1937.
NISBET, J. *Burmah under British Rule and Before*, 2 vols. London, 1901.
PEARN, B. R. *Judson of Burma*. London, 1962.
PURCHAS, S. *Hakluytus Posthumus, or Purchas his Pilgrimmes*, 20 vols. Glasgow, 1905–7.
ROBERTS, F. E. (Field-Marshal Lord Roberts of Kandahar). *Forty-one Years in India*, 2 vols. London, 1897.
ROSEBERY, A. P. P. (fifth Earl of). *Lord Randolph Churchill*. London, 1906.
SCOTT, SIR J. G. *Burma from the Earliest Times to the Present Day*. London, 1924.
SINGHAL, D. P. *The Annexation of Upper Burma*. Singapore, 1960.
SLIM, W. J. (Field-Marshal Viscount Slim) *Defeat into Victory*. London, 1956.
SNODGRASS, J. J. *A Narrative of the Burmese War*. London, 1827.
SYMES, M. *An Account of an Embassy to the Kingdom of Ava*. London, 1800.
The Book of Helen's Tower (privately printed). Belfast, n.d.
The Times, The History of, vols. ii and iii. London, 1935–1952.
TINKER, H. *South Asia, a Short History*. London, 1966.
TRANT, T. A. *Two Years at Ava*. London, 1828.
WARNER, O. *Captain Marryat, a Rediscovery*. London, 1953.
WHITE, SIR HERBERT THIRKELL. *Burma*. Cambridge, 1923.
WOODMAN, DOROTHY. *The Making of Burma*. London, 1962.
WRIGHT, S. F. *Hart and the Chinese Customs*. Belfast, 1950.
YOUNG, L. K. *British Policy in China, 1895–1902*. Oxford, 1970.
YULE, SIR HENRY *A Narrative of a Mission sent by the Governor-General of India to the Court of Ava in 1855*. London, 1858.

INDEX

213

INDEX

INDEX

INDEX

INDEX

INDEX

INDEX

INDEX